40 Days Through GENESIS

RON RHODES

HARVEST HOUSE PUBLISHERS
EUGENE, OREGON

Unless otherwise indicated, all Scripture quotations are from The ESV® Bible (The Holy Bible, English Standard Version®), copyright © 2001 by Crossway, a publishing ministry of Good News Publishers. Used by permission. All rights reserved.

Verses marked NIV are taken from the Holy Bible, New International Version®, NIV®. Copyright © 1973, 1978, 1984, 2011 by Biblica, Inc.® Used by permission. All rights reserved worldwide.

Verses marked NASB are taken from the New American Standard Bible®, © 1960, 1962, 1963, 1968, 1971, 1972, 1973, 1975, 1977, 1995 by The Lockman Foundation. Used by permission. (www.Lockman.org)

Verses marked NKJV are taken from the New King James Version®. Copyright © 1982 by Thomas Nelson, Inc. Used by permission. All rights reserved.

All italicized emphasis in Scripture quotations is added by the author.

Cover by Dugan Design Group, Minneapolis, Minnesota

Cover photos © Dugan Design Group; yurakp / Fotolia

40 DAYS THROUGH GENESIS

Published by Harvest House Publishers
Eugene, Oregon 97408
www.harvesthousepublishers.com

Library of Congress Cataloging-in-Publication Data
Rhodes, Ron.
40 days through Genesis / Ron Rhodes.
pages cm
Includes bibliographical references.
ISBN 978-0-7369-6096-0 (pbk.)
ISBN 978-0-7369-6098-4 (eBook)
1. Bible. Genesis—Devotional use. I. Title.
BS1235.54.R46 2015
222'.1106—dc23

2014021861

Printed in the United States of America

21 22 23 24 25 26 27 / BP-JC / 10 9 8 7 6 5 4 3

To Kerri
with love and appreciation

Acknowledgments

Kerri, David, and Kylie
Words are inadequate to express my continued gratitude
for your enduring love and support.
I am truly blessed!

All my friends at Harvest House Publishers
Thanks for your collective hard work.
You are hugely appreciated!
It is always a delight to partner with you.

Contents

Introduction

Thank you for joining me on this exciting journey through the book of Genesis. You are in for a spiritually uplifting time! My hope and prayer is that as you read *40 Days Through Genesis*, you will make many discoveries. For example...

- Genesis is a book of beginnings, including the beginnings of the universe and humankind.
- God is a personal being who personally interacts with His people.
- God is sovereign, and He providentially controls the universe and human history.
- God not only makes promises but also is a relentless promise keeper.
- God blesses righteous living.
- God's people need to maintain faith in Him regardless of what outward circumstances may look like.
- God can providentially bring good out of evil.
- The Bible in general and the book of Genesis in particular are completely trustworthy.

I want to let you know right up front that the book of Genesis is absolutely foundational to a proper understanding of the rest of the Bible. After all, Genesis not only tells us about the origins of the universe and humankind but also informs us where human sin, suffering, and death came from. God's work of redemption, as recorded throughout the rest of Scripture, would make little sense if we did not first understand these foundational truths in the book of Genesis. So we might say that Genesis sets the stage for all that follows in the rest of Scripture.

As we begin our journey together, I wish to address a few things that will lay a foundation for better understanding the book of Genesis. Let's look at the big picture first, and then we will zero in on the details in subsequent chapters.

Two Primary Streams of Thought in Genesis

The book of Genesis is based on two streams of thought:

- Genesis 1–11 documents the creation of the universe and humankind, and then it broadly traces the peoples and nations as they turn away from God.
- In Genesis 12–50, God zeroes in on one family—Abraham, Isaac, Jacob, and Joseph and his brothers. This family will become the nation of Israel, through which all the other nations of the earth are to be blessed.

I will provide a more detailed outline below, but these two broad concepts help us to easily conceptualize the book of Genesis in broad terms.

The Author and Date of Genesis

Moses is the author of the book of Genesis. This is confirmed throughout the rest of the Old Testament (see Exodus 17:14; Numbers 33:1-2; Deuteronomy 31:9; Joshua 1:7-8; 1 Kings 2:3; 2 Kings 14:6; Ezra 6:18; Daniel 9:11-13; Malachi 4:4) as well as the New Testament (Matthew 19:8; Mark 12:26; John 5:46-47; Romans 10:5).

One might naturally wonder how Moses could know the universe was created if he wasn't there to witness it. The answer is simple. The book of Genesis is a book of divine revelation. God Himself gave special revelation to Moses regarding how He created the universe. The book was written between 1445 and 1405 BC.

The Truth of Genesis

Liberal critics typically argue that the book of Genesis is mythological and does not contain real truth. They note that similar creation accounts have been discovered among the Babylonians, Sumerians, Greeks, Hindus, Chinese, and many others. Here are a few examples.

- The Ebla Tablets—a library of 16,000 cuneiform clay tablets discovered at Tell Mardikh, Syria—contain an account of the creation that is strikingly close to Genesis. It speaks of one being who created the heavens, earth, moon, and stars, all out of nothing.
- The Atrahasis Epic, a Babylonian document, contains many details that are similar to the biblical account of both the creation and the flood.
- The Enuma Elish presents a Mesopotamian account of the creation.

Such facts, however, do not mean that Genesis is mythological. The truth of the matter is that Genesis gives the original story, and the other versions—all dated later—contain elaborations, thereby introducing corruptions into the original account.

Later Bible writers confirmed that Genesis is not full of myths. They interpreted its contents literally, including...

- the creation of the universe (Exodus 20:10-11)
- the creation of Adam and Eve (Matthew 19:6; 1 Timothy 2:13)
- the fall of Adam and his resulting death (Romans 5:12,14)
- Noah's flood (Matthew 24:38)

The verses in Matthew indicate that Jesus Himself took the events in Genesis as literally true. Therefore, Christians should not allow their faith to be shaken by the claims of liberal critics who seek to undermine a literal interpretation of Genesis.

The Title of the Book

Genesis literally means "beginning." This book contains an account of the beginning of the world, the universe, and humankind. It also contains an account of the beginning of human sin, suffering, death, and redemption.

A Summary Outline of Genesis

1. The Creation and the Fall (1–3)

God created the entire universe, including the earth and human beings (1:26-27). Even in a perfect living environment, Adam and Eve sinned against God and catapulted the entire human race into sin (3).

2. The Family of Adam and Eve (4–5)

The name Adam derives from a Hebrew word meaning "humanity," which is appropriate because he represents humanity (1:26-27; 2:7,22-23). Eve means "giver of life" (3:20; 4:1). Cain, their firstborn (4:1), murdered his righteous brother Abel out of resentment that God accepted Abel's sacrifice but not his (4:1-16). Cain was consequently exiled from Eden (4:10-15). Adam and Eve had many other children (4:25; 5:3-4).

3. Noah and the Flood (6–9)

The flood came because humankind became filled with violence and corruption (6). Noah was the only one who honored God (6:8-9). Noah's ark was about 450 feet long, 75 feet wide, and 45 feet high. In this vessel, a remnant of humanity (Noah and his family) and two of each species of animals were preserved from the flood (6:14–9:18).

4. The Early Nations and the Tower of Babel (10–11)

After the flood, some of the descendants of Noah through his son Ham developed a wicked kingdom centered at the tower of Babel. This tower was a pagan effort to observe and worship the heavens. God confounded the people, causing them to speak different languages. This gave rise to the name Babel, meaning "confusion." This confusion caused them to scatter (11:1-9).

5. Abram and Sarah (12–25)

God commanded Abram to leave Ur and go to Canaan. He also gave Abram a promise—a great nation, as numberless as the stars, would emerge out of his offspring. God changed Abram's name to Abraham, meaning "father of a multitude" (17:5). God also promised to give this nation the land of Canaan and promised that this nation would bring blessing to all the other nations of the world (12:3). The problem was, by now Abraham was 100 years old, and Sarah was 90. How would they bear a son? In unbelief, Sarah offered Abraham her younger handmaiden Hagar, through whom Ishmael was born. But this was not the child of promise. God's promise was eventually fulfilled when Isaac was born to them.

6. Isaac and Rebekah (26:1–27:45)

Isaac married Rebekah. God reaffirmed His covenant with Isaac on two occasions (26:3-5,24-25). God reiterated that Isaac's descendants would be as numberless as the stars, inherit the land of Canaan, and bring blessing to the world.

7. Jacob and Esau (27:46–36:43)

Isaac had twin sons—Esau and Jacob. The blessing rightfully belonged to Esau, the firstborn (and hairier) son. When it came time to confer the blessing, a vision-impaired Isaac was deceived into conferring the blessing on a deceptively hair-enhanced Jacob instead. Jacob's wives Leah and Rachel (and their concubines) bore him 12 sons and a daughter.

8. Joseph (37–50)

Joseph was Jacob's favorite son, but his brothers hated him. They sold him to a group of Ishmaelite traders en route to Egypt. Joseph's brothers soaked his robe in goat blood and took it to Jacob, implying Joseph was now dead. While in Egypt, a faithful Joseph was elevated to a prominent position in Potiphar's house. When Joseph resisted the sexual advances of Potiphar's lustful wife, she falsely accused him of improper actions, and he was imprisoned. Two years later, he was released from prison after accurately interpreting Pharaoh's dreams regarding seven years of prosperity followed by seven years of famine. Pharaoh elevated Joseph to great authority so he could prepare for the famine.

Canaan was also hit by the famine. Jacob's sons (except for Benjamin) came to Egypt for food and bowed before Joseph without recognizing him. Eventually, Joseph revealed his identity to them, and the family was reconciled (45:1-15). Joseph knew God had orchestrated his earlier painful circumstances to bring him to Egypt (50:20).

Genesis ends with Joseph's death and his family's promise to take his bones with them when they are restored to the Promised Land.

The Centrality of Faith in Genesis

One of the most exciting aspects of the book of Genesis is that a number of the people it mentions are heroes of faith. Two examples come immediately to mind.

- Abraham's faith was especially evident when he was being obedient to God's command to sacrifice his own son Isaac (Genesis 22:1-19). God stopped him just in the nick of time.
- Joseph, too, showed great faith, knowing that even though his brothers treated him cruelly, God was with him and was providentially working in his painful circumstances (50:20). In the end, God elevated Joseph to a supreme position in Egypt.

There are quite a number of other examples. I urge you to constantly be on the lookout for examples of faith in the book of Genesis.

How to Use this Book

As you begin each chapter, pray something like this:

> *Lord, I ask You to open my eyes and enhance my understanding so that I can grasp what You want me to learn today* [Psalm 119:18]. *I also ask You to enable me, by Your Spirit, to apply the*

truths I learn to my everyday life and to be guided moment by moment by Your Word [Psalm 119:105; 2 Timothy 3:15-17]. *I thank You in Jesus's name. Amen.*

Following this short prayer, you can read the assigned section of the book of Genesis using your favorite Bible. With your Bible still in hand, you can then go verse by verse through your Bible again, but this time, after reading each verse, also read the appropriate notes in the book.

You'll notice that some of the biblical phrases I comment on are in quote marks and some aren't. Quote marks are used only when someone is speaking, whether God, Abraham, or someone else.

After the insights on each verse in the passage, I provide four brief summaries:

- *Major Themes.* These topical summaries will help you learn how to think theologically as you study the Bible.
- *Digging Deeper with Cross-References.* These will help you discover relevant insights from other books of the Bible.
- *Life Lessons.* This is where you learn to apply what you have read to your everyday life. You will discover that the book of Genesis is rich in transforming truths!
- *Questions for Reflection and Discussion.* Use these for your personal journaling or for lively group interactions.

Lord, by the power of Your Spirit, please enable my readers to understand and apply truth from the book of Genesis. Please excite them with Your Word and instill in them a sense of the majestic awesomeness of God. I thank You in Jesus's name. Amen.

Day 1

God's Creation of the Earth

Genesis 1:1–2:3

Scripture Reading and Insights

Begin by reading Genesis 1:1–2:3 in your favorite Bible. Read with the anticipation that the Holy Spirit has something important to teach you today (see Psalm 119:105).

In the introduction, we noted that the book of Genesis is a book of beginnings, including the beginnings of the universe and humankind. In this chapter, we will begin to explore these beginnings. With your Bible still accessible, consider the following insights on the biblical text.

Genesis 1:1-2

In the beginning (1:1): This refers not to the beginning of all eternity, but rather the beginning of the creation.

God (1:1): God's prior existence is presumed. The Hebrew term for God is *Elohim*. This name means "Strong One," and it indicates fullness of power. It pictures God as the powerful and sovereign Governor of the universe. The form of the word is plural (the *-im* ending). Hebrew grammarians categorize it as a plural of majesty. This points to the majesty, dignity, and greatness of God.

Created (1:1): God created the universe instantaneously and *ex nihilo* (out of nothing). Psalm 33:6 tells us, "By the word of the Lord the heavens were made, and by the breath of his mouth all their host" (see also verse 9). Hebrews 11:3 likewise tells us, "The universe was created by the word of God."

The heavens and the earth (1:1): The entire universe.

Without form and void (1:2): God first created the "stuff" (or matter) of creation, which at this point was yet unorganized and uninhabited. God would soon remedy this by molding this "stuff" into the earth and the universe.

Spirit of God (1:2): This is the Holy Spirit, who has the attributes of deity, including omnipresence (Psalm 139:7), omniscience (1 Corinthians 2:10), omnipotence (Romans 15:19), holiness (Romans 1:4), and eternity (Hebrews 9:14). He played a significant role in the creation of the universe (see Job 33:4; Psalm 104:30).

Genesis 1:3-31

God said (1:3): God merely spoke, and things came into existence out of nothing (see Psalm 148:5).

"Light" (1:3): This light existed prior to the creation of the sun (which was on day four). There are a number of sources of light in the universe. Even God Himself is a source of light (Revelation 21:23; 22:5). This was apparently a temporary light until the permanent light of the sun was created.

God separated (1:4): This is the first of three separations God engaged in. Here God separated the light from the darkness. In verse 7 God separates the waters below the sky (on earth) from the waters above the sky (around the earth). In verse 9 God separates the land from the seas. By so doing, God gave form to the previously formless creation. Likewise, by creating sea, air, and land creatures to fill the earth (see below), the earth was no longer void (or, more literally, empty).

Day...Night (1:5): This would seem to be a literal 24-hour day, not an age and not a day separated by an age. See Major Themes below.

"Expanse" (1:6): This is the atmosphere, or sky, appearing to be a shiny dome or canopy from the perspective of earth.

Waters that were under the expanse (1:7): The oceans.

Waters that were above the expanse (1:7): A vast layer of water vapor surrounding the earth that created a greenhouse effect on the earth.

This may account for the great longevity among the patriarchs (see Genesis 5). It may also relate to the deluge of water in Noah's flood (Genesis 6–9).

"Waters... dry land" (1:9-10): God separated the land from the waters. When God looked out over the earth and seas, He saw that the arrangement was good—ideal for life on earth.

God called (1:10): In ancient Semitic thought, whoever names something has authority over it (see Genesis 17:5,15; 41:45).

"According to its kind" (1:11-12): God created the initial kinds of vegetation, plants, and fruit trees, and then each species reproduced "according to its kind." This implies there are fixed reproductive boundaries among each of the kinds. (An apple tree does not produce oranges.)

"Lights" (1:14): God created the stars, planets, and moons in their solar systems and galaxies.

"For signs and for seasons, and for days and years" (1:14): Some suggest that interstellar lights are signs in the sense of helping people navigate and get their bearings (north, south, east, and west). Others suggest that the interstellar lights are signs in the sense of pointing to God's power and majesty (see Psalm 19:1). In any event, the rotation of the earth (in relation to the sun and moon) helps people keep track of days, seasons, and years.

Two great lights (1:16): The sun and the moon now replace the temporary light source that emerged on day one.

To rule (1:17-18): The sun rules the day, and the moon rules the night. In ancient times, pagans believed the sun, moon, and other celestial bodies were deities, and they worshipped them. But our text indicates that in reality the sun and moon serve the one true God.

"Living creatures" (1:20): This includes small sea creatures and giant sea creatures, apparently including marine dinosaurs (see Job 40:15–41:1).

According to their kinds (1:21): Each kind of creature reproduces after its kind. The genetic pool of DNA in each kind of sea creature and bird sets developmental parameters beyond which the kind cannot go. For example, the DNA in a goldfish prohibits it from evolving into a shark.

"Be fruitful and multiply" (1:22): God earlier created a "good" earth suitable for habitation. Now God creates a variety of creatures to inhabit this good earth.

"Living creatures" (1:24): Just as God created a variety of living creatures to inhabit the sea, so now He creates a variety of living creatures to inhabit the land. The whole earth is being populated with life. It is no longer empty.

"According to their kinds" (1:24-25): The genetic pool of DNA in each kind of land creature sets developmental parameters beyond which the kind cannot go. The DNA includes developmental possibilities within that kind, such as the various colors of fur, colors of eyes, and body sizes. But each respective kind never evolves into a different kind.

"In our image, after our likeness" (1:26): "Image" and "likeness" are synonymous in Scripture (see 1 Corinthians 11:7; Colossians 3:10; James 3:9). Notice the plural pronouns ("us," "our"). Hebrew grammarians tell us that the plural pronouns are a grammatical necessity. The plural pronouns "us" and "our" are required by the plural ending of *Elohim*: "Then God [*Elohim*, plural] said, 'Let us [plural] make man in our [plural] image.'"

"Dominion" (1:26): We find an interesting nuance of the term "image" in biblical times. Whenever a king conquered a new territory, he set up an image of himself in that territory to represent his sovereignty over it. Interestingly, when God created human beings, He created them in His image and then commanded them, "Fill the earth and subdue it, and *have dominion* over the fish of the sea and over the birds of the heavens and over the livestock and over all the earth and over every creeping thing that creeps on the earth."

Man (1:27): The word is used generically here, including both males and females. God provides the specifics of humankind's creation in Genesis 2.

"Be fruitful and multiply" (1:28): Just as the sea creatures were to multiply to fill the sea and the birds were to multiply to fill the sky, so God now instructs that human beings are to multiply to fill the earth.

"Subdue it, and have dominion" (1:28): This relates to human beings as created in the image of God (see *"Dominion" [1:26]* above).

"Food" (1:29): Humans were apparently vegetarians at first. After Noah's flood, God gives humans permission to eat meat (Genesis 9:3).

It was very good (1:31): Individual items in the creation have previously been called good (see Genesis 1:4,10,12,18,21,25). But now the entire creation as a whole is called "very good."

Genesis 2:1-3

Host (2:1): This term is used in different ways in different contexts. The word can refer to stars in outer space (Nehemiah 9:6) or to angels (1 Kings 22:19). In the present context, the term seems to refer to all the various things God just created.

God...rested (2:2): The Hebrew word translated "rest" communicates the idea of ceasing from activity. God completed His work of creation and then stopped. There was nothing further to do.

Blessed the seventh day (2:3): The Hebrew term translated Sabbath is the noun form of the word translated "rest." Later, Moses's instructions on the Sabbath were based on the creation week (see Exodus 20:8-11).

Major Themes

1. *The Trinity and creation.* Many Old Testament references to the creation attribute it simply to God (Genesis 1:1; Psalm 96:5; Isaiah 37:16; 44:24; 45:12; Jeremiah 10:11-12). Other verses relate the creation specifically to the Father (Psalm 102:25), the Son (John 1:3; Colossians 1:16; Hebrews 1:2), or the Holy Spirit (Job 26:13; 33:4; Isaiah 40:12-13). First Corinthians 8:6 reveals that the Father is the Creator in a broad, general sense, and the Son is the actual agent or mediating Cause of creation. The Holy Spirit's role was apparently to give life to the creation (Psalm 104:30).
2. *The days of creation.* There are four primary views on the days of creation.
    - The days were simply revelatory days—that is, they were days during which God revealed the creation

scene to Moses. (Exodus 20:11, however, seems to contradict this view.)

- Each day represents an age. Some Bible verses portray a day as a long period of time (Psalm 90:4; 2 Peter 3:8).
- The days are literal solar days, but each day was separated by a huge time gap. This allegedly accounts for the apparent long geological ages that science has discovered.
- The days are literal solar days with no time gap between them. This is my view. In support of this view, the Genesis account refers to evening and morning (Genesis 1:5). God created the sun to rule the day and the moon to rule the night (verse 16). Further, Exodus 20:11 plainly states that "in six days the Lord made heaven and earth." Moreover, whenever a number (such as six) is used with the Hebrew word for day (*yom*), it always refers to a literal solar day.

Digging Deeper with Cross-References

The Holy Spirit's role in creation—Job 26:13; 33:4; Psalm 104:30; compare with Luke 1:35

The power of God's spoken word—Psalms 33:6; 148:5; Isaiah 55:11; Hebrews 11:3

Life Lessons

1. *Human sexuality in the marriage relationship.* A sexual relationship is restricted to the confines of marriage (between a man and woman) (1 Corinthians 7:2). Sex within marriage is good (Genesis 2:24; Matthew 19:5; Ephesians 5:31). Sexual intercourse was actually one of God's first commands to Adam and Eve: "Be fruitful and multiply and fill the earth" (Genesis 1:28). So important is sex in the marriage relationship, the apostle Paul said,

that husbands and wives should always be available to each other (1 Corinthians 7:1-5). The apostles urged all Christians to abstain from fornication (Acts 15:20; 1 Corinthians 6:13,18).

2. *The importance of rest.* The principle of rest is first laid out early in the Genesis account: "On the seventh day God finished his work that he had done, and he rested on the seventh day from all his work that he had done" (Genesis 2:2). In Exodus 20:9-10, God instructs His people, "Six days you shall labor, and do all your work, but the seventh day is a Sabbath to the Lord your God. On it you shall not do any work." Even though we do not have a Sabbath-day requirement today, as did the ancient Jews, the principle of rest is still important (see Hebrews 4:9-11). Jesus urged His followers to take time to rest (Mark 6:31-32; see also Psalm 23:2; Matthew 11:26-30; Philippians 4:6-7).

Questions for Reflection and Discussion

1. God is the Strong One (*Elohim*). What does that mean to you personally?
2. You are created in the image of God. What does that mean to you? What difference might that make in how you live your life?
3. Do you make an effort to honor God's principle of rest each week? Why or why not? How do you do that?

Day 2

God's Creation of Adam and Eve

Genesis 2:4-25

Scripture Reading and Insights

Begin by reading Genesis 2:4-25 in your favorite Bible. Read with the anticipation that the Holy Spirit has something important to teach you today (see Psalm 119:105).

In yesterday's reading, we focused on God's six days of creation. In this chapter we will focus specifically on God's creation of human beings. With your Bible still accessible, consider the following insights on the biblical text.

Genesis 2:4-6

These are the generations (2:4): Means "This is the history of..." or "This is the account of..." Note that chapter 2 is not intended as a second account of the creation. Rather, it is a further expansion of the creation account in Genesis 1.

In the day that the Lord God (2:4): Means "when the Lord God."

No bush...no small plant (2:5): Green plants appeared on the third day (1:11-12), so this reference to bushes and small plants must refer specifically to those that require cultivation to grow.

The Lord (2:4): This is the term *Yahweh*, which occurs more than 6800 times in the Old Testament. The name conveys the idea of eternal self-existence (see Exodus 3:14-15). *Yahweh* never came into being at a point in time, for He has always existed. He was never born, and He will never die. He does not grow older, for He is beyond the realm of time. To know *Yahweh* is to know the Eternal One. The name is often used in contexts of God's covenant faithfulness to His people.

No man (2:5): This sets the stage for what is to come. A large part of the rest of Genesis 2 deals with the creation of the first man and woman.

To work the ground (2:5): Adam is assigned work prior to the Fall. This means that working is not a penalty for sin. God intended Adam to work from the very beginning.

A mist was going up (2:6): This may refer to the condensation and evaporation that takes place during temperature changes from night to day. Or perhaps it refers to subterranean springs that rise to ground level. If the second view is correct, "mist" may better be translated as "flow."

Genesis 2:7-17

Formed (2:7): Just as a potter fashions and molds clay, so God fashioned and molded man. The word pictures a master craftsman working to shape a work of art to which he gives life (1 Corinthians 15:45).

Dust of the ground (2:7): There is a word play here. The Hebrew word for "man" is *adam*, and the ground is *adama*. It reads like this: "God formed the *adam* (man) out of dust from the *adama* (ground)."

Breath of life (2:7): Man's life came directly from God. Just as man came alive as a result of God's imparting of the breath of life, so the animals too have the breath of life in them (see Genesis 1:21,24). The difference between human beings and animals is that human beings were created in the image of God and are therefore the noblest part of God's creation (Genesis 1:26).

Garden in Eden (2:8): Eden literally means "luxurious," "pleasurable," "delightful," or "bliss." God placed Adam and Eve in the garden for both divine fellowship and physical blessing. Eden is likely in the general area of modern Iraq (ancient Mesopotamia). Two of the four rivers mentioned in our passage—the Tigris and the Euphrates—help us make this identification. See Major Themes.

In the east (2:8): East from the perspective of the author of Genesis (Moses).

Tree of life (2:9): A real tree that has special properties that sustain one with eternal life (see Genesis 3:22-24). We encounter the tree of life again in the future eternal city of heaven known as the New Jerusalem (Revelation 22:2). That Adam and Eve had access to the tree of life indicates that God's original design for them was life.

Tree of the knowledge of good and evil (2:9): This carries the idea, "the tree of the knowledge of the difference between good and evil." It refers to moral or ethical knowledge.

A river flowed out of Eden (2:10): This river that flowed out of Eden split into four rivers. Interestingly, other verses in Scripture use water and rivers as symbolic of God's presence (see Psalm 46:4; Ezekiel 47:1-12; Zechariah 14:8; Revelation 22:1-2). This may be the case with the rivers mentioned in the garden of Eden.

Pishon (2:11): An unknown territory.

Havilah (2:11): An unknown territory that is apparently rich in gold and bdellium and onyx. Pishon and Havilah and other such localities relate to pre-flood geology. Following the flood, the terrain was significantly altered, so we no longer know precisely where they are located.

Bdellium (2:12): A precious and sweet-smelling resin similar to myrrh.

Onyx stone (2:12): A precious jewel. Gold and onyx were later used for decorating both the tabernacle and the temple (see Exodus 25:3-9; 1 Chronicles 29:2).

Gihon (2:13): A small stream in the Jerusalem area (1 Kings 1:33).

Land of Cush (2:13): Likely refers to a geographical territory somewhere in Mesopotamia (Genesis 10:7).

Tigris (2:14): A major river in Mesopotamia.

Assyria (2:14): A nation of Semitic people who lived along the Tigris River in what is now the northern part of Iraq (ancient northern Mesopotamia).

Euphrates (2:14): A river in Mesopotamia. Also called "the river" (see the ESV footnote at Exodus 23:31) and "the great river" (Deuteronomy 1:7), it is almost 1800 miles long. It begins in modern-day Turkey, heads toward the Mediterranean Sea, and then turns south, flows more than 1000 miles to eventually converge with the Tigris River, and flows into the Persian Gulf. Many ancient cities, including Ur and Babylon, were located along the river.

Work it and keep it (2:15): God instructed Adam to cultivate the garden, keep it (guard over it), eat its fruit (except from the tree of the knowledge of good and evil), and name the animals.

The Lord God commanded the man (2:16): The tasks assigned to Adam were not optional. God, as the Creator, has the right to command the creature.

"You shall surely die" (2:17): This refers to immediate spiritual death (separation from God). Physical death would come later.

Genesis 2:18-25

"It is not good that the man should be alone" (2:18): This is God's first negative statement about the creation (compare with 1:31). This statement indicates that man was created by God as a social creature. He was never intended to go it alone. He needs companionship.

"Helper" (2:18): A partner or ally (see 1 Corinthians 11:9). See Major Themes.

"Fit for him" (2:18): "Suitable for him," or "corresponding to him." She is to be a perfect complement to him, made in the image of God just as he was (Genesis 1:26-27).

He would call them... The man gave names (2:19-20): The naming of things in biblical times implied one's authority over them. That Adam named the various animals implies his position over them (see Genesis 1:26).

Deep sleep (2:21): Adam was knocked out cold before he woke up and saw his knock-out wife. (The Hebrew is particularly strong about Adam's response when he first saw the woman.)

Rib (2:22): This Hebrew word can be translated "side." In the present context, however, it clearly means "rib." The fact that Eve was created from a rib of Adam is a metaphorical picture of the unity and side-by-side nature of their marriage relationship.

"Bone of my bones and flesh of my flesh" (2:23): Adam was asleep when God took out his rib, so God must have told Adam what had transpired.

"Woman" (2:23): There is a word play here. "Woman" is the Hebrew term *'ishshah*, while man is *'ish*. Our text says something like this: "I will call her *'ishshah* (woman) because she was taken out of *'ish* (man)."

Man shall leave his father and his mother (2:24): A man's primary loyalty in life is now to his wife, not his parents. The man leaves one family to start another. This is not intended as disrespect to parents, for one can still respect parents while making one's wife the object of primary loyalty.

One flesh (2:24): Husband and wife are intimately identified in marriage. It is the closest possible union. Notice that marriage is between one man and one woman. Marriage is thus to be monogamous and heterosexual. Jesus indicated the marriage relationship was intended to be permanent—an inseparable union (Mark 10:9).

Naked and were not ashamed (2:25): Shame did not surface until they sinned against God. They were in a state of moral innocence until they sinned.

Major Themes

1. *Helper*. The woman was created as a helper to man (Genesis 2:18). Contrary to what some have said, the term "helper" does not refer to a servant. After all, the Holy Spirit is called a helper in the New Testament (John 14:16,26; 15:26; 16:7). The word carries the idea of "one who supports." Adam was incomplete and inadequate in himself. He needed a life-companion, a helper, and an equal to walk side by side with him. Woman was made by God to meet man's deficiency.
2. *God dwelling among us*. God walked with Adam and Eve in the Garden of Eden (Genesis 1–3). Once sin entered the world, God dwelt among the Israelites by means of the Jewish tabernacle (Exodus 40:34) and later the temple (2 Samuel 22:7). In New Testament times, God lived (or "tabernacled") among us in the person of Jesus (John 1:14). Today, Christians are the temple of the Holy Spirit

(1 Corinthians 3:16; 6:19). In the New Jerusalem, God will dwell with His people face-to-face (Revelation 22:4).

3. *Death from disobedience.* In Genesis 2:17 God warned Adam that he would die the same day he ate of the forbidden fruit. This does not contradict Genesis 5:5, which tells us that Adam lived to the age of 930 years. When Adam and Eve sinned, they did not die that day physically, but they did die spiritually. The word "death" carries the idea of separation. Spiritual death involves the separation of the human being from God. When Adam and Eve ate the forbidden fruit, they were immediately spiritually separated from God. The moment of their sin, they became "dead in…trespasses and sins" (Ephesians 2:1-3). Their spiritual separation from God eventually led to their physical deaths.

Digging Deeper with Cross-References

God's creation of human beings—Genesis 1:26; 5:2; Deuteronomy 32:6; Job 10:8; 33:4; Psalms 8:5; 95:6; 100:3; 119:73; 139:13; Ecclesiastes 12:1; Isaiah 42:5; 44:2; 45:12; 64:8; Jeremiah 1:5; Malachi 2:10; Matthew 19:4; Mark 10:6; Acts 17:26

The breath of life—Genesis 6:17; 7:22; Job 27:3; 33:4; Ecclesiastes 3:19; Isaiah 2:22; 42:5; Lamentations 4:20; Ezekiel 37:5,9; Acts 17:25

Life Lessons

1. *God's call to obedience.* God called Adam and Eve to obedience, just as He calls you and me to obedience. Scripture reveals that obedience to God brings blessing (Luke 11:28), long life (1 Kings 3:14; John 8:51), happiness (Psalms 112:1; 119:56), peace (Proverbs 1:33), and a state of well-being (Jeremiah 7:23; see also Exodus 19:5; Leviticus

26:3-4; Deuteronomy 4:40; 12:28; 28:1-14; Joshua 1:8; 1 Chronicles 22:13; Isaiah 1:19). As James put it, "Be doers of the word, and not hearers only, deceiving yourselves" (James 1:22). Obedience to God's Word is nonnegotiable.

2. *The marriage relationship*. Scripture says much about the nature of the marriage relationship. For example, men are to be understanding of their wives, showing them honor (1 Peter 3:7). Men are to love their wives as Christ loved the church (Ephesians 5:25), "hold fast" to their wives (verse 31), and love their wives as they love themselves (verse 33). The husband "should give to his wife her conjugal rights, and likewise the wife to her husband" (1 Corinthians 7:3). Wives are the helpers of their husbands (Genesis 2:18). Wives are to be subject to their husbands (1 Peter 3:1), for "the husband is the head of the wife" (Ephesians 5:23). Husbands and wives—indeed, all Christians—are to be "submitting to one another out of reverence for Christ" (verse 21).

Questions for Reflection and Discussion

1. You were directly created by God instead of evolving from apes. How does that affect the way you live your life?
2. If you are married, how does the fact that you are "one flesh" with your spouse affect the way you live (for example, in terms of fidelity)?
3. If you are married, how do you and your spouse view the term "helper" in the wife's role in marriage? Has what you've learned today help clarify things? If so, how?

Day 3

Temptation, Sin, and Judgment

Genesis 3

Scripture Reading and Insights

Begin by reading Genesis 3 in your favorite Bible. As you read, remember that the Word of God is alive and working in you (Hebrews 4:12).

In yesterday's reading, we were introduced to God's creation of human beings. In today's lesson, we will focus our attention on the temptation, fall, and subsequent judgment of the first man and woman. With your Bible still accessible, consider the following insights on the biblical text.

Genesis 3:1-7

The serpent (3:1): The serpent is characterized by treachery, deceitfulness, venom, and murderous proclivities. Satan speaks through the serpent (2 Corinthians 11:3,14; Revelation 12:9; 20:2). See Major Themes.

More crafty (3:1): Means "more shrewd," or "more cunning."

"Did God actually say?" (3:1): Satan is a master at twisting Scripture. He used the same technique when trying to tempt Jesus to sin in Matthew 4 but failed.

"We may eat" (3:2): Eve did not faithfully reflect God's words when speaking with the serpent. God's reference to "surely eat" (2:16) became "may eat" in Eve's words. She also added "neither shall you touch it" to God's command against eating the forbidden fruit.

"Lest you die" (3:3): When Adam and Eve sinned, they did not die that day physically, but they did die spiritually (see Ephesians 2:1-3). The Hebrew word translated "death" carries the idea of separation. Spiritual death involves the separation of the human being from God. When Adam and Eve partook of the forbidden fruit, they were immediately separated from God in a spiritual sense. Their consequent action of trying to hide from God in the Garden of Eden indicates their awareness of this spiritual separation.

"Surely not die" (3:4): The serpent was crafty. In one sense he was right—Adam and Eve would surely not physically die if they partook of the fruit. However, as noted above, Adam and Eve did die spiritually when they ate the fruit. Notice also that Satan (through the serpent) earlier questioned God's word—"Did God actually say?" Now he outright denies it: "You will not surely die."

"God knows that when you eat of it your eyes will be opened, and you will be like God" (3:5): The serpent implies that God is sinister—that He is abusing Eve. He's trying to hold her back. He suggests that eating the fruit will bring a great advantage—"You will be like God."

Good for food...a delight to the eyes...desired to make one wise (3:6): Notice the close connection here with 1 John 2:16. The woman saw that the fruit of the tree was good for food (this involves the desires of the flesh). The fruit was pleasing to the eye (the desires of the eyes). The fruit was desirable for gaining wisdom (the pride of life). Times may have changed, but the nature of temptation has not.

She took of its fruit (3:6): One would think that such a noble creature as man would do no wrong. But soon after their creation, Adam and Eve sinned against God and catapulted the entire human race into sin (Romans 5:12).

She took of its fruit and ate...and he ate (3:6): Note that Eve was deceived into eating the fruit (2 Corinthians 11:3; 1 Timothy 2:14; Revelation 12:9), whereas Adam sinned knowingly (see 1 Timothy 2:14-15).

The eyes of both were opened (3:7): Their new knowledge was that of their own nakedness.

Loincloths (3:7): The loincloths they designed were sufficient to cover their bodies but not their shame.

Genesis 3:8-13

Heard the sound of the LORD God (3:8): The almost casual way in which God walked in the garden may indicate that this was not the first time He had done this. The assumption that God had repeatedly visited the garden is quite feasible. An appearance of God in Old Testament times is called a theophany.

Hid themselves (3:8): When Adam and Eve sinned, they immediately sensed an alienation from God. They hid from God not because God had changed in any way. Rather, they were the ones who had changed. They chose to disobey God. Eden had been a place of joy and fellowship with God. Now it became a place of fear and hiding from God.

The LORD God called to the man (3:9): As he was walking along, the Lord called to Adam and Eve, "Where are you?" God in His omniscience knew where they were. But he was nevertheless appealing to them, seeking through tenderness and love to draw them out. The real question was, why were they hiding?

"I was afraid" (3:10): Previously Adam enjoyed a carefree life of fellowship with God. Now, following sin, he was afraid and felt alienated. Sin always exacts a high price!

"Who told you?" (3:11): A rhetorical question. God is omniscient and already knew what was going on. God was drawing Adam out on what he had done.

"The woman whom you gave" (3:12): Adam passed the buck (or blame) to Eve, who had given him the fruit. Adam has now committed three wrong choices. First he knowingly ate of the forbidden fruit. Then he chose to hide from God. Now he tries to blame Eve. Adam is woefully off track at this point.

"What is this that you have done" (3:13): Adam and Eve were held responsible for their free choice to sin.

"The serpent deceived me" (3:13): Like Adam, Eve passed the buck (or blame) by saying, "The serpent deceived me, and I ate."

Genesis 3:14-19

"Enmity...between your offspring and her offspring" (3:15): The

serpent's offspring are the spiritual descendants of Satan (John 8:44; Ephesians 2:2). The woman's offspring refers to people in the family of God. A single person from the woman's offspring—the divine Messiah, Jesus Christ—would deal a death blow to Satan's head at the cross of Calvary (see John 12:31; 16:11; see Hebrews 2:14; 1 John 3:8). Satan, however, would succeed in bruising Christ's heel—that is, Satan would cause Christ to suffer.

"Multiply your pain in childbearing" (3:16): The woman's judgment related to that which is unique to women alone—the bearing of children. From this time forward, pain would predominate in the delivery process.

"Your desire shall be for your husband" (3:16): Some believe this refers to the wife's attraction to her husband, including sexual attraction. A more likely and more widely held view is that the wife will have a desire to control her husband.

"He shall rule over you" (3:16): This means, "Though your desire will be to control or 'lord it over' your husband, he in fact will rule over you by divine design." God's judgment of Eve pertains to two things most fulfilling to a woman—the roles of wife and mother. As a wife, she will have a desire to control her husband but instead will be ruled by him. As a mother, she will experience painful childbirths. The twofold judgment involves servitude and pain.

"Because you have listened to the voice of your wife" (3:17): One of Adam's failures in the Fall was his abdication of responsibility for leadership. Instead of obeying God and leading his wife, he disobeyed God and followed his wife's lead (by eating the fruit). In the Fall, then, God's intended order of authority was reversed. Eve listened to the serpent instead of Adam. Adam listened to Eve instead of God.

"Cursed is the ground" (3:17): The Fall had consequences not only for humanity. The entire cosmos was affected. The ground (or earth) was cursed. This is the reason for Paul's statement in Romans 8:20, "The creation was subjected to futility."

"In pain" (3:17): Man's work would now be exhausting. He would experience more pain in his work. Adam would be able to work and eat only "by the sweat of his brow."

"Till you return to the ground" (3:19): Adam was to sustain life from the ground by working the garden to produce food. Now, as a result of sin, he will die and be placed in the ground, returning to the dust from which he was created.

Genesis 3:20-24

Called his wife's name Eve (3:20): To name someone or something in ancient times implied having authority over the one named (see Genesis 17:5; 2 Kings 23:34; Daniel 1:7). Adam names his wife Eve, thereby demonstrating his headship over her.

"Tree of life" (3:22): This is a tree that bestows continuing life (Genesis 2:9; 3:22-24; see also Revelation 22:2).

God sent him out from the garden of Eden (3:23): God confirmed His mercy to Adam and Eve by driving them out of the garden—a judgment for sin to be sure, but an act of mercy as well. How horrible it would have been to eat of the tree of life and live forever in bodies of sin.

Placed the cherubim (3:24): The cherubim are depicted in Scripture as powerful and majestic angelic creatures who surround God's throne and defend His holiness from any contamination by sin (Exodus 25:18,20; Ezekiel 1:1-18). They are portrayed as being indescribably beautiful and powerful spirit-beings of the highest order (Ezekiel 28:12-13,17).

Major Themes

1. *Serpent.* The word "serpent" literally means "snake." The book of Revelation informs us that the serpent is Satan (12:9; 20:2; see also 2 Corinthians 11:3). Since Satan, as the serpent, tempted our first parents, we infer that Satan's fall from heaven took place before Adam and Eve appeared in the garden of Eden. Yet it must have also taken place sometime later than Genesis 1:31, where we are told that the entire creation was good. This means that Satan fell sometime between Genesis 1:31 and 3:1. Based on Isaiah 14:13-14 and Ezekiel 28:11-15, we conclude that Satan's fall

was rooted in self-inflated pride as he sought to challenge the authority of God Himself.

2. *God and judgment.* God is a God of love, grace, and mercy, but He is also a God of judgment in the face of unrepentant sin. Judgment fell on Adam and Eve because of their disobedience to God (Genesis 3). In the New Testament, judgment fell on the Jews for rejecting Christ (Matthew 21:43), on Ananias and Sapphira for lying to God (Acts 5), on Herod for self-exalting pride (Acts 12:21-23), and on Christians in Corinth for irreverence regarding the Lord's Supper (1 Corinthians 11:29-32; 1 John 5:16). Christians will one day stand before the judgment seat of Christ (1 Corinthians 3:12-15; 2 Corinthians 5:10). Unbelievers will be judged at the great white throne judgment (Revelation 20:11-15).

Digging Deeper with Cross-References

The work of Satan—Genesis 3:1-5; John 8:44; Acts 5:3; 1 Corinthians 7:5; 2 Corinthians 11:14; 1 Timothy 3:6; James 3:13-16; 1 Peter 5:8; Revelation 12:10

The effects of sin—Psalms 9:16; 141:10; Proverbs 3:35; 5:22; 12:13,21; 13:5-6; 29:6; Isaiah 57:21; Romans 5:12; 6:23; 7:14-15; 1 Corinthians 3:3; Ephesians 4:17-19

Life Lessons

1. *Alienation following sin.* One of the natural results of sin is a sense of alienation from God. Our text tells us that when Adam and Eve sensed God approaching in the garden of Eden, they "hid themselves from the presence of the Lord God among the trees of the garden" (Genesis 3:8). This hiding was rooted in shame, remorse, confusion, guilt, and fear that accompanies rebellion against God. We tend to respond in the same way. Of course, there is no place to

hide from God (Psalm 139:1-2,7-8). The single best step to take after falling into sin is to confess that sin to God so that fellowship with God is restored (1 John 1:9).

2. *Making excuses.* People tend to make excuses when they sin. When God confronted Adam about his sin, Adam said, "The woman whom you gave to be with me, she gave me fruit of the tree, and I ate" (Genesis 3:12). When God confronted Eve, she said, "The serpent deceived me, and I ate" (verse 13). We tend to make excuses as well (see Luke 14:16-24). When we sin, the best thing to do is to be honest before God and admit our failures (see Psalms 32:5; 51:3-4,6).

Questions for Reflection and Discussion

1. Do you ever struggle with the desires of the flesh, the desires of the eyes, or the pride of life? What steps do you want to take today to deal with any specific issues?
2. Do you presently feel any sense of alienation from God? If so, what immediate steps could you take to put an end to it?
3. Have you ever been tempted to pass the buck after doing something wrong? Give an example.

Day 4

The Beginnings of Human Civilization

Genesis 4–5

Scripture Reading and Insights

Begin by reading Genesis 4–5 in your favorite Bible. As you read, remember that the Word of God is alive and working in you (Hebrews 4:12).

In the previous lesson, we studied the temptation, fall, and subsequent judgment of the first man and woman. In today's lesson, we focus attention on Cain's murder of Abel as well as the genealogy from Adam to Noah. With your Bible still accessible, consider the following insights on the biblical text.

Genesis 4:1-7

Knew Eve his wife (4:1): A euphemism for sexual relations.

Cain (4:1): The firstborn son of Adam and Eve. Cain's name apparently means "spear."

"I have gotten" (4:1): There is a Hebrew play on words in this verse. "Cain" is the Hebrew *qayin.* "I have gotten" is the Hebrew *qaniti.* We might put it this way: "She conceived and bore *qayin* (Cain), saying *qaniti* (I have gotten) a man."

"With the help of the Lord" (4:1): Eve recognized that God is the ultimate source of life (see Acts 17:25).

Abel (4:2): The second son of Adam and Eve. His name means "breath" or "vanity," reflecting the transitory nature of his existence (see Ecclesiastes 1:2).

Keeper of sheep... worker of the ground (4:2): Both honorable professions in biblical days.

An offering of the fruit of the ground (4:3): Cain apparently brought this offering with an attitude of unbelief, which was displeasing to God (see Hebrews 11:4,6).

Abel and his offering (4:4): Abel gave not only the firstborn of his flock but even the choicest of the firstborn. In other words, Abel gave the "best of the best" that was in his possession. Abel also offered his offering by faith.

The Lord had regard for Abel (4:4): The Lord looked favorably upon Abel.

Cain and his offering (4:5): Cain brought an offering of "the fruit of the ground" (verse 3). One gets the feeling that Cain routinely gathered some fruit and offered it to the Lord to fulfill his obligation. God had apparently given special revelation regarding the type of offerings He expected. Cain may have ignored God's directions on the matter and brought what he wanted to bring. Some expositors suggest that perhaps an offering from the ground was unacceptable because the ground had just been cursed as a result of Adam and Eve's sin (Genesis 3:17-19).

Had no regard (4:5): The Lord did not look favorably on Cain or his offering.

Cain was very angry (4:5): Cain showed his sinful state by being angry at God. All would have been well had Cain repented and then offered the animal sacrifices God had evidently required. But his heart seems to have been hardened toward God in bitterness.

His face fell (4:5): The expression on Cain's face showed what he was feeling on the inside.

The Lord said to Cain (4:6): God had earlier sought out Adam and Eve when they sinned. Now God seeks out Cain for the same reason. Adam and Eve had given evasive answers when God asked them questions, and now Cain does the same thing.

"Will you not be accepted?" (4:7): Cain had a choice to make. If he responded properly and appropriately, his fellowship with God would

be restored. However, sin was crouching nearby, ready to pounce like a lion attacking its prey. The Hebrew word for "crouching" is identical to a Babylonian word used to describe an evil demon crouching at the door of a building, ready to pounce on the people inside. One wonders whether Cain was even now pondering the possibility of murdering Abel.

Genesis 4:8-16

Cain... killed him (4:8): Sin overcame Cain, and he murdered his own brother. This is the first instance in the Bible of one human being taking the life of another. How awful that this first murder was the result of a conflict about religious practice. See Matthew 23:35; Luke 11:51; Hebrews 12:24; 1 John 3:11-12; and Jude 11.

"Am I my brother's keeper?" (4:9): Cain compounded his sin. He not only murdered Abel but also lied to God about it. Cain's indifference to the murder shows the depth of his sinful attitude. In Cain, sin ran its full gamut. Notice also that there is a play on words in this verse. Abel had been the keeper of the sheep. Now Cain asks if he is his brother's keeper.

"Blood is crying to me" (4:10): A figure of speech indicating that the all-knowing God knew exactly what had transpired.

"Cursed from the ground" (4:11): This would have been particularly devastating to Cain—a farmer.

"Whoever finds me will kill me" (4:14): By now the earth's population had increased. Cain would be a wanderer, so many people might be willing to prey on him.

The Lord put a mark on Cain (4:15): This mark represented God's sovereign protection of Cain. (We read about other protective marks in Exodus 12:13; Ezekiel 9:4-6; and Revelation 7:3.)

Land of Nod (4:16): The word Nod resembles a Hebrew word meaning "wanderer" or "one in exile."

Genesis 4:17-26

Cain knew his wife (4:17): Where did Cain get his wife? Adam and Eve had other children after the births of Cain, Abel, and Seth. Genesis

5:4 tells us, "The days of Adam after he fathered Seth were 800 years; and he had other sons and daughters." Eight hundred years is a long time to be fruitful and multiply (Genesis 1:28)! Adam and Eve were the first man and woman, and God had commanded them (and their descendants) to be fruitful and multiply, so we can reasonably conclude that Cain married one of his many sisters. And given their long life spans, he could have married a niece or even a grandniece. Apparently, in the early years of the human race, no genetic defects had yet developed as a result of the fall of man. By the time of Abraham, God had not yet declared this kind of marriage to be contrary to His will (see Genesis 20:12). Laws governing incest did not become enacted until the time of Moses (Leviticus 18:7-17; 20:11-12,14,17,20-21).

Lamech took two wives (4:19): Lamech was the fifth in descent from Cain. He feared neither God nor man (see Genesis 5:28-29). This is the first recorded instance of bigamy in the Bible.

"Seventy-seven fold" (4:24): Lamech was an ungodly boaster. He indicated that unlike Cain, he didn't need any help from God. If anyone tried to kill him, the response from Lamech would be catastrophic. Notice the contrast between Lamech's arrogant pronouncement of seventy-sevenfold revenge and Jesus's seventy-sevenfold policy on forgiveness (Matthew 18:21-22).

Seth (4:25): The third son of Adam and Eve (Genesis 5:3). Eve considered him a replacement for Abel, her son whom Cain had killed. Seth means "the appointed one"—that is, the substitute for the now-dead Abel. God gave Adam and Eve a godly son through whom He would carry on the redemptive line leading to Jesus's birth (Luke 3:38).

Call upon the name of the Lord (4:26): With sin escalating planet-wide, many called on the Lord for mercy and grace.

Genesis 5:1-32

Book of the generations (5:1): A written family history. Chapter 5 mentions ten families. This essentially records the messianic line from Adam to Noah. Notice how God's earlier command to be fruitful and multiply is being fulfilled (Genesis 1:28).

Fathered a son in his own likeness (5:3): Because of the fall in the garden of Eden, the likeness was now sinful.

All the days that Adam lived were 930 years (5:5): There was great longevity in these early Bible times. Nothing in the context of Genesis 5 indicates that this chapter is to be taken less than literally. We are left to conclude that people really did live that long during the early years of humanity. Why this was the case? Many have suggested that prior to the flood, a water canopy surrounded the earth, protecting its inhabitants from harmful radiation in outer space. Also, before the flood, people were primarily vegetarians rather than meat eaters (see Genesis 9:3), and perhaps this too contributed to the longer lives. All of this points to the truth that human beings are "fearfully and wonderfully made" (Psalm 139:14).

Seth...Enosh...Kenan...(5:6-32): For each of the remaining patriarchs, we are told four things: his name, his age when his first son was born, the length of his remaining life, and his age at the time of death.

Enoch (5:22-24): The one exception to "and he died" is Enoch. The eldest son of Jared, Enoch walked (lived day by day) with God. Enoch bypassed death and was taken up by God into heaven. (Other divine "takings" are referenced in 2 Kings 2:1,11; Psalms 49:15; 73:24.)

Methuselah (5:27): He holds the distinction as the longest-living human being—969 years.

Major Themes

1. *Longevity.* There was great longevity in early biblical times. Adam lived to the age of 930 years, Seth lived 912 years, Lamech lived 777 years, Noah lived to 950 years, and Shem lived 600 years (see Genesis 5). Notice, though, that a bit later Abraham lived to only 175 years and Moses lived only 120 years. Why the shortened life spans? Many theologians attribute it to the Fall (Genesis 3). After the Fall, each successive generation seems to have had shorter and shorter life spans. This clearly shows a connection between sin and death (see Romans 6:23; 8:22). Others

attribute the shorter life spans to the removal of the water canopy that surrounded the earth prior to the Flood.

2. *Calling on the name of the Lord.* Genesis 4:26 reveals that as people recognized their inherent sinfulness and no human means of appeasing God's wrath against sin, some began to call on the Lord for mercy and grace. In Bible times people called on the Lord for various reasons. They called on Him for salvation (Romans 10:13), for help in times of trouble (Psalm 50:15), and for deliverance from enemies (2 Samuel 22:4). One could call on the Lord for whatever reason (Deuteronomy 4:7). By the time of the flood, however, sin had run rampant on a global basis, and Noah and his family were the only ones deemed worthy of salvation.

Digging Deeper with Cross-References

Death—Genesis 2:16-17; 3:19; 49:33; Deuteronomy 31:16; Job 18:13-14; 30:23; Psalms 23:4; 116:15; Ecclesiastes 3:1-2; 7:2; 8:8; Isaiah 25:8; Ezekiel 18:23; 33:11; Luke 12:20; Romans 5:12; 6:23; 1 Corinthians 15:26,56; Philippians 1:21; Hebrews 9:27; Revelation 1:18; 21:3-4

God's attitude toward offerings—1 Samuel 15:22; Psalm 51:17; Proverbs 21:3; Amos 5:21; see also Romans 12:1; Hebrews 13:15

Life Lessons

1. *Sin crouching at the door.* Genesis 4:7 refers to sin crouching at the door. Here sin is personified, waiting to pounce on a victim like a wild beast, such as a lion. It lies in wait for precisely the right moment to strike. We can infer an important lesson from this verse—we always need to have our spiritual radar on, watching for the sudden and unexpected attack of the temptation to sin. We must be on guard against sin.

2. *Walking with God.* Genesis 5:22 tells us, "Enoch walked with God." The only other man in the Bible that enjoyed this kind of intimacy with God was Noah (see Genesis 6:9). We may not walk with God in the same sense as Enoch and Noah, but Scripture says much about our spiritual walk. We ought to walk honestly (1 Thessalonians 4:11-12) and in a way that is worthy of the Lord (Colossians 1:10). We should walk humbly with God (Micah 6:8). We should have a godly walk characterized by integrity (Proverbs 20:7). We should walk in dependence on the Holy Spirit (Galatians 6:8) and seek to walk as Jesus Himself walked (1 John 2:6).

Questions for Reflection and Discussion

1. What have you learned about the nature of sin in this lesson that motivates you to put up your guard?
2. Have you personally embraced Jesus's seventy-sevenfold policy on forgiveness in your lifestyle? Do you want to make any resolutions in this regard?
3. What steps do you need to take to enhance your personal walk with God?

Day 5

God Instructs Noah to Build an Ark

Genesis 6

Scripture Reading and Insights

Begin by reading Genesis 6 in your favorite Bible. As you read, remember that those who hear and obey the Word of God are truly blessed (Psalm 119:2; Luke 11:28; Revelation 1:3).

In yesterday's reading, we studied the account of Cain's murder of Abel as well as the genealogy from Adam to Noah. In today's lesson, we focus attention on the emergence of great wickedness during Noah's time and Noah's instruction from God to build an ark. With your Bible still accessible, consider the following insights on the biblical text.

Genesis 6:1-8

Man began to multiply (6:1): The population of humanity on earth had increased greatly, due in no small part to the tremendous longevity of human beings during those early biblical times.

The sons of God... the daughters of man (6:2): See Major Themes. The sons of God could be...

- evil angels cohabiting with human women
- evil angels possessing human men who then cohabit with women
- godly men intermingling with ungodly women
- kings enjoying their royal harems

"My Spirit shall not abide in man forever" (6:3): This is a difficult verse. It is more often translated, "My Spirit shall not contend with man forever," or "My Spirit shall not strive with man forever." Perhaps the best interpretation is that the Holy Spirit was striving to call people to repentance and righteousness, particularly through human vessels such as Enoch and Noah. We know that the Spirit of Christ—that is, the Holy Spirit—spoke through all the Old Testament prophets (1 Peter 1:11). This being so, perhaps Genesis 6:3 is telling us that the Holy Spirit's preaching through the prophet Noah would not last forever, especially for the people of Noah's day, for the flood that would destroy the wicked would arrive in 120 years.

"His days shall be 120 years" (6:3): Refers not to man's life span, but to the time God would allow before He sent the flood on humankind. God thus provided plenty of time for humans to repent before sending judgment. This was a period of grace before the flood was to commence (Isaiah 55:6-7). Unfortunately, during the 120-year period of Noah's time, only Noah and his family were righteous.

One cannot avoid relating all this to the Olivet discourse, where Jesus speaks of the future. He affirmed, "As were the days of Noah, so will be the coming of the Son of Man" (Matthew 24:37; see also Luke 17:26). The analogy is a good one, for people were carousing and remaining unprepared for 120 years in the days of Noah, just as people will be prior to the second coming of Christ. Just as it was in the days of Noah, people living in the days prior to the second coming will be engaged in life as usual, having no concept that a judgment is imminent. Just as Noah had warned the people of his day and was ignored (2 Peter 2:5), so Christian leaders today warn people about the future and are ignored.

Nephilim (6:4): Mighty men, perhaps mighty military men, with great size and great strength. See Major Themes.

Wickedness of man... every intention of the thoughts of his heart was only evil continually (6:5): The sin of humankind was both extensive and intensive. That is, it was global, and the sins were particularly vile. Humankind had passed a critical threshold of degradation. Notice the reference to thoughts. Sin is first conceived in the mind. It begins in the thought life. As Jeremiah 17:9 puts it, "The heart is deceitful above all things, and desperately sick; who can understand it?" Jesus likewise said that sin emerges "out of the abundance of the heart" (Matthew 12:34). Jesus also said, "For from within, out of the heart of man, come evil thoughts, sexual immorality, theft, murder, adultery, coveting, wickedness, deceit, sensuality, envy, slander, pride, foolishness. All these evil things come from within, and they defile a person" (Mark 7:21-23).

The Lord regretted (6:6): The Lord was sorry. He was deeply troubled and sorrowful. See Major Themes.

"I will blot out" (6:7): God would exterminate sinful humanity and all animals.

Noah found favor (6:8): The Hebrew word for "favor" is typically used in contexts of a superior, strong person showing favor to a weaker, inferior person. Noah likely found favor with God because he was righteous and blameless and walked with God (verse 9).

Genesis 6:9-16

Generations (6:9): The family record of Noah and his sons—Shem, Ham, and Japheth (verse 10).

Noah was a righteous man, blameless (6:9): Noah was not sinless (no man is—Romans 3:23; 5:12-14), but he was a man of spiritual integrity. He sought to obey God in all things. That he was righteous means that he lived by God's righteous standards. He "walked with God," meaning that he fellowshipped and obeyed God on a day-to-day basis.

Corrupt...corrupt...corrupted (6:11-12): This kind of repetition in biblical literature is significant. Humanity had truly become corrupt in the time of Noah.

"End of all flesh" (6:13): All living beings on the face of the earth would be killed except Noah, his family, and the animals brought aboard the ark.

"I will destroy them with the earth" (6:13): Just as the sin of Adam and Eve led to their expulsion from the garden of Eden (Genesis 3), so now the unrestrained sins of humanity would lead to their expulsion from the earth.

"Ark" (6:14-15): The ark was probably constructed from either cypress or pine ("gopher wood" in the Bible) according to the specifications God gave Noah (6:14-16). It was a rather large vessel—about 450 feet long, 75 feet wide, and 45 feet high. It had three stories, which means it had plenty of room to carry a large body of animals (verse 16). Noah had to build the ark by faith because no catastrophe of this magnitude had yet occurred in earth's history. Interestingly, the Hebrew word for "ark" was also used in reference to the basket that the babe Moses would later be put in. Moses's basket was coated with pitch, just as Noah's ark had been (see Exodus 2:3).

"Make a roof" (6:16): To prevent the water from coming into the ark and sinking it.

"Finish it to a cubit above" (6:16): Perhaps the ark had a series of small widows encircling its perimeter. This would allow light and air into the ark.

Genesis 6:17-22

"Flood of waters" (6:17): This flood was universal, covering the whole face of the earth (see Genesis 7:19-20; more on this in the next chapter). Interestingly, some pagan accounts of a universal flood add embellishments to the biblical account. For example, tablet 11 of the Gilgamesh Epic (discovered in ancient Mesopotamia and named after the principal character, King Gilgamesh) speaks of a great flood that came on the earth by wrathful gods. It also speaks of an individual who was instructed to build a large boat that would house him and every kind of animal on the earth.

"To destroy all flesh in which is the breath of life under heaven" (6:17): Convincing global evidence indicates that Noah's flood really did occur. This sudden worldwide flood upset normal geological processes on a catastrophic scale, causing mass extinction of animals and their subsequent fossilization in layer upon layer of sedimentary rock around the globe. The waves of this flood would have swept up all forms of life, and the mud into which these various forms of life finally settled solidified into rock as a result of the tremendous pressure of the water. The

flood produced wave after wave after wave, eventually forming rock strata after rock strata full of fossils of dead animals and plants.

"I will establish my covenant with you" (6:18): After God rescued Noah and his family from the universal flood, He established a relationship with them based on a covenant that stipulated both provisions and protection. This is the first mention in the Bible of a covenant. The particulars of the Noahic covenant are addressed in Genesis 9:8-17.

"Every living thing...two of every sort...male and female" (6:19): Following the flood, the male and female of each animal would be able to reproduce and repopulate the earth.

Noah...did all that God commanded him (6:22): Not surprising for a man who was righteous and blameless and walked with God (6:9).

Major Themes

1. *The sons of God and the daughters of man.* Who are the sons of God and daughters of man referenced in Genesis 6:2? This is a much-debated issue. A common view is that some evil angels cohabited with human women. There are three supportive evidences for this view: (1) Some manuscript copies of the Septuagint (the Greek translation of the Old Testament) have the phrase "angels of God" instead of "sons of God." (2) The Hebrew phrase for "sons of God" elsewhere refers to angels (Job 1:6; 2:1; 38:7). (3) Perhaps this view explains why some angels are presently bound in prison and others are not (2 Peter 2:4).

   Another view is that some fallen angels possessed human men who then cohabited with "the daughters of man." This view has the merit of providing a good explanation of how angels who are bodiless (Hebrews 1:14) and sexless (Matthew 22:30) could cohabit with humans.

   Another common interpretation is that these "sons of God" are the godly (human) line of Seth who intermingled with the godless women of Cain. Still another possibility is that the "sons of God" were kings who were interested in establishing royal harems (daughters of men) for themselves.

It is best not to be dogmatic regarding this verse.

2. *The Nephilim.* Contrary to popular misconceptions, the Nephilim (Genesis 6:4) were not the offspring of the "sons of God" and "daughters of men." After all, our text tells us that these beings "were on the earth in those days." That is, they were already on the earth. Most scholars take the term Nephilim to refer to mighty men, or men of great stature (see Numbers 13:33). Perhaps they were military leaders. It is possible that they contributed to the violence that filled the earth in those days.

Digging Deeper with Cross-References

Noah's flood—Isaiah 54:7-10; Matthew 24:37-39; Luke 17:26-27; Hebrews 11:7; 1 Peter 3:20; 2 Peter 2:5

God grieved by human sin—Deuteronomy 5:29; Psalms 78:40; 81:13; 95:10; 119:158; Isaiah 48:18; 63:10; Ezekiel 33:11; Luke 19:41-42; Ephesians 4:30; Hebrews 3:10,17

Life Lessons

1. *Avoid worldliness.* Apparently the people of Noah's day had no fear of the Lord and were completely entrenched in worldly living. We learn a lesson here. Christians ought not have a worldly character, a character focused only on the things of this earth. One of the best ways to avoid worldliness is to regularly feed on the Word of God and allow it to do its transforming work in our lives. As the apostle Paul put it, "Do not be conformed to this world, but be transformed by the renewal of your mind" (Romans 12:2).

2. *Finding favor with God.* There are many in biblical times who found favor with God. "Noah found favor in the

eyes of the Lord" (Genesis 6:8). "The Lord was with Joseph...and gave him favor" (Genesis 39:21). "The boy Samuel continued to grow both in stature and in favor with the Lord" (1 Samuel 2:26). "David became greater and greater, for the Lord, the God of hosts, was with him" (2 Samuel 5:10). In the New Testament, the angel said to Mary, "Do not be afraid, Mary, for you have found favor with God" (Luke 1:30). Do you want to find favor with God? If so, then live righteously and be obedient to Him (see Proverbs 12:2).

Questions for Reflection and Discussion

1. Do you feel spiritually and morally prepared for the second coming of Jesus Christ during these days, which seem similar to the days of Noah? What steps can you take to be more prepared?
2. Hebrews 11:7 commends Noah for his faith and his reverent fear of God. How can you demonstrate your reverent fear for God?
3. How can Christians be blameless (like Noah)? See Philippians 1:9-11 and 2:12-14.

Day 6

The Ark and the Flood

Genesis 7–8

Scripture Reading and Insights

Begin by reading Genesis 7–8 in your favorite Bible. As you read, remember that those who hear and obey the Word of God are truly blessed (Psalm 119:2; Luke 11:28; Revelation 1:3).

In yesterday's lesson, great wickedness emerged during Noah's time, and God instructed Noah to build an ark. In today's lesson, God sends a universal flood as a judgment against sinful humankind. With your Bible still accessible, consider the following insights on the biblical text.

Genesis 7:1-10

"Go into the ark" (7:1): A repeat of God's earlier instruction (see 6:18-20).

"You are righteous before me" (7:1): Noah conforms himself to God's law. In the New Testament, Noah is called a "herald of righteousness" (2 Peter 2:5).

"Clean animals... not clean" (7:2): Only clean animals could be sacrificed as burnt offerings (see 8:20). Later on, we will see that only clean animals can be eaten (see Leviticus 11; Deuteronomy 14). But God saved both the clean and the unclean animals on the ark.

"Seven pairs" (7:2-3): There's a good reason that Noah was commanded to include seven pairs of every kind of clean animal but only a pair of the unclean animals. More of the clean animals were needed

because they'd have to not only reproduce and repopulate the earth but also be used for burnt offerings that Noah would sacrifice (8:20). As well, in Genesis 9:3, human beings are no longer required to be vegetarians but are given the okay to eat animals. Only clean animals could be eaten.

"In seven days" (7:4): God allowed an additional week for any last-minute sinners to repent. But alas, there were none.

"Forty days and forty nights" (7:4): The fact that rain could fall continuously for 40 days and 40 nights assumes a vast amount of moisture above the earth. Genesis 1:7 refers to "the waters that were above the expanse."

Waters of the flood... waters of the flood (7:6,10): Ancient epic literature often used repetition.

Went into the ark... went into the ark (7:7,9): The importance of the ark cannot be overstated. Salvation is inside the ark. Only destruction is outside the ark. Because sin had so infected every aspect of human life, nothing short of a new beginning would suffice. This beginning would take place through the ark survivors.

His sons and his wife and his sons' wives (7:7): We are not provided information on the character of Noah's family. Their salvation is apparently due to Noah and his favor with God.

Genesis 7:11-24

The fountains of the great deep burst forth (7:11): The flood apparently began with the displacement of large volumes of subterranean waters. Some suggest the possibility that earthquakes may have played a role, or perhaps the sinking of large land masses, thus causing the subterranean waters to surface.

The windows of the heavens were opened (7:11): Following the release of vast amounts of subterranean water, rain fell from the sky for 40 days.

Forty days and forty nights (7:12): The number 40 is sometimes associated with trials or punishment (for example, Exodus 16:35; Judges 13:1; Ezekiel 4:6; Jonah 3:4).

Every beast (7:14): The animals that entered the ark included "every beast...all the livestock...every creeping thing...and every bird." These are the exact creatures that are listed in the creation account, with one exception—sea creatures, which would naturally survive the flood.

God...the Lord (7:16): Notice that "God" commanded Noah and the others to enter the ark, but "the Lord" shut them in. Some suggest that the term "the Lord" is more personal and that He would personally be watching out for Noah and his family while on the ark.

Shut him in (7:16): Once Noah, his family, and the animals were aboard the ark and the Lord shut them in, there was no hope for the rest of humankind or the animal kingdom. God personally protected those in the ark and annihilated those outside the ark. God is sovereign over matters of life and death (see Deuteronomy 32:39).

The waters increased (7:17): This is literally, "the waters multiplied." Earlier in Genesis, humankind multiplied (the same Hebrew word is used in Genesis 1:22,28).

The high mountains under the whole heaven were covered (7:19). This seems to indicate a worldwide flood instead of a local flood in Noah's territory. See Major Themes.

The breath of life (7:22): God gave every creature the breath of life at the original creation. It was His gift to all creatures (1:30; 2:7). That gift was revoked in judgment because of human sin.

The waters prevailed on the earth 150 days (7:24): This extended time—about five months—includes the 40 days of rainfall. So the rain fell for 40 days, and then another 110 days transpired before the floodwaters began to diminish.

Genesis 8:1-19

God remembered Noah (8:1): When the Bible says God remembered, it doesn't mean He had forgotten or that something suddenly popped into His mind. Rather, the phrase always indicates that God is concerned and is about to act on someone's behalf. In the present case, God remembered Noah by causing a wind to blow over the earth so the waters would subside.

A wind (8:1): Notice the parallel between Genesis 8 and the creation account in Genesis 1. We read of the Spirit hovering over the waters in Genesis 1. Now we read of the wind blowing over the waters of the earth as the waters subside ("Spirit" and "wind" are translations of the same Hebrew word). Genesis 1 records the original beginning of humankind. Genesis 8 is a new beginning for humankind through Noah and his family.

The mountains of Ararat (8:4): Ararat contains a range of mountains, not just a single mountain.

Sent forth a raven (8:7): Until this time, Noah had responded step-by-step to God's revelations, doing everything God commanded him. In a sense, Noah took a passive role. He simply responded obediently to God. But now Noah becomes more active. He chose to send a raven to determine whether the waters had sufficiently receded. The raven did not return to the ark. This is not surprising because the raven is a scavenger. It would easily have found something to eat, assuming the waters had sufficiently receded.

The dove... returned (8:8-9): The dove is much pickier than a raven about what it will eat and where it will land. Obviously unsatisfied, it returned to the ark.

He sent forth the dove... a freshly plucked olive leaf (8:10-11): Noah sent the dove out a second time. The dove returned with a freshly plucked olive leaf. This was significant because olives do not grow at high elevations. The dove would have had to fly down to a valley to find this olive leaf. This was a sign to Noah that the water had receded significantly.

"Go out from the ark" (8:16): Just as God had instructed Noah to go into the ark, so God now instructed Noah to go out of the ark. God is the commander in chief.

"The earth" (8:17): The water canopy was no longer above the earth. (The waters fell on the earth for 40 days.) Longevity among human beings decreased. The land surface had changed due to the catastrophic flood (for example, new mountains had formed). There was apparently more seismic activity. This environment was harsher than it was before the flood.

"Be fruitful and multiply on the earth" (8:17): Just as living beings in

the original creation were to be fruitful and multiply, so the people and animals in this new beginning were to do the same.

Genesis 8:20-22

Noah built an altar to the Lord (8:20): Noah built an alter to worship God and thank Him for sparing him and his family. This is the first mention of an altar in the Bible.

Pleasing aroma (8:21): The Lord "smelled" Noah's offering and took delight in it. It was pleasing to Him. This, of course, is anthropomorphic language—that is, it is a metaphorical description of God using human terms (compare with Exodus 29:18; Leviticus 1:9; Numbers 15:3). Certain things in the New Testament are also said to be pleasing sacrifices to God, including Christ's sacrifice on the cross (Ephesians 5:2) and the Philippians' gift to Paul (Philippians 4:18).

"I will never again curse the ground...Neither will I ever again strike down" (8:21): Regardless of how sinful humankind would become in the future, God would never again destroy life the way He did in early Genesis.

"Seedtime and harvest, cold and heat, summer and winter, day and night, shall not cease" (8:22): The continuity of seasons is evidence of God's continued forbearance.

Major Themes

1. *A universal flood.* Some have held that Noah's flood was a local flood. The evidence, however, points to a universal flood. The biblical text indicates that "the waters prevailed so mightily on the earth that all the high mountains under the whole heaven were covered" to a depth of more than 20 feet (7:19-20). The Bible also affirms that every living thing that moved on the earth perished (verses 22-23). Still further, the universal view best explains the worldwide distribution of diluvia deposits. A universal flood would also explain the sudden death of many woolly mammoths frozen in Alaskan and Siberian ice. Investigation shows

that these animals died suddenly by choking or drowning and not by freezing. Finally, a universal flood is mentioned in the many flood legends (more than 270) among people of various religious and cultural backgrounds all over the world.

2. *Sudden destruction.* We often find sudden destruction falling on the wicked in the Bible. For the people living during Noah's time, the flood was sudden and catastrophic. Proverbs 6:15 warns, "Therefore calamity will come upon him suddenly; in a moment he will be broken beyond healing." Proverbs 24:22 warns that disaster "will arise suddenly." Isaiah 47:11 warns that "ruin shall come upon you suddenly, of which you know nothing." God affirms in Jeremiah 15:8, "I have made anguish and terror fall upon them suddenly."

Digging Deeper with Cross-References

God's attitude toward the righteous—Psalms 33:18-19; 34:15; Proverbs 10:6-7,9; 11:4-8; 15:28-29; Isaiah 3:10-11; Romans 1:17; Philippians 2:15-16; James 5:16; 2 Peter 2:5-9

Burnt offerings—Exodus 29:13-34; Leviticus 1; 6:13,22; Psalms 51:19; 66:13; see also Amos 5:21-24

Life Lessons

1. *God remembered.* Genesis 8:1 tells us that "God remembered Noah and all the beasts and all the livestock that were with him in the ark." The word "remembered" in such contexts is an action word. That is, it carries the idea that God remembers and therefore acts. When the Bible says God remembers someone, He is about to take action on behalf of that person. In Genesis 8, God is about to act on behalf of Noah and the animals by bringing them to dry land. Elsewhere in the Bible, when God

says, "I will remember my covenant" (Genesis 9:15), He is indicating He will act to fulfill His covenant. When God "remembered Rachel" (Genesis 30:22), He was about to end her barrenness by giving her a child. God remembers you and me too. He regularly takes action on our behalf. He promises us, "I will never leave you nor forsake you" (Hebrews 13:5).

2. *Avoid partial obedience*. Genesis 7:5 tells us, "Noah did all that the Lord had commanded him." Like Noah, our goal ought to be to do all that the Lord tells us. Partial obedience won't cut it. God blesses total obedience. As Psalm 119:1-3 puts it, "Blessed are those whose way is blameless, who walk in the law of the Lord! Blessed are those who keep his testimonies, who seek him with their whole heart, who also do no wrong, but walk in his ways!" If you've been holding back from God, why not rectify the situation this very moment?

Questions for Reflection and Discussion

1. Obedience to God's word was a big deal to Noah. Is the Word of God a big deal to you? Would you say your life is characterized more by complete obedience or partial obedience to God's Word?
2. God "will never leave you nor forsake you." What does that mean to you personally?
3. What is your personal attitude toward worship?

Day 7

God's Covenant with Noah

Genesis 9

Scripture Reading and Insights

Begin by reading Genesis 9 in your favorite Bible. As you read, keep in mind that just as we eat food for physical nourishment, so we need the Word of God for spiritual nourishment (1 Corinthians 3:2; Hebrews 5:12; 1 Peter 2:2).

In the previous lesson, God sent a universal flood as a judgment against sinful humankind. In this chapter, God makes a post-flood covenant with Noah, and a curse is placed on Canaan. With your Bible still accessible, consider the following insights on the biblical text.

Genesis 9:1-7

"Be fruitful and multiply" (9:1): At humankind's beginning, God instructed humans to be fruitful and multiply. Now, at humankind's new beginning, God repeats the instruction.

"The fear of you and the dread of you" (9:2): Previously, humans and the animal kingdom had enjoyed a sense of harmony. But now, animals would experience a natural fear of humans. Some Bible expositors suggest that animals would dread humans now because God allows human beings to eat animals.

"Blood" (9:4): God's only stipulation for eating animals is that they could not be eaten with the blood of the animal. Some may wonder why God made this dietary regulation. Bible scholar H.C. Leupold explains.

> These restrictions are given in view of the ordinances that are later to govern the use of blood in sacrifices. This provision, then, of Noah's time prepares for the sacrificial use of blood, and that which is to be sacred in sacrifice...should hardly be employed that a man may glut his appetite with it. In fact, it is not an overstatement of the case to remark that ultimately this restriction is made in view of the sanctity of the blood of our Great High Priest, who is both priest and sacrifice.[1]

The pagan nations surrounding Israel ate blood on a regular basis. Sometimes they did this as part of the worship of false gods; at other times they did this because they thought it might bring them supernatural power. The prohibition against eating blood set Israel apart from such ungodly nations (see Leviticus 7:26-27; 17:11-12; Acts 15:28-29).

"I will require a reckoning: from every beast" (9:5): Human life is of such worth and is so precious that God is very protective of it. Later in Israel's history, any animal that took the life of a human being was to be stoned to death (Exodus 21:28-32).

"Whoever sheds the blood of man" (9:6): God now institutes a law of retributive justice: If a person takes the life of another human being, the penalty will match the crime—the murderer's life must now be taken. A life for a life. This stringent law is intended as a deterrent to murder.

The underlying basis for this severe punishment is that human beings are made in the image of God (Genesis 1:26-27). Humans are so valuable that anyone who tampers with their sacred right to live must face the consequences of losing his or her own life.

The death penalty was eventually incorporated into the Mosaic code (Exodus 21:12; Numbers 35:16-31). Likewise, in Romans 13:1-7, the apostle Paul taught that human government has a God-given right to use force in its resistance of evil. Romans 13:4 indicates that the government has the right to take the life of a criminal.

"Be fruitful and multiply" (9:7): God again instructs that human beings are to be fruitful and multiply. When God repeats something,

He is speaking about something important. Note the contrast with the previous verse: Instead of the human population being depleted as a result of murder, God's desire is that human life multiply and replenish the earth.

Genesis 9:8-17

"I establish my covenant with you" (9:9): This is the Noahic covenant. This is the only covenant God made with human beings where He stipulated that He would *not* do something. The Noahic covenant is the first of five Scriptural covenants that are called "everlasting." The others are the Abrahamic (Genesis 17:7), priestly (Numbers 25:10-13), Davidic (2 Samuel 23:5), and new covenants (Jeremiah 32:40). See Major Themes.

"Never again" (9:11): God promised He would never again destroy *all* flesh by a global flood. Notice the specific words used in this covenant: This is an "everlasting covenant" (verse 16) that is "for all future generations" (verse 12).

Liberal critics claim that if there is a God, He did not keep His promise. After all, many deadly floods have occurred since the time of Noah. Notice, however, that God promised that never again "shall all flesh be cut off" by a global flood. This promise does not pertain to localized floods with limited casualties. Besides, even though God caused Noah's flood, we cannot assume He causes all floods in the world.

"The sign of the covenant" (9:12): In Bible times, signs commonly accompanied covenants. A sign is a memorial and reminder of the covenant. For example, the sign of the Abrahamic covenant was circumcision (Genesis 17). Abraham gave Abimelech seven ewe lambs as "a witness" to their covenant (Genesis 21:30). Baptism is the sign of the new covenant (Romans 6:3-4; Colossians 2:9-12). The sign of the Noahic covenant was a rainbow.

"My bow in the cloud" (9:13-15): This is a rainbow. The context seems to indicate that rainbows had not previously existed. Perhaps the flood caused new cloud and atmospheric conditions that caused

the appearance of the rainbow. This sign served as a guarantee that "all flesh" would never again be destroyed by a universal flood.

Genesis 9:18-29

Shem, Ham, and Japheth (9:18): From Noah's three sons descended all the world's people. This anticipates the table of nations in Genesis 10.

Noah...a man of the soil (9:20): Noah planted a vineyard and made wine from its fruit.

Became drunk (9:21): Even though this is the first reference to wine in the Bible, this is not the first occasion of drinking: "In those days before the flood they were eating and drinking, marrying and giving in marriage, until the day when Noah entered the ark" (Matthew 24:38). Some Bible expositors suggest that Noah was likely aware of the effects of drinking wine and was therefore culpable in his choice to drink too much. Elsewhere in the Bible, wine is said to cheer the heart (Judges 9:13; Psalm 104:15) and alleviate pain (Proverbs 31:6).

Lay uncovered (9:21): When one is under the control of wine, natural inhibitions wane. Note the contrast in Noah's life. Earlier in Genesis we read that Noah walked with God in righteousness (6:9). Now we read that he lays drunkenly in shame. This is just another evidence that all people have been infected by sin (Romans 5:12).

Ham...saw the nakedness (9:22): The Hebrew of this verse indicates that Ham "gazed with satisfaction" at his father's nakedness. Ham subsequently gossiped to his brothers about Noah instead of covering Noah's shame. The better policy is to "honor your father and mother" (Exodus 20:12).

Shem and Japheth...covered the nakedness (9:23): Unlike Ham, Shem and Japheth showed respect for their father by not only covering his nakedness but also averting their eyes.

"Cursed be Canaan" (9:25): When Noah awoke and knew what Ham had done, he said "cursed be Canaan" (Ham's son). We are not told what Canaan did, but apparently he was involved in his father's disrespectful act. Did he join Ham in gazing at the naked Noah with satisfaction? Did he first see Noah naked and then tell Ham? We don't

know. Another option is that this is simply an illustration of the "eye for an eye" principle of justice. Noah may have reasoned, "Since I have been disgraced by my son Ham, so now Ham will be disgraced by his own son Canaan." Canaan's offspring would later be pagan enemies of Israel.

"Blessed be the LORD, the God of Shem" (9:26): Unlike Canaan, the son of Ham, Shem is blessed. It is interesting to observe that Jews are of Semitic descent. The word "Semitic" comes from "Shem."

"May God enlarge Japheth" (9:27): Japheth's name sounds like the Hebrew word for "enlarge." Japheth's descendants would multiply all over the earth.

Days of Noah were 950 years (9:29): Noah enjoyed great longevity. Human life spans decrease steadily from this point forward.

Major Themes

1. *The Noahic covenant*. In Genesis 9:12-15, God instituted the Noahic covenant, which included these stipulations: (1) God would never again destroy humanity by a flood, and (2) the memorial token of the covenant is a rainbow. This was the first covenant God made with a human being. God says, "I will remember my covenant...I will see it and remember the everlasting covenant" (verses 15-16). This means that the covenant is a sure thing. God will make sure it is fulfilled just as promised. This is why it is called an everlasting covenant.
2. *The origin of human government*. God is a God of order. This order is evident in the authority structures He set up among people. For example, in the family unit, God has instituted an ordered structure with the man as the head of the house and then both parents over the children (1 Corinthians 11:3; Ephesians 6:1). In the church, God has assigned elders to bring order to the church (1 Timothy 5:17). In the same way, God is clearly the author of human government (Romans 13:1-6), which first emerges in

Genesis 9. Human government is intended to restrain evil on the earth (Genesis 9:6).

Digging Deeper with Cross-References

Murder—Genesis 9:5-6; Exodus 20:13; Numbers 35:16,30-31; Deuteronomy 5:17; Psalm 5:6; Matthew 15:19; 1 John 3:15

No devouring of lifeblood—Leviticus 3:17; 7:26; 17:10-14; 19:26; Deuteronomy 12:16,23; 15:23; 1 Samuel 14:32-34; Ezekiel 33:25; Acts 15:20,29; 21:25

Drunkenness—Genesis 19:33; 1 Samuel 25:36; 2 Samuel 11:13; 1 Kings 16:9; 20:16; Esther 1:10; Isaiah 56:12; Hosea 7:5; Joel 3:3; Luke 12:45-46; 1 Corinthians 11:21; Ephesians 5:18

Life Lessons

1. *Blessing others and being blessed.* Genesis 9:1 tells us, "God blessed Noah and his sons." God's blessing is a wonderful thing. The biblical pattern seems to be that God blesses us so that we can bless others. In Genesis 12:2 God instructs Abraham, "I will bless you and make your name great, so that you will be a blessing." It also seems to be true that when our goal is to bless other people, God Himself blesses us. There is a reciprocal relationship. In Luke 6:38 Jesus says, "Give, and it will be given to you." Do you want to find out more about being blessed? Check out Jesus's beatitudes in Matthew 5:1-12.

2. *God keeps His promises.* Our God is a promise keeper—including God's promise in the Noahic covenant. Numbers 23:19 asserts, "God is not a man, that he should lie, or a son of man, that he should change his mind. Does he speak and then not act? Has he said, and will he not do it? Or has he spoken, and will he not fulfill?" Prior to his death, an aged Joshua declared, "Now I am about to go the

way of all the earth. You know with all your heart and soul that not one of all the good promises the Lord your God gave you has failed. Every promise has been fulfilled; not one has failed" (Joshua 23:14 NIV; see also Joshua 21:45). Solomon later proclaimed, "Praise be to the Lord, who has given rest to his people Israel just as he promised. Not one word has failed of all the good promises he gave through his servant Moses" (1 Kings 8:56 NIV).

Questions for Reflection and Discussion

1. Do you believe in capital punishment? Why or why not?
2. Noah was righteous and walked with God, yet he fell into sin. How would you relate this to Paul's comments in Romans 7:15-20? How would you relate it to your own life?
3. Has your view of the importance of honoring parents changed any as a result of this lesson? Why or why not?

Day 8

Noah's Descendants and the Tower of Babel

Genesis 10:1–11:9

Scripture Reading and Insights

Begin by reading Genesis 10:1–11:9 in your favorite Bible. As you read, keep in mind that just as we eat food for physical nourishment, so we need the Word of God for spiritual nourishment (1 Corinthians 3:2; Hebrews 5:12; 1 Peter 2:2).

In yesterday's reading, we focused attention on God's post-flood covenant with Noah and the curse on Canaan. Now let's find out more about the emergence of nations from Noah's line as well as the tower of Babel. With your Bible still accessible, consider the following insights on the biblical text.

Genesis 10:1-32

The generations of the sons of Noah, Shem, Ham, and Japheth (10:1): The genealogy of Noah's family.

The sons of Japheth (10:2): Fourteen nations emerged out of the line of Japheth. His descendants spread over a wide geographical area, with many settling around the Black Sea and Caspian Sea.

Each with his own language…clans…nations (10:5): Until now, everyone spoke the same language. Following the incident at the Tower of Babel, however, there would be peoples with many languages. This verse is speaking from the perspective of the situation following the Tower of Babel.

The sons of Ham (10:6): Thirty nations emerged out of the line of Ham, most of which ended up in southwestern Asia and northeastern Africa. Many of them became enemies of Israel.

Nimrod (10:8): A descendant of Cush who had a reputation as a mighty hunter and a powerful leader. His name means "rebel." This rebel-warrior was an enemy of Israel.

Babel (10:10): Babel is the former name of Babylon. It was situated on the Euphrates River, a little more than 50 miles south of modern Baghdad. Because of its ideal location, Babylon was an important commercial and trade center in the ancient world. Like other pagan nations of the ancient Near East, those who lived in this territory believed in many false gods and goddesses. Divination was common. For example, astrologers often observed the movements of the stars to obtain information about the will of the gods (see Daniel 1:20; 2:2,10,27; 4:7; 5:7,11,15). Babylon is often represented in Scripture as being arrayed against God and His people (2 Kings 24:10).

Assyria...Nineveh (10:11): The Assyrians were a Semitic people who lived along the Tigris River in what is now the northern part of Iraq. They became a primary enemy of the Israelites. The Assyrians were pagans, believing in many gods. Assyrian art often exalted the Assyrian gods, who were believed to be the key to military victory. The national god of Assyria was Ashur, the king of the gods. Ashur and various other deities were believed to control all natural phenomena, including the sun, the moon, and the weather. The patron god or goddess of each city was worshipped in a local temple. Assyrians also practiced divination, consulted astrologers, and engaged in other forms of occultism, attempting to predict the future.

Clans of the Canaanites...territory of the Canaanites (10:18-19): The Canaanites were possessors of the land God promised to Israel (the Promised Land). God would later instruct His people to conquer the Canaanites and drive them from the land.

To Shem (10:21): Twenty-six nations emerged out of the line of Shem. Shem was the oldest of Noah's sons. His descendants were the Semites.

For in his days the earth was divided (10:25): A preview of God's dispersion of the nations at Babel (see 11:1).

Genesis 11:1-9

The whole earth had one language (11:1): Increasing archaeological evidence indicates that the world once had a single language. Sumerian literature alludes to this several times. One clay tablet discovered has remarkable similarities to the account of the Tower of Babel and its destruction in Genesis 11.

God created human language for a purpose. When God created Adam in His own rational image, He gave Adam the gift of intelligible speech. This enabled him to communicate objectively with his Creator and with other human beings through words (Genesis 11:1,7). Scripture shows that God sovereignly chose to use human language as a medium of revelation, often through "thus saith the Lord" pronouncements of the prophets (Isaiah 7:7; 10:24; 22:15; 28:16; 30:15; 49:22; 51:22; 52:4; 65:13). There was a single language at the time of the Tower of Babel incident. Language—the gift of communication—was abused by these sinful people. Language formerly enabled humankind to enjoy unity, but God would shortly use language as a tool to divide.

People migrated (11:2): The migration of people presumes that by now humanity had been successful at multiplying and being fruitful.

The land of Shinar (11:2): A plain located between the Tigris and Euphrates rivers.

"Make bricks" (11:3): Because this Babylonian plain had few stones, the people resorted to making bricks. Nothing is wrong with making bricks, but these bricks were to be used for an ungodly purpose.

"Build ourselves a city and a tower...make a name for ourselves" (11:4): The tower the people wanted to build was probably a ziggurat. This was a seven-staged tower that pagans typically erected to study the gods as well as the stars. (An incipient form of astrology emerged in what would later become Babylon.)

All this reminds one of Lucifer's sin—pride (Isaiah 14:14; Ezekiel 28:11-19; 1 Timothy 3:6). In his pride, Lucifer defied the one true God. As a result, God judged him. In this chapter, the people at Babel sought to pridefully build a tower and make a name for themselves. They did this in defiance of the one true God. Just as God judged Lucifer, so He would judge those participating at the Tower of Babel.

"With its top in the heavens" (11:4): They wanted to build a tower so high, so magnificent, that it would bring great glory to themselves. They sought self-glory instead of God's glory. This, too, reminds one of Lucifer, whose desire for glory motivated him to exalt himself to God's level (Isaiah 14:14; Ezekiel 28:11-19).

The Lord came down (11:5): Notice the irony here. The people in their arrogance wanted to build a skyscraper. But from the Lord's perspective, it was so small that He had to "go down" to see it (see verse 7).

"Nothing...will now be impossible for them" (11:6): God knew that if they succeeded here, they would continue their relentless pursuit of glory and fame. There would be no limit to their unrestrained rebellion against God. They would seek to build a human kingdom to the exclusion of God's kingdom.

"Let us go down and there confuse their language" (11:7): Notice the contrast: The people had earlier said, "Come, let us build" (verse 4). Now God says, "Come, let us...confuse their language" (11:7). God answers the arrogance of these people.

Some Bible expositors interpret "let us" as an Old Testament reference relating to the doctrine of the Trinity. In favor of this view is verse 5, which tells us that "the Lord came down to see the city and the tower." Since the Lord alone came down, "let us" must be a reference to Him alone. Others, however, believe God was addressing an angelic assembly in heaven, inviting them to participate in the judgment against those involved at the Tower of Babel. In verse 7, God states, "Let us go down and there confuse their language." Since they must "go down," God must still be in heaven with the angels. In any event, the ultimate goal is the same: Human languages would now be confused so that people could not communicate with each other. These people had sought worldwide fame. Now they would experience worldwide humiliation.

The Lord dispersed them (11:8): These sinful humans unified themselves in defiance of God. Now God judged them by breaking their unity. He dispersed them. Following this, they spread all over the earth (see Genesis 10:5,32).

Its name was called Babel (11:9): The word Babel is rooted in a Hebrew word meaning "to confuse."

The Lord dispersed them (11:9): God had instructed them to fill the earth. Instead, they congregated in the land of Shinar and defied God. Now God forced them to fill the earth by confusing their language and dispersing them.

Major Themes

1. *The table of nations.* Genesis 10–11 contains what is known as the table of nations. It contains a list of the patriarchs of 70 nations that descended from Noah through his three sons, Shem, Ham and Japheth. As Genesis 10:32 puts it, "These are the clans of the sons of Noah, according to their genealogies, in their nations, and from these the nations spread abroad on the earth after the flood."
2. *God is triune.* God is a Trinity. The doctrine of the Trinity is based on three lines of evidence.
   - There is only one true God (see Isaiah 44:6; 46:9; John 5:44; 17:3; Romans 3:29-30; 16:27; 1 Corinthians 8:4; Galatians 3:20; Ephesians 4:6; 1 Timothy 2:5; James 2:19).
   - There are three persons who are recognized as God—the Father (1 Peter 1:2), Jesus (John 20:28; Hebrews 1:8), and the Holy Spirit (Acts 5:3-4).
   - There is three-in-oneness within the one God (Matthew 28:19; 2 Corinthians 13:14).

   The doctrine of the Trinity may be reflected in the plural pronouns used of God in Genesis (1:26; 3:22; 11:6-7).

Digging Deeper with Cross-References

Babylon—Isaiah 13:1–14:23; 47; Jeremiah 20:1-6; 25:1-14; 50–51; Revelation 18

God can judge by confounding—Job 5:12-13; 12:20; Psalms 2:4; 33:10; Acts 2:4-11

Life Lessons

1. *The danger of ambition.* Unbridled ambition can be dangerous. Scripture reveals that ambition certainly played a role in the fall of Lucifer, who was ambitious to take God's place (see Isaiah 14:13). Ambition also played a role in the fall of humankind (see Genesis 3:6). In the New Testament, a mother was ambitious for the glory of her two sons in the coming kingdom (Matthew 20:21). Jesus rebuked the unbridled ambition of the Pharisees: "Woe to you Pharisees! For you love the best seat in the synagogues and greetings in the marketplaces" (Luke 11:43). Jesus likewise warned, "Beware of the scribes, who like to walk around in long robes, and love greetings in the marketplaces and the best seats in the synagogues and the places of honor at feasts" (Luke 20:46). In the future, the antichrist's ambition will drive him to claim deity for himself (see 2 Thessalonians 2:3-4). First John 2:16 appropriately warns, "All that is in the world—the desires of the flesh and the desires of the eyes and pride of life—is not from the Father but is from the world."
2. *Humility—the better way.* Corrie ten Boom was once asked if it was difficult for her to remain humble. She replied simply, "When Jesus rode into Jerusalem on Palm Sunday on the back of a donkey, and everyone was waving palm branches and throwing garments on the road, and singing praises, do you think that for one moment it ever entered the head of that donkey that any of that was for him?" Her point was, "If I can be the donkey on which Jesus Christ rides in His glory, I give Him all the praise and all the honor."[2] The Scriptures tell us that those who want to please God must walk in humility. Not only that, but God

exalts the humble: "Humble yourselves before the Lord, and he will exalt you" (James 4:10; see also Luke 1:52). King David humbled himself, and God exalted him greatly (2 Samuel 7:18-21). The apostle Paul humbled himself, and God exalted him too (1 Timothy 1:15-16). It is in our best interest to clothe ourselves with humility (1 Peter 5:5).

Questions for Reflection and Discussion

1. Do you ever struggle with the temptation to be prideful? What steps can you take today to deal with this temptation?
2. Read James 4:13-17. How does James's instruction contrast with the rebels' mindset at the Tower of Babel? What do you learn from James that you can implement in your life?
3. Contrast the unity humans sought at Babel with the unity Christians have in Christ. What does being unified with the body of Christ mean to you personally?

Day 9

The Call of Abram

Genesis 11:10–12:20

Scripture Reading and Insights

Begin by reading Genesis 11:10–12:20 in your favorite Bible. As you read, remember that storing God's Word in your heart can help you to avoid sinning (Psalm 119:9,11).

In the previous lesson, we learned about the emergence of nations from Noah's line as well as the tower of Babel. Now let's examine God's call of Abram and Abram's trip to Egypt. With your Bible still accessible, consider the following insights on the biblical text.

Genesis 11:10-26

Generations of Shem (11:10): The genealogy of Shem. Hebrew genealogies do not necessarily list every single generation.

Fathered... lived after he fathered... had other sons and daughters (11:10-25): Here we have a listing of Shem's descendants. Notice how human life spans are greatly reduced following the flood. We are told when each person's first son was born, the son's name, how long the father lived after the son's birth, and that the father had other sons and daughters.

Genesis 11:27-32

Generations of Terah (11:27): The genealogy of Terah.

Terah fathered Abram (11:27): Abram's name means "exalted father."

This exaltation is rooted in the fact that he is the father of God's chosen people, the Jews. His name would later be changed to Abraham ("father of a multitude").

Haran fathered Lot (11:27): Lot was Abram's nephew.

Ur of the Chaldeans (11:28): An ancient Mesopotamian city near the mouth of the Euphrates. The city was heavily populated and enjoyed great prosperity. Paganism was predominant.

Abram's wife was Sarai (11:29): Sarai means "princess" in Hebrew. Unfortunately, she was infertile.

Went forth... to Haran (11:31): Abram chose the easier of two routes to Canaan. He could have dragged his entourage straight through the Arabian desert. But his herds and flocks probably wouldn't survive that kind of trip because of limited water sources. Abram instead traveled along the Euphrates river down to Haran—a city known for its worship of the moon. From there he traveled to Canaan.

Genesis 12:1-9

The LORD said to Abram (12:1): The Abrahamic covenant is addressed through much of Scripture. It is first introduced here. The covenant is formally stated and enacted in Genesis 15:18-21. It is reaffirmed in Genesis 17:1-21 and then renewed with both Isaac (26:2-5) and Jacob (28:10-17). It is an everlasting covenant (Genesis 17:7-8; 1 Chronicles 16:17; Psalm 105:7-11; Isaiah 24:5). On day 11 we will address the unconditional nature of this covenant. Specific elements of the covenant are listed below.

"Go from your country... to the land that I will show you" (12:1): God instructed Abram to leave Haran and make his way to Canaan. With God's call of Abram, a shift in emphasis occurs. Prior to this time, God had focused broadly on humankind. Now God narrows the focus to Abram and his descendants. This is the beginning of the Jewish people, from whom the Messiah would one day be born (Luke 3:34).

"I will make of you a great nation" (12:2): This was a remarkable promise from Abram's perspective. After all, he and Sarai had not yet had a son. That the Jewish nation would emerge from him and his

wife seemed unlikely at best. With God, however, all things are possible (Mark 10:27).

"I will bless you and make your name great" (12:2): Looking back, God obviously blessed Abram and made his name great. In Old Testament times Abram became very rich (13:2), was greatly blessed with material goods (24:35), was heavily favored by God (21:22), and was considered a "prince of God" (23:6).

"I will bless those who bless you, and him who dishonors you I will curse" (12:3): Recall Jesus's teaching in Matthew 25:31-46 that to feed His brothers was akin to feeding Him. To give His brothers water was akin to giving Him water. To visit them in jail was akin to visiting Him in jail. In much the same way, Genesis 12 implies that to bless Abram was to bless God, and to curse Abram was to curse God (compare with Genesis 20:2-18; 21:22-34; 23).

"In you all the families of the earth shall be blessed" (12:3): All the families of the earth were blessed when Abram's seed, Jesus Christ, was born as the Savior of humankind (Galatians 3:8,16).

Abram went...and Lot went with him...and Abram took Sarai his wife (12:4-5): Abram was an obedient servant of the Lord. The Lord commanded, and Abram obeyed in faith (Hebrews 11:8; see also Genesis 17:23; 21:14; 22:3). God considered him righteous because of his faith (see Genesis 15:6; see also Romans 4:3; Galatians 3:6; James 2:23).

By this time Lot's father was dead. He therefore came under Abram's wing and traveled with Abram and Sarai to Canaan. Some Bible expositors suggest that because Sarai was infertile, unable to give birth to an heir, Lot was apparently next in line.

Shechem (12:6): An ancient fortified city in the central part of Canaan, located between Mount Ebal and Mount Gerizim, about 30 miles north of Jerusalem. Much later, it became the first capital of the northern kingdom of Israel (see Genesis 33:18; 1 Chronicles 7:28).

"To your offspring I will give this land" (12:7): God made specific land promises to Abram. We read of the actual territories of the Promised Land in Genesis 15:18-21: "On that day the Lord made a covenant with Abram, saying, 'To your offspring I give this land, from the river of Egypt to the great river, the river Euphrates, the land of

the Kenites, the Kenizzites, the Kadmonites, the Hittites, the Perizzites, the Rephaim, the Amorites, the Canaanites, the Girgashites and the Jebusites'" (see Psalm 105:8-11; see also Genesis 26:3-4; 28:13-14).

Built there an altar to the LORD (12:7): The Hebrew noun for "altar," *mizbeah*, means "place of sacrifice." Altars played a prominent role in the religious history of the Israelites. Abram's altar is the first place of sacrifice—indeed, the first place of worship—to appear in the Promised Land. Abram built these altars and worshipped as a means of proclaiming the one true God at these cities of false worship.

The hill country...with Bethel on the west and Ai on the east (12:8): Abram settled in the hill country between Bethel and Ai. Bethel, a name meaning "house of God," is a city north of Jerusalem. Ai was a Canaanite city east of Bethel.

He built an altar to the LORD (12:8): Another act of worship on Abram's part, this time in the hill country.

Genesis 12:10-20

Famine in the land (12:10): In biblical times, threats to the food supply were common—even in Palestine, the land of milk and honey (Exodus 13:5). An enemy might invade and destroy all the crops. Locusts might swoop in out of nowhere and consume the crops in less than an hour. Without enough rain, the crops would not grow. Because of such factors, famines often occurred in biblical times.

Abram went down to Egypt to sojourn there (12:10): The famine caused Abram to trek to Egypt, which was well known for plentiful food supplies. Because of Egypt's close proximity to the Nile River, the irrigation of crops was much more dependable there than in other parts of the ancient biblical world.

"Say you are my sister" (12:13): Sarai was a beautiful woman. Even though she was 65 years old, she had maintained her attractive appearance. Sarai lived to be 127, so she was apparently still in her prime at age 65. Abram therefore feared that if Pharaoh wanted Sarai for his harem, Pharaoh would think nothing of disposing of Abram as her husband. Abram decided to stretch the truth by telling Pharaoh that Sarai was his sister. (She was actually his half sister—see Genesis 20:12.) Deception

would later plague his family throughout the rest of Genesis (26:1-11; 27:1-29; 29:15-30; 30:34-36; 31:6-11; 37:18-35; 39:7-20).

Pharaoh...dealt well with Abram (12:15-16): Pharaoh's officials beheld Sarai's beauty and promptly arranged for her to be taken into Pharaoh's house. In appreciation, Pharaoh bestowed significant material wealth on Abram.

The LORD afflicted Pharaoh and his house (12:17): Trouble soon began for Pharaoh and his house. Great plagues fell on them. Abram had lied to protect himself, but now the Lord intervened to protect Sarai.

"What is this you have done to me?" (12:18-20): Archaeological discoveries reveal that truthfulness was a high virtue among the ancient Egyptians. Pharaoh rightly wanted to know why Abram had lied.

We are not told how Pharaoh came to know of Sarai's true identity as Abram's wife after the plagues fell. Did she say something to Pharaoh's officials? Did God appear to Pharaoh in a dream? We don't know. In any event, Pharaoh took quick action to remedy the situation by delivering Sarai back to Abram and sending them on their way. Abram no doubt left Egypt ashamed for what had occurred.

Major Themes

1. *Covenants in Bible times.* A covenant is simply an agreement between two parties. Covenants were used among the ancients as treaties or alliances between nations (1 Samuel 11:1), treaties between individuals (Genesis 21:27), friendship pacts (1 Samuel 18:3-4), and agreements between God and His people. In the Bible, God made specific covenant promises to a number of people, including Noah (Genesis 9:8-17), Abram (Genesis 15:12-21; 17:1-14), the Israelites at Mount Sinai (Exodus 19:5-6), David (2 Samuel 7:13; 23:5), and God's people in the new covenant (Hebrews 8:6-13). God is a God of promises.
2. *The Promised Land.* In the covenant God made with Abram, God promised to give him and his descendants the

land of Canaan "for an everlasting possession" (Genesis 17:8). After the wilderness sojourn—yet future from the perspective of Genesis—the entrance into the Promised Land became a reality, but only for a handful of the original Exodus crowd (most of the disobedient Israelites perished during the sojourn). Many passages in the Old Testament speak of inheriting the Promised Land. You may wish to consult Psalm 37 for an extended discussion of who gets to inherit the Promised Land. The land promises will find final and ultimate fulfillment in Christ's future millennial kingdom.

Digging Deeper with Cross-References

Lying and deception in the book of Genesis—Genesis 12:13; 20:2; 26:7; 27:19; 31:35

Plagues—Leviticus 14:34,43,54; 26:21; Numbers 8:19; 11:33; 14:37; 16:46; 25:9; 31:16; Deuteronomy 28:27,59; Joshua 22:17; 1 Samuel 5:6,11; 2 Samuel 24:25; Psalm 106:29; Zechariah 14:12,15,18; Revelation 15:1; 16:21; 18:8; 21:9; 22:18

Life Lessons

1. *God's command to Abram called for a step of faith.* Just as Abram had to exercise faith in following God, so must you and I. The Bible defines faith as "being sure of what we hope for and certain of what we do not see" (Hebrews 11:1). The big problem for most people is that they tend to base everything on what the five senses reveal. The spiritual world is not subject to any of these, so many people's faith is often weak and impotent. The eye of faith, however, perceives this unseen reality. The spiritual world lies all about us, enclosing us, embracing us, altogether within our reach. Do you want a stronger faith? The key is to

saturate your mind with God's Word (see Romans 10:17; John 20:31).

2. *Worship—the right response to God.* Worship involves reverencing God, adoring Him, praising Him, venerating Him, and paying homage to Him, not just externally (with rituals and songs) but in our hearts as well (Isaiah 29:13; see also 1 Samuel 15:22-23). The Hebrew word for worship, *shaha*, means "to bow down" or "to prostrate oneself" (see Genesis 22:5; 42:6). Likewise, the New Testament word for worship, *proskuneo*, means "to prostrate oneself" (see Matthew 2:2,8,11). Such worship is the proper response of a creature to the divine Creator (Psalm 95:6). Worship can be congregational (1 Corinthians 11–14) or individual (see Romans 12:1).

Questions for Reflection and Discussion

1. Do you consider yourself an honest and truthful person? Considering all the deception we witness in Genesis, what resolutions might you make in this regard?
2. Two of Abram's character traits are obedience and faith. How can you express your obedience to God and faith in Him today?
3. The people at Babel sought to make their name great. God told Abram that He'd make his name great. What's the difference between the people of Babel and Abraham?

Day 10

The Adventures of Abram and Lot

Genesis 13–14

Scripture Reading and Insights

Begin by reading Genesis 13–14 in your favorite Bible. As you read, remember that storing God's Word in your heart can help you to avoid sinning (Psalm 119:9,11).

In yesterday's reading, we examined God's call of Abram and Abram's trip to Egypt. Now let's learn about Abram's separation from Lot as well as Abram's military victory over an invading force. With your Bible still accessible, consider the following insights on the biblical text.

Genesis 13:1-18

The Negeb (13:1): The desert region south of Palestine.

Rich in livestock (13:2): The size of Abram's flocks and herds was an indication of his great wealth. In fact, Abram departed from Egypt with more material wealth than he previously possessed. We find a parallel with what would happen to the Jews enslaved in Egypt much later. They, too, would depart Egypt with much of Egypt's wealth (see Exodus 3:22; 12:36).

Between Bethel and Ai (13:3): Abram decided to revisit familiar territory. Following the fiasco in Egypt (where he lied to Pharaoh about his wife), he went to the place between Bethel and Ai where he had built an altar. In an apparent recommitment to the Lord, Abram "called upon the name of the Lord" (verse 4).

Lot...also had flocks and herds and tents (13:5): Lot was also a wealthy man.

The land could not support both of them dwelling together (13:6): Abram's and Lot's herds overtaxed the land.

Strife between the herdsmen (13:7): Massive herds and limited grazing space led to conflict among Abram's and Lot's herdsmen. Things got a little too close for comfort.

The Canaanites and the Perizzites (13:7): The Canaanites were the pagan inhabitants of Canaan. The Perizzites were a Canaanite tribe (see Genesis 34:30; Deuteronomy 7:1; Judges 1:4; 3:5-6; 1 Kings 9:20-21; Ezra 9:1).

"Let there be no strife...Separate yourself from me" (13:8-9): In Egypt Abram had been self-centered, watching out only for himself. Now, however, Abram is other-centered. In an effort to end any conflict with Lot, Abram let Lot choose whatever land he wanted. Abram would then take the remaining land. Abram was the elder in the family, so the land was actually his to choose and allocate. But he condescended in allowing Lot to choose.

"For we are kinsmen" (13:8): Abram and Lot were close relatives.

"Jordan Valley" (13:10-11): By eyeballing the landscape, Lot saw that the Jordan Valley appeared very inviting. It seemed like a no-brainer to him. He chose this territory because it appeared to be premium real estate. The problem was, it was near to Sodom, a heinously wicked city (19:1-25). This was a big risk for Lot—getting a little too close to temptation's door. Recall from Genesis 4:7 that sin can be like an animal "crouching at the door." Sin is like a predator ready to pounce on its prey. By moving close to Sodom, Lot made himself vulnerable.

Lot's choice had another downside. By choosing to depart and live in the Jordan Valley, he parted ways with the recipient of God's covenant promises. His greatest chance of being blessed would have been to stay close to Abram.

Land of Canaan (13:12): This is the Promised Land, which God promised to Abram in the Abrahamic covenant.

The men of Sodom (13:13): The occupants of Sodom were "wicked, great sinners against the Lord." Sodom's wickedness and moral depravity became proverbial (Romans 9:29; Revelation 11:8).

"Northward and southward and eastward and westward" (13:14): After Lot moved to his new territory, God reaffirmed the land promises of the Abrahamic covenant. So vast was the land that Abram could look in all directions and walk in all directions to measure it.

"I will make your offspring as the dust of the earth" (13:16): God promised all of this land to Abram's descendants, whose number would be so great that they would be like dust. That is, they would be innumerable (from a human perspective). Abram's offspring are elsewhere described as numerous "as the stars of heaven and as the sand that is on the seashore" (22:17).

Oaks of Mamre, which are at Hebron (13:18): Abram settled in the plain of Mamre, named after Mamre the Amorite, who owned a large grove of trees. This was located at Hebron, about 22 miles south of Jerusalem.

Built an altar to the Lord (13:18): As he traditionally did, Abram continued in his regular worship of the Lord.

Genesis 14:1-16

These kings made war (14:2-10): Genesis 14:1-12 describes a number of kings and their armies who engaged in war with each other. James 4:1-2 offers this insight on war and fighting: "What causes quarrels and what causes fights among you? Is it not this, that your passions are at war within you? You desire and do not have, so you murder. You covet and cannot obtain, so you fight and quarrel." These kings desired and coveted what the others had, so they engaged in lots of fighting. It is noteworthy that in ancient times, more powerful kings often joined forces in order to subjugate smaller kings and kingdoms. In the present case, four powerful kings from the east launched an assault against five lesser Palestinian kings.

The enemy took all the possessions of Sodom and Gomorrah (14:11): Sodom and Gomorrah were in the battle zone and were overthrown. In the process, Lot—by then a resident of Sodom—was taken captive.

Lot...who was dwelling in Sodom (14:12): Life was not easy for Lot in Sodom. As 2 Peter 2:8 puts it, "He was tormenting his righteous soul over their lawless deeds that he saw and heard."

Abram the Hebrew (14:13): Abram is the first person in the Bible to be referred to as a Hebrew. The term came to describe the Jewish people, who descended from Abram and settled in the land of Canaan (Exodus 1:15; 9:13).

When Abram heard (14:14): A survivor of the battles fled from the invaders and managed to tell Abram what had happened. Abram was both wealthy and well known. The survivor probably located him without effort.

Trained men (14:14): Only a wealthy man would have a large number of trained men as part of his entourage. The phrase "trained men" has military overtones. These would be good fighters in Abram's little militia. Abram needed people he could count on. All the men in his force were men he knew personally and could trust. They would also fully trust his military leadership. They set out in pursuit of Lot's captors.

He and his servants...defeated them (14:15): After a 150-mile pursuit, Abram with his military prowess overcame the enemy and rescued his nephew Lot.

He brought back all the possessions (14:16): Abram brought back not only Lot but also all the material goods that the invading forces had plundered.

Genesis 14:17-24

Melchizedek king of Salem (14:18): Melchizedek's name is made up of two words meaning "king" and "righteous." He was also a priest. Ancient kings often served as priests. This was the case with Melchizedek. See Major Themes.

Bread and wine (14:18): This has nothing to do with the New Testament doctrine of communion. The food was for the troops after an exhausting victory.

"God Most High" (14:18): This is *El Elyon* in Hebrew. We learn much about God from the names ascribed to Him in the Bible. These names

are not man-made—God used these names to describe Himself. They describe His characteristics, each name making known something new about Him. The name *El Elyon* depicts God's strength and sovereignty.

Abram gave him a tenth of everything (14:20): This was a voluntary 10 percent offering derived from the spoils of the battle. This is the first time that giving 10 percent is mentioned in the Bible. In ancient times, a tenth was traditionally considered the king's share of the booty (see 1 Samuel 8:15,17). By offering a tenth, Abram was acknowledging Melchizedek's kingship in Salem.

"Give me the persons, but take the goods for yourself" (14:21): Abram didn't want any wealth from Melchizedek. He didn't want to be obligated to Melchizedek in any way. The Lord alone brought Abram blessing and wealth, and no other. Abram just wanted his servants back.

"I have lifted my hand" (14:22): A standard way of taking an oath in Bible times (Deuteronomy 32:40; Revelation 10:5-6).

Major Themes

1. *Was Melchizedek the preincarnate Christ?* Some today believe Melchizedek was a preincarnate appearance of Christ. Hebrews 7:3 is offered in support of this view: "He is without father or mother or genealogy, having neither beginning of days nor end of life, but resembling the Son of God he continues a priest forever." No human being, it is argued, can be described in such terms, so this must be the preincarnate Christ.

   Other scholars counter by suggesting that this verse simply means that the Old Testament Scriptures have no record—no account—of Melchizedek's parents or birth. Seen in this light, the silence of Scripture on these matters is divinely intended, thereby rendering Melchizedek an ideal *type* of Christ. (A type may be defined as a figure or representation of something yet to come.) Note that Melchizedek is described as being *like* the Son of God, not as *being* the Son of God (Hebrews 7:3). It seems best to conclude that Melchizedek was an actual historical person who served as a type of Christ, prefiguring Christ as a righteous King-Priest.

2. *The wickedness of Sodom.* Genesis 13:13 tells us that "the men of Sodom were wicked, great sinners against the Lord." A comparison of Genesis 13–14 with Genesis 19 reveals that the sin of Sodom was homosexuality. They wanted to "know" the men in Lot's house. The Hebrew word translated "know" (*yada*) does not always mean "to have sex with"; nonetheless, in Genesis it clearly has this meaning. Ten of the twelve times the word *yada* is used in Genesis, it refers to sexual intercourse (for example, Genesis 4:1,25). Lot himself refers to his two virgin daughters as not having "known" (or *yada*-ed) a man (Genesis 19:8), which is an obvious sexual use of the word. Lot thus implored the men not to act wickedly by "knowing" the men in his house in a sexual sense (Genesis 19:7; see also 2 Peter 2:7-10; Jude 7).

Digging Deeper with Cross-References

Oath-taking in the Bible—Leviticus 19:12; Numbers 30:2; Deuteronomy 23:21-23; Jeremiah 11:5; Matthew 5:33-37; James 5:12

Treaties in Bible times—Genesis 21:22-32; Deuteronomy 7:2; 1 Samuel 18:3-4; 23:18; 1 Kings 5:12-18; Jeremiah 34:8-20

Life Lessons

1. *God's people and personal wealth.* God does not condemn possessions or riches. To be wealthy is not a sin! Some very godly people in the Bible—Abram and Job, for example—were quite wealthy. But God does condemn a love of possessions or riches (Luke 16:13; 1 Timothy 6:10; Hebrews 13:5). The apostle Paul warned that those "who

desire to be rich fall into temptation, into a snare, into many senseless and harmful desires that plunge people into ruin and destruction" (1 Timothy 6:9). Jesus warned, "Do not lay up for yourselves treasures on earth, where moth and rust destroy and where thieves break in and steal, but lay up for yourselves treasures in heaven, where neither moth nor rust destroys and where thieves do not break in and steal" (Matthew 6:19-20; see also John 6:27).

2. *Take steps to avoid quarreling.* Genesis 13:8 reveals that some strife had developed between Abram's and Lot's herdsmen. Quarrelsomeness is a common problem among God's people. It is best to disarm troublesome situations before they become quarrels. As Proverbs 17:14 (NASB) puts it, "Stop contention before a quarrel starts." Second Timothy 2:24 urges us, "The Lord's servant must not be quarrelsome but kind to everyone." It is best to "seek peace and pursue it" (Psalm 34:14). Indeed, we should "strive for peace with everyone" (Hebrews 12:14).

Questions for Reflection and Discussion

1. Do you presently have any relationships characterized by strife? What have you learned in this lesson that might help you make things better?
2. What have you learned in this lesson about the importance of distancing yourself from sinful opportunities?
3. God is *El Elyon*—the strong and sovereign One. What does that mean to you personally?

Day 11

God's Covenant with Abram

Genesis 15

Scripture Reading and Insights

Begin by reading Genesis 15 in your favorite Bible. As you read, remember that the Word of God teaches us, trains us, and corrects us (2 Timothy 3:15-17).

In the previous lesson, we examined Abram's separation from Lot as well as Abram's military victory over an invading force. Today let's focus our attention on the Abrahamic covenant. With your Bible still accessible, consider the following insights on the biblical text.

Genesis 15:1-6

The word of the Lord came to Abram in a vision (15:1): As we have seen before in Genesis, God is the aggressor in communicating revelation to His people. It was particularly necessary in patriarchal times for God to communicate directly because people did not yet have Bibles. Visions were a common means of God's communications in biblical times.

"Fear not, Abram, I am your shield" (15:1): God is Abram's protector. God is often called the shield of His people. For example, "You, O Lord, are a shield about me" (Psalm 3:3). "He is a shield for all those who take refuge in him" (Psalm 18:30). "The Lord is my strength and my shield" (Psalm 28:7). Because God was Abram's shield, Abram didn't need to fear anything—including retaliation from the kings he had just overcome to rescue Lot (Genesis 14).

"Your reward shall be very great" (15:1): There are differing views as to what is meant here. Some believe that the reward relates to the countless descendants that would come from Abram's line. Others believe the reward is God Himself. In this line of thought, Abram's most precious treasure was God Himself (see also Deuteronomy 10:9).

"Lord God" (15:2): This is the Hebrew name *Adonai Yahweh*. *Adonai* means "Master" or "Lord" or "Sovereign One." *Yahweh* is God's covenant name that communicates eternal self-existence. *Adonai Yahweh* is thus the eternal, self-existent, sovereign Lord of the universe. This is the God who would fulfill the promises of the Abrahamic covenant.

"What will you give me, for I continue childless?" (15:2): Abram had received God's promises that he would have countless descendants (13:16). He had heard God's promises about a great nation emerging from his descendants (12:2). And yet no child of promise had been born. How could all this possibly come about?

"Eliezer of Damascus...a member of my household will be my heir" (15:2-3): Abram was not seeing God acting to fulfill what He had promised, so Abram pondered that maybe the solution was in his household servant, Eliezer of Damascus. Eliezer may have been "his servant, the oldest of his household" mentioned in Genesis 24:2. Perhaps he could be the heir of promise by proxy. In biblical days, a servant sometimes became an heir if no son had been born in the family.

"Your very own son shall be your heir" (15:4): God rejected Abram's solution, reiterating that Abram's very own son would be the heir of promise.

"Look toward heaven, and number the stars...So shall your offspring be" (15:5): God reaffirmed to Abram that his descendants would be as numberless as the stars (see Genesis 22:17; 26:4; Exodus 32:13). One should not miss the significance of this. God Himself called the starry universe into being. God said, "Let there be lights in the expanse of the heavens" (Genesis 1:14). And it was so. The same God who created the countless stars now tells Abram that his descendants would be as countless as the stars. Thus, in Romans 4:18 we read of Abram, "In hope he believed against hope, that he should become the father of many nations, as he had been told, 'So shall your offspring be.'"

He believed the Lord, and he counted it to him as righteousness (15:6): Here we have one of the most inspiring verses in all of Scripture. Abram believed God, and God therefore counted him as righteous. This verse is quoted in Romans 4:3,9,22; Galatians 3:6; and James 2:23. Romans 4:11 tells us that Abram is "the father of all who believe." See Major Themes.

Genesis 15:7-16

"I am the Lord" (15:7): Ancient royal covenants typically began with the king's self-identification, followed by a prologue stating the purpose of the covenant. God's covenant with Abram follows this format.

"Land to possess" (15:7): Abram would have countless descendants, and they would live in a land chosen by God Himself. We will see in verses 18-21 that God specifies the territories to be possessed by His people.

"How am I to know?" (15:8): Abram believed God and knew God was fully capable of bringing about what He promised. But Abram still wanted assurance about the land promises.

Cut them in half (15:9-10): In answering Abram, God initiates a covenant ceremony that involved cutting animals in half. This was a common covenant ritual in biblical times. Parties agreeing to a covenant used this ritual to say, "May this happen to me if I go back on my promise" (see Jeremiah 34:18-19).

Birds of prey came down on the carcasses (15:11): Many Bible expositors believe that this relates to God's revelation recorded in verse 13 that before entering the promised land, Abram's descendants would be enslaved in Egypt for 400 years.

Deep sleep fell on Abram (15:12): The interesting thing here is that God put Abram to sleep so that only God participated in the ritual of promise. God alone was the Promiser. The whole covenant hinged on Him and not Abram. This was an unconditional covenant. See Major Themes.

Dreadful and great darkness fell upon him (15:12): This darkness pointed forward to the enslavement of the Jews in Egypt described in verse 13.

"Your offspring will be sojourners in a land that is not theirs" (15:13): God now informed Abram of a hard truth. His descendants would definitely possess the land. But before this happens, his descendants would be detoured in Egypt for some 400 years. They would "be servants there" and "be afflicted." That is, they would be enslaved. Note that Bible expositors say the number 400 is intended as an approximation, a rounded-off number. Exodus 12:40 provides the exact number of 430 years.

"I will bring judgment...they shall come out with great possessions" (15:14): God would bring Egypt to its knees in judgment. God's people would depart Egypt with much of the Egyptians' wealth.

"You shall go to your fathers" (15:15): God now assures Abram that he would die in old age in a state of peace. He would go to his fathers, meaning that he would join those who preceded him in death in the afterlife. Note that Abram is portrayed as alive and well in the afterlife in one of Jesus's parables (Luke 16:19-31). Moreover, Jesus, in speaking about the Old Testament saints Abram, Isaac, and Jacob, said that God "is not God of the dead, but of the living" (Luke 20:38). In effect, Jesus was saying, "Abram, Isaac, and Jacob, though they died physically many years ago, are actually living today. For God, who calls Himself the God of Abraham, Isaac, and Jacob, is not the God of the dead but of the living."

"The iniquity of the Amorites is not yet complete" (15:16): The Jews, after departing Egypt, would come back to the Promised Land in the fourth generation. In Old Testament times, the length of a generation was considered to be the age of a man at the time his firstborn son was born. Abram would be 100 years old when his firstborn would be born, so a generation would be 100 years in his case. The fourth generation would be after 400 years.

The Amorites are Canaanites, presently living in Canaan. Archaeological discoveries reveal that the sin of the Amorites included such things as child sacrifice and religious prostitution. Once the iniquity of the Amorites reached the breaking point, God would judge them, and Israel would possess the land. This would take place when Israel under Joshua conquered Palestine.

Genesis 15:17-21

A smoking fire pot and a flaming torch (15:17): Fire often symbolizes God's presence in the Bible. Recall the burning bush that Moses saw (Exodus 3:2) and the pillar of fire that led the Israelites out of Egypt (Exodus 13:21). The smoking fire pot and flaming torch represent God's presence passing through the animal pieces, thereby indicating that this was an unconditional covenant that depended on God alone for its fulfillment.

The Lord made a covenant with Abram (15:18): This is literally, "cut a covenant." God here provides more precise details regarding the boundaries of the Promised Land. Other specific descriptions of the land are found in Numbers 34:1-12; Joshua 15:1-2; and Ezekiel 47:15-20.

Major Themes

1. *The Abrahamic covenant is unconditional.* A conditional covenant has an "if" attached. It demands that the recipient meets certain obligations or conditions before God is obligated to fulfill His promise. On the other hand, an unconditional covenant has no "ifs" attached. Whatever God promises, He sovereignly gives to the recipient of the covenant apart from the recipient's merit. According to ancient custom, the two parties of a conditional covenant divided animals into two equal parts and then walked between them, indicating they were mutually responsible to fulfill the obligations of the covenant (see Jeremiah 34:18-19). In the case of the Abrahamic covenant, however, God put Abram into a deep sleep and passed between the parts alone. This indicates that God made unconditional promises to Abram in this covenant (Genesis 15:17).
2. *God's eternal purpose.* Human history in all its details, even the most minute, is but the outworking of God's eternal purposes. What has happened in the past, what is happening today, and what will happen in the prophetic future are all evidence of the unfolding of a purposeful

plan devised by the wondrous, personal God of the Bible (Ephesians 3:11; 2 Timothy 1:9). God used covenants to Old Testament personalities like Noah, Abram, and David to accomplish His eternal purpose.

Digging Deeper with Cross-References

Visions in Bible times—Genesis 46:2; Numbers 12:6; Psalm 89:19; Daniel 2:19; 4:5,13; 10:7; Hosea 12:10; Joel 2:28; Luke 1:22; Acts 2:17; 10:3; 11:5; 16:9; 18:9; 2 Corinthians 12:1

Abraham's descendants promised throughout Genesis—Genesis 13:16; 15:5,18; 16:10; 17:6,20; 22:17; 26:4,24; 28:14; 35:11; 46:3; 48:4,19

Life Lessons

1. *"Fear not."* God appeared to Abram in a vision and said, "Fear not, Abram, I am your shield" (15:1). God also tells us to "fear not." Proverbs 3:25 tells us that we need not be afraid of sudden terror. The psalmist affirms, "The LORD is my light and my salvation; whom shall I fear? The LORD is the stronghold of my life; of whom shall I be afraid" (Psalm 27:1). We are assured that God has given us "a spirit not of fear but of power and love and self-control" (2 Timothy 1:7). Our beloved Savior, Jesus Christ, instructs us, "Peace I leave with you; my peace I give to you. Not as the world gives do I give to you. Let not your hearts be troubled, neither let them be afraid" (John 14:27).

2. *Justification by faith.* Genesis 15:6 tells us that Abram "believed the LORD, and he counted it to him as righteousness." This is justification by faith. The word "justified" is a legal term. Negatively, the word means that one is once-for-all pronounced not guilty before

God. Positively, the word means that one is once-for-all pronounced righteous. Abram believed the Lord and was thus both acquitted of sin and pronounced righteous before God. The same is true of you and me. When a person trusts in Christ for salvation, he or she is pronounced not guilty and once-for-all righteous (Romans 3:25,28,30). It is a singular and instantaneous judicial act of God (Romans 3:25,28,30; 8:33-34).

Questions for Reflection and Discussion

1. What does it mean to you personally that you have been justified by faith (Genesis 15:6; Romans 3:28)? Do you ever make the mistake of thinking that you can make God like you more by engaging in good works?
2. Are you facing any circumstances that are producing anxiety? Can you imagine God saying to you today, "Fear not"?
3. How is Abram a model for us?

Day 12

Ishmael Is Born

Genesis 16

Scripture Reading and Insights

Begin by reading Genesis 16 in your favorite Bible. As you read, remember that the Word of God teaches us, trains us, and corrects us (2 Timothy 3:15-17).

In yesterday's reading, we focused attention on the Abrahamic covenant. Now let's find out about the birth of Ishmael. With your Bible still accessible, consider the following insights on the biblical text.

Genesis 16:1-6

Sarai...no children (16:1): Sarai was barren, or infertile. At this point, Abram and Sarai had been childless for a decade since receiving the promise. This was especially difficult for Sarai, for ancient society placed a heavy premium on having children. To not have children was taken by some as a sign of God's disfavor. See Major Themes.

Hagar (16:1): Sarai's Egyptian handmaiden, probably first acquired while Abram and Sarai were in Egypt (12:10-20).

"The Lord has prevented me from bearing children" (16:2): Sarai's impatience seems to be simmering. She may have thought the Lord was not keeping His promise. That being so, Abram and Sarai now began to act on their own to bring about the line of promise.

"Go in to my servant" (16:2): This is a euphemism for sexual intercourse (see Genesis 6:4; 30:3; 38:8-9; 39:14). Archaeology sheds some

interesting light on a man "going into" his wife's servant. Twenty thousand baked clay tablets discovered at Nuzi (east of the Tigris River) contain a plethora of information on customs, stories, and history, shedding light on the book of Genesis. These legal tablets indicate that an infertile wife had the prerogative of giving her maidservant to her husband in order to provide him an heir who could then be adopted by the wife. This is what Sarai did in suggesting that Abram impregnate Hagar. If a husband (such as Abram) said to a handmaiden's son whom he impregnated, "You are my son," then the boy became an adopted son and heir.

At this time, Abram is 85 years old. From a human perspective, it would seem that his child-bearing years are rapidly running out. It would have been infinitely better, of course, for Sarai to pray to the God who opens women's wombs (see Psalm 113:9; see also 1 Samuel 1; Luke 1).

Abram listened to the voice of Sarai (16:2): At this point it seems that Abram is listening to his wife more than he is listening to God. This seems to represent a desire to accomplish by human means something that God had promised to accomplish by divine means.

One cannot help noticing a parallel here between Abram and Adam. Adam had listened to his wife instead of listening to God, and humankind fell as a result. Abram listened to Sarai instead of God, causing disruption between Sarai and Hagar as well as strife between their descendants. We might also observe that like Eve, Sarai passed the buck and blamed someone else for the results of her act—namely, Abram (verse 5). A theme is emerging—it is always best to do things God's way.

Sarai...gave her to Abram (16:3-4): Despite God's earlier assurance that an heir would be born to him (see 15:2-5), Abram went along with Sarai's scheme to produce an heir who could be adopted into the family.

She looked with contempt on her mistress (16:4): After Hagar discovered she was pregnant, she looked on Sarai with contempt, and Sarai became upset. When Sarai suggested Hagar as a solution to her infertility, she had not considered the possibility of such contemptuous behavior. Abram's camp included hundreds of people, and everyone likely knew that Sarai was barren. Now, with the pregnancy of Hagar, Sarai probably felt some sense of public humiliation. Moreover, in the eyes of society, Hagar—because she bore a child—might be considered by others in the camp as the primary wife, in place of Sarai. Hagar's contempt would have been exceedingly hurtful to Sarai.

"May the wrong done to me be on you" (16:5): Sarai promptly confronted Abram and expressed her displeasure. She apparently wanted Abram to intervene and set Hagar straight.

"May the Lord judge between you and me" (16:5): This was a common way of expressing personal offense, hostility, and suspicion about the motives of another.

"Behold, your servant is in your power" (16:6): Abram passed the responsibility right back onto Sarai's shoulders. Abram told her to do as she pleased with Hagar. Sarai laid it on so thick with Hagar that Hagar up and left.

Genesis 16:7-16

The angel of the Lord (16:7): Literally, the "angel of *Yahweh*." This is the first of 48 references to the Angel of the Lord in the Old Testament. The Angel of the Lord was an appearance of God (a theophany). Notice that the Angel spoke with God's authority and made promises to Hagar that only God could keep. For example, He said, "I will surely multiply your offspring so that they cannot be numbered for multitude" (16:10). No ordinary angel could make such a promise, for the promise itself required the exercise of omniscience, and fulfilling the promise would require omnipotence. It is noteworthy that Hagar expressed an awareness of the Angel's deity, for she acknowledged that she had seen God (verse 13). Many Bible expositors believe that this appearance of God was actually the preincarnate Christ (that is, a Christophany). See Major Themes.

A spring of water (16:7): Hagar found this pool on her way to Shur, a sandy desert between Palestine and Egypt. Hagar apparently wanted to make her way back to Egypt, where she could reunite with old friends or perhaps even some relatives (see 25:18).

"Where have you come from and where are you going?" (16:8): The

divine Angel asks questions not because He doesn't know the answers but as a means of drawing Hagar out. Hagar indicated she just wanted to get away from Sarai. Hagar may have been running away from Sarai, but she ran into God. God was watching out for her!

"Return to your mistress and submit to her" (16:9): God told Hagar to return and submit. From God's perspective, the mistress–servant relationship was not dissolved. Her place was not to rebel.

"I will surely multiply your offspring" (16:10): God gave this servant girl an amazing promise. He informed her that she would be the mother of a multitude. This means that Abram would be the father of two different lines, each with innumerable descendants. We find this promise of a line through Ishmael reaffirmed in Genesis 17:20, where God says, "As for Ishmael...I have blessed him and will make him fruitful and multiply him greatly. He shall father twelve princes, and I will make him into a great nation." We find a genealogy of Ishmael in Genesis 25:13-16.

"You are pregnant...call his name Ishmael" (16:11): God instructed her to name her son Ishmael. The name means "God hears." It commemorates God's response to her cry of desperation after she fled from Sarai.

"Wild donkey of a man" (16:12): Literally, "wild ass of a man." Ishmael would be aggressive and independent, just like an untamed wild donkey.

"He shall dwell over against all his kinsmen" (16:12): Today Arabs claim Ishmael as their forefather (see Genesis 17:20; 25:12-18). Of course, there has been a longstanding hostility between the descendants of Ishmael (Arabs) and those of Isaac (the Jews).

"You are a God of seeing" (16:13): I noted previously that in Bible times, names always meant something. A name was considered as equivalent to whoever or whatever bore it. A person's entire internal and external pattern of behavior was gathered up into his name. Indeed, knowing a person's name amounted to knowing his essence. Hagar thus called God "a God of seeing." After all, God had seen her affliction and responded with help.

Beer-lahai-roi (16:14): Hagar named the well at that (unknown) location Beer-lahai-roi, or "well of the Living One who sees me." In ancient times, people often named places based on circumstances that occurred there.

Abram called the name of his son...Ishmael (16:15): Abram named his son as God instructed Hagar. Some Bible expositors suggest that Abram may have felt rebuke after hearing that the child was to be named "God hears." After all, Abram himself had earlier heard God's promise about a son, and yet he succumbed to his wife's plan to produce an heir through a handmaiden. In any event, with this epilogue, Abram now seems to be taking responsibility for Ishmael.

Major Themes

1. *Infertility in Bible times*. Infertility in biblical times brought great reproach and was sometimes even considered a punishment from God (1 Samuel 1:6; Isaiah 47:9; 49:21; Luke 1:7,25). Bible expositors suggest that the reproach attached to infertility—especially among the Hebrews—was likely due to the fervent hope and expectation of the Messiah being born of a Hebrew woman or from her line. Hebrew women everywhere hoped for this awesome privilege.
2. *The Angel of the Lord*. Many theologians believe that appearances of the Angel of the Lord in Old Testament times were actually preincarnate appearances of Jesus Christ. ("Preincarnate" means "before becoming a human being.") When the word "Angel" is used in reference to Christ in the Old Testament, the word indicates not a created being (like other angels), but—true to its Hebrew root—a messenger, or one who is sent. Christ as the Angel of the Lord was sent by the Father as a messenger to accomplish specific tasks in Old Testament times. Three lines of evidence identify Christ as the Angel of the Lord:
   - The Angel of *Yahweh* is God (Exodus 3:6).

- The Angel of *Yahweh* is distinct from *Yahweh* (Zechariah 1:12).
- The Angel of Yahweh and Jesus share notable parallels. For example, just as Jesus was sent into the world by the Father in New Testament times (John 3:16-17), so the Angel of *Yahweh* was sent into the world by *Yahweh* in Old Testament times (Judges 13:8-9).

Digging Deeper with Cross-References

God as a Judge—Genesis 16:5; 18:25; 30:6; 31:53; 1 Chronicles 16:33; Psalms 7:8; 50:4; 58:11; 67:4; 75:7; Ecclesiastes 12:14; Isaiah 2:4; Micah 4:3; 1 Peter 1:17; Revelation 20:11-15

Seeing God—Genesis 32:30; Exodus 24:10; Numbers 12:8; 14:14; Judges 6:22; 13:22; Job 19:27; 42:5; Psalms 27:4; 141:8; Isaiah 6:5; 33:17; Matthew 5:8; John 14:9

Life Lessons

1. *Trust God even when it hurts.* After Hagar was mistreated by Sarai, she fled and felt all alone in her problems. She was rescued by the Lord. She trusted in what the Lord said to her. You and I learn a good lesson here. Sometimes our problems may be so severe that we just feel like withdrawing and hiding from them. But God calls us to trust Him: "Call upon me in the day of trouble; I will deliver you, and you shall glorify me" (Psalm 50:15). "Trust in him at all times...God is a refuge for us" (Psalm 62:8). "It is better to take refuge in the LORD than to trust in man" (Psalm 118:8). "Trust in the LORD with all your heart, and do not lean on your own understanding. In all your ways acknowledge him, and he will make straight your paths" (Proverbs 3:5-6).

2. *Seeing God.* After the Lord appeared to Hagar, she said, "Truly here I have seen him who looks after me" (Genesis 16:13). We will likely never experience the Lord appearing to us. But we can look forward to one day seeing God face-to-face, and we will be with Him forever. Revelation 21:3 affirms, "Behold, the dwelling place of God is with man. He will dwell with them, and they will be his people, and God himself will be with them as their God" (see also 1 Corinthians 13:12; 1 John 3:2; Revelation 22:4).

Questions for Reflection and Discussion

1. Are you ever tempted to force your own solution onto a difficulty or circumstance instead of waiting for God to act? Has today's passage provided you any insights on this?
2. Have comments or suggestions from well-meaning relatives ever drawn you away from what you consider to be God's will for your life?
3. What does it mean to you personally that God is a "God of seeing" and a "God of hearing"?

Day 13

Abraham Is Circumcised

Genesis 17

Scripture Reading and Insights

Begin by reading Genesis 17 in your favorite Bible. As you read, never forget that you can trust everything that is recorded in the Word of God (Matthew 5:18; John 10:35).

In yesterday's reading, we focused attention on Ishmael's birth. Today we shift attention to the covenant sign of circumcision. With your Bible still accessible, consider the following insights on the biblical text.

Genesis 17:1-8

The Lord appeared to Abram (17:1): God often appeared to people in patriarchal times. This was His primary means of special revelation to His people. In the present context, God renewed and expanded His covenant with Abram.

"I am God Almighty" (17:1): In ancient covenants, the one making the covenant often begins by identifying himself. God calls himself "God Almighty" (*El Shaddai*). Some 56 times Scripture declares that God is Almighty. Scripture portrays God as being all-powerful (Jeremiah 32:17). No one can hold back His hand (Daniel 4:35). Nothing is impossible with Him (Matthew 19:26; Mark 10:27; Luke 1:37).

"Walk before me, and be blameless" (17:1): The obligations of the covenant fall on God alone, but this does not give Abram license to live

any way he wishes. God calls on him to live in keeping with the reality that he and his descendants would be the covenant people of God.

"That I may make my covenant between me and you" (17:2): God introduced His covenant with Abram in Genesis 12 and then provided details of it in Genesis 15. Earlier, Abram thought that maybe God would fulfill His promise through Ishmael. But that was not to be the case. At this point, 13 years have passed since Ishmael was born (see 16:16; 17:24-25).

Abram fell on his face (17:3): People often fell on their faces in Bible times when God appeared to them. When Manoah and his wife saw the Angel of the Lord (an appearance of God, likely the preincarnate Christ), "they fell on their faces to the ground" (Judges 13:20). When Ezekiel saw the glory of God, he fell on his face (Ezekiel 3:23; 43:3; 44:4). The apostle John saw Christ in His glory and "fell at his feet as though dead" (Revelation 1:17).

"You shall be the father of a multitude of nations" (17:4): A primary promise of the covenant relates to the many nations that would emerge from Abram's line. This promise is restated in the verses that follow.

"No longer...Abram, but...Abraham" (17:5): The Hebrew word transliterated Abraham means "father of a multitude" (see Romans 4:17).

"For I have made you the father of a multitude of nations" (17:5): God here repeats the reason for Abraham's name change—perhaps because Abram has had a few lapses of faith regarding the promised multitude of descendants.

"Kings shall come from you" (17:6): Individual nations and individual kings would come from Abraham (including David and Solomon). This points to the reality that Israel would one day become a monarchy (see Genesis 35:11; 36:31; Numbers 24:7; Deuteronomy 17:14-18; 28:36).

"I will establish my covenant" (17:7): God refers to the covenant as "my covenant." He is the one who set it up. He is the one making the promises, and He is the one who will fulfill them.

"To be God to you and to your offspring" (17:7): This is the very heart of God's covenant promise to Abraham and his descendants. God's

people cannot truly experience the blessings of the covenant without also experiencing the presence of the Blesser, who would watch over and care for them.

"I will give to you...all the land of Canaan" (17:8): This is yet another reaffirmation of the land-promise stipulations of the covenant.

"For an everlasting possession" (17:8): The Promised Land would be Abraham's descendants' everlasting possession. The final fulfillment of these land promises will take place in Christ's future millennial kingdom—that is, His future 1000-year reign following His second coming (see Revelation 20).

"I will be their God" (17:8): This sets Abraham and his descendants apart from all the pagan nations the Jews would encounter, for they all worshipped false gods that in fact were not true gods at all. The one true God would be the God of the Jews.

Genesis 17:9-14

"You shall keep my covenant" (17:9): Again, the obligations of the covenant fall on God alone, but this does not give Abraham license to live any way he wishes. God calls him to live in keeping with the reality that he and his descendants would be the covenant people of God. He was to remain faithful.

"Every male among you shall be circumcised" (17:10): The Old Testament ceremony of circumcision consisted of cutting away the foreskin of the male organ with a sharp knife or stone (Exodus 4:25; Joshua 5:2). Circumcision constituted an oath that said something like this: "If I do not honor the covenant, may the Lord cut me off as I have cut off the foreskin." See Major Themes.

"Sign of the covenant" (17:11): In Bible times, a sign commonly accompanied a covenant. It was to be a memorial and reminder of the covenant. For example, the sign of the Noahic covenant was a bow in the clouds (9:13). Abraham gave Abimelech seven ewe lambs as a "witness" to their covenant (Genesis 21:30). Baptism is the sign of the new covenant (Romans 6:3-4; Colossians 2:9-12).

"Eight days old" (17:12): This age requirement is repeated in Leviticus 12:3.

"Whether born in your house or bought with your money" (17:12): Any member of the covenant community must abide by covenant stipulations, including the covenant requirement of circumcision.

"Any uncircumcised male who is not circumcised" (17:14): To refuse the cutting off of the foreskin results in being cut off from God's people. This means that one loses all the benefits of being a part of God's chosen nation, a nation led by God, a theocracy.

Genesis 17:15-27

"Your wife... not... Sarai, but Sarah" (17:15): Sarai's name (meaning "my princess") is now changed to Sarah ("princess"). The name is appropriate since she would be the ancestress of multitudes—of nations and kings.

"I will give you a son by her" (17:16): This was no doubt astonishing news to Abraham. How could an old woman who had long been infertile give birth? Abraham was now learning that "with man this is impossible, but with God all things are possible" (Matthew 19:26).

"She shall become nations; kings of peoples shall come from her" (17:16): Not only would Sarah give birth, but a multitude of peoples would come from her.

Abraham fell on his face and laughed (17:17): Abraham fell on his face again, which, as noted previously, is an appropriate response. However, Abraham then laughed and expressed incredulity. Abraham responded this way because not only would he (an old man) be the father of many nations, but his infertile wife, Sarah, would be their mother.

"Oh that Ishmael might live before you" (17:18): Abraham thought that perhaps Ishmael could become the son of promise.

"Sarah your wife shall bear you a son" (17:19): God repeated the promise to Abraham. If I might put it in modern vernacular, Abraham was a bit slow to believe, so God said to him, "Abraham, read My lips! Sarah will bear the child of promise. It's a done deal—it's a lock."

"You shall call his name Isaac" (17:19): This name means "he laughs." The name would be a perpetual reminder to Abraham of how he first responded to the news that he and Sarah would bear a son.

"I will establish my covenant with him" (17:19): God left no doubt in

Abraham's mind. The covenant would not be fulfilled through Ishmael. Isaac would be the son of promise.

"As for Ishmael" (17:20): God affirmed that He would bless Ishmael and make him fruitful. Genesis 25:12-16 reveals that God indeed did make Ishmael fruitful, as promised.

"But I will establish my covenant with Isaac" (17:21): Archaeological discoveries reveal that among the ancients, a natural son would become the heir of the family, even if born far after the son of a slave-wife.

God went up from Abraham (17:22): God's special revelation to Abraham was complete. He therefore departed Abraham's presence.

Every male... of Abraham's house... he circumcised (17:23): Abraham did not delay in fulfilling the covenant stipulation of circumcision. "All the men of his house" (verse 27) were circumcised.

Abraham was ninety-nine years old (17:24): Abraham's obedience came at a cost. It was no doubt difficult for a ninety-nine-year-old man to experience circumcision. But Abraham obeyed without hesitation.

Ishmael his son was thirteen years old (17:25): Circumcision was no doubt a difficult experience for a young lad just entering puberty.

Major Themes

1. *Old Testament names for God.* God's names are not man-made; God Himself used these names to describe Himself. The name *Yahweh* reveals that God is eternally self-existent (Exodus 3:14-15). The name *Yahweh-Nissi* means that the Lord is our protective banner. The name *Elohim* means that God is a Strong One who has fullness of power (Genesis 1:1). The name *El Shaddai* indicates that God is not only mighty but also full of compassion, grace, and mercy. The name *Adonai* means that God is Lord and Master.
2. *Circumcision in Bible times.* "Circumcision" comes from the Greek word *peritome*, which means a "cutting around." The Old Testament ceremony of circumcision consisted of

cutting away the foreskin of the male organ with a sharp knife or stone (Exodus 4:25; Joshua 5:2). The son's father usually performed the ritual, although any Israelite could do it (but never a Gentile). After God made a covenant with Abraham (Genesis 15), He commanded that every male should be circumcised as a token of the covenant. Everyone not so circumcised was to be "cut off from his people" as having broken the covenant (Genesis 17:10-14). Circumcision fell into disuse during the wilderness sojourn because the disobedient nation was forbidden to use the sign of the covenant. However, when Israel entered Canaan, Joshua circumcised the generation that had been born in the wilderness (Joshua 5:3). Christians in New Testament times were exempt from having to be circumcised (Acts 15:5; Galatians 5:2).

Digging Deeper with Cross-References

Appearances of God—Genesis 12:7; 18:1; 26:2; 35:7,9; Exodus 3:16; 1 Kings 3:5; 9:2; 11:9; 2 Chronicles 3:1; Micah 1:3; Habakkuk 3:3; Acts 7:2

God is Almighty—Genesis 17:1; Psalm 91:1; 2 Corinthians 6:18; see also Matthew 19:26; Mark 10:27

Life Lessons

1. *"Walk before me, and be blameless."* When God appeared to Abraham, He instructed him, "Walk before me, and be blameless" (Genesis 17:1). God desires that we too walk blamelessly before Him—"pure and blameless for the day of Christ" (Philippians 1:10). We are called to be "blameless and innocent, children of God without blemish in the midst of a crooked and twisted generation, among whom [we] shine as lights in the world" (Philippians 2:15; see also 1 Thessalonians 5:23).

Day 14

Sodom and Gomorrah Are Destroyed

Genesis 18–19

Scripture Reading and Insights

Begin by reading Genesis 18–19 in your favorite Bible. As you read, never forget that you can trust everything that is recorded in the Word of God (Matthew 5:18; John 10:35).

In the previous lesson, we examined the covenant sign of circumcision. Now let's find out the details of God's visit to Abraham, Abraham's intercession for Lot's survival, and the destruction of Sodom. With your Bible still accessible, consider the following insights on the biblical text.

Genesis 18:1-21

Oaks of Mamre (18:1): Named after Mamre the Amorite, who owned a large grove of trees. This was located at Hebron, about 22 miles south of Jerusalem.

Three men (18:2): One of these men was actually *Yahweh*, the Lord. The other two were angels (see 19:1). When angels appear as men, their resemblance to men can be so realistic that they are actually taken to be human beings (see Hebrews 13:2).

"If I have found favor in your sight" (18:3): Abraham may not yet have known he was in the presence of *Yahweh*, who had taken on a humanlike appearance. Abraham was hospitable and invited them to stay and eat.

He stood by them under the tree while they ate (18:8): People often shared meals when making covenants in ancient times (see Exodus 24:9-11; Matthew 26:17-30).

"Where is Sarah your wife?" (18:9): God knew where she was, but He used the question to introduce an important topic of discussion related to the covenant.

"This time next year" (18:10): Previously God had given Abraham a general promise of a son. Now God gives a specific time frame for the birth of the child of promise.

Sarah was listening... Sarah laughed (18:10-12): Sarah may have been unaware of the promise God made to Abraham that she would bear a son (see 17:19). Or perhaps Abraham told her but she didn't believe it. Whichever view is correct, Sarah laughed inwardly.

The Lord said to Abraham, "Why did Sarah laugh?" (18:13): One of the three men displayed omniscience, thereby revealing His true identity as *Yahweh*, who alone is all-knowing. Psalm 147:5 affirms that God's understanding is beyond measure. His knowledge is infinite (Psalms 33:13-15; 139:11-12; 147:5; Proverbs 15:3; Isaiah 40:14; 46:10).

"Is anything too hard for the Lord?" (18:14): This is a rhetorical question. The answer is obvious—nothing is too hard for the Lord. Notice that the visitor here identifies Himself as the Lord. The Lord God is all-powerful (Jeremiah 32:17) and Almighty (Revelation 19:6). Nothing is impossible for Him (Matthew 19:26; Mark 10:27; Luke 1:37).

"At the appointed time" (18:14): God has a timetable for the outworking of His sovereign plan. In New Testament times, Jesus was born "when the fullness of time had come" (Galatians 4:4).

Sarah denied it (18:15): Sarah denied that she laughed, but the truth could not be hidden from the omniscient Lord, who knows the human heart (Psalm 69:5; Proverbs 20:27; Hebrews 4:13).

They looked down toward Sodom (18:16): The look was ominous. It was a look that said, "And now I must act."

"Shall I hide from Abraham what I am about to do?" (18:17): Abraham—and the covenant God made with him—played a central role in the outworking of God's plan on earth. For this reason, God made him aware of His intention to destroy Sodom and Gomorrah.

"Because the outcry against Sodom and Gomorrah is great" (18:20): So awful were the sins of Sodom and Gomorrah that they metaphorically cried out to heaven, begging for punishment.

"I will go down to see" (18:21): God is omniscient. He knew of the transgressions transpiring in Sodom. The two angels were likely sent to investigate Sodom so there would be no question among observing humans that God was right to destroy an entire city.

Genesis 18:22-33

Abraham still stood before the Lord... "Will you indeed..." (18:22-23): Abraham begins his work of intercession, pleading to the Lord on behalf of any righteous people who may yet be in the cities.

"Shall not the Judge of all the earth do what is just?" (18:25): This is a rhetorical question. Abraham knew that God was absolutely just—He carries out His righteous standards justly and with equity. God never shows any partiality or unfairness in His dealings with people (Zephaniah 3:5; Romans 3:26).

"Fifty righteous" (18:26): One of the 50 was Abraham's nephew Lot. Abraham pondered the possibility that other righteous people might be in the city.

"I who am but dust and ashes" (18:27): Abraham recognizes that he is but a creature speaking with the divine Creator. His reference to himself as "dust and ashes" shows his humility before God.

"Fifty... Forty-five... forty... thirty... twenty... ten" (18:28-32): Abraham continued to humbly ask the Lord whether He would destroy the city if decreasing numbers of righteous people were found there. God conceded that He would not destroy the city even if only ten righteous people were found. The fact that only Lot and his family were evacuated shows that the number was indeed less than ten (19:14).

Genesis 19:1-22

The two angels came to Sodom (19:1): These are the same two angels that visited Abraham along with *Yahweh* (the "three men" of chapter 18).

When Lot saw them, he... bowed (19:1): Bowing was a common form of greeting in ancient times. Lot may have invited the visitors to stay with him not only out of common courtesy but also to prevent homosexual rape.

"Where are the men" (19:5): The men of the city were homosexuals. When they asked, "Where are the men?" they were seeking sexual gratification.

"Know them" (19:5): "Know them" is a euphemism for sexual intercourse. These men wanted to engage in sex with the men in Lot's house.

"Do not act so wickedly" (19:7): Lot knew homosexuality was a wicked sin. He urged the men to back off.

"Two daughters" (19:8): Lot's offer boggles the mind. Why would he allow his daughters to be sexually abused? Some Bible expositors suggest that Old Testament hosts commonly felt absolutely responsible to watch after visitors to their homes, and that is why Lot offered up his daughters. Lot urged the men not to act wickedly, but by offering his daughters in an attempt to rescue his guests, he acted wickedly himself.

Struck with blindness (19:11): This is an ironic twist. Lot tries to protect the visitors, but the visitors end up protecting Lot.

"We are about to destroy this place" (19:13): With wickedness confirmed beyond any doubt, judgment was now irrevocable and imminent.

Sons-in-law (19:14): His sons-in-law thought Lot was kidding. Their failure to take him seriously was a lethal mistake.

"Escape for your life. Do not look back" (19:17): There is great urgency in these words. The idea is, "Run for your life!"

"This city is near enough to flee to" (19:20): The city of Zoar is a small town near the Dead Sea.

"I grant you this favor" (19:21): Apparently Zoar had been slated for judgment along with Sodom and Gomorrah. But it is a small city and would now be spared in order to accommodate Lot's request.

Genesis 19:23-29

The Lord rained on Sodom and Gomorrah sulfur and fire (19:24): Archaeologists have discovered abundant deposits of asphalt, petroleum, and natural gas in Sodom. If these combustible materials were ignited, brimstone and fire would explode and rain on the city.

Lot's wife...looked back (19:26): Lot's wife disregarded the angel's warning against looking back (verse 17). Disobedience brought immediate judgment. She became encased in salt.

God remembered Abraham and sent Lot out (19:29): Lot was rescued because of God's affection for Abraham. We might say that Lot was rescued because he had a friend in high places (see James 2:23).

Genesis 19:30-38

Afraid to live in Zoar (19:30): Perhaps some in Zoar thought Lot had something to do with Sodom's destruction. Lot and his daughters had no place to go but into a cave.

"Make our father drink wine...lie with him...became pregnant" (19:32-36): Lot's daughters got him drunk on different nights, shamelessly engaged in incest, and became pregnant by him. Lot's daughters had lived long enough in Sodom for their sense of morality to become debased. As one Bible expositor put it, it was hard to remove Lot and his family from Sodom, but it was harder still to remove Sodom from the hearts of his family.

Moab (19:37): The name Moab literally means "from the father." He became the father of the Moabites, who dwelt east of the Dead Sea. They would become enemies of Israel.

Ben-ammi (19:38): A name meaning "son of my people"—the child's father and mother were in the same family (but not by marriage). He became the father of the Ammonites, who dwelt northeast of the Dead Sea. They too would be enemies of Israel.

Major Themes

1. *God protects His people.* God has a long history of protecting His people from judgment. Enoch was transferred to heaven before the judgment of the flood. Noah and his family were safe in the ark throughout the flood. Lot was taken out of Sodom before judgment fell

on the city. The firstborn among the Hebrews in Egypt were sheltered by the blood of the Paschal Lamb before judgment fell. Likewise, the spies were safely out of Jericho and Rahab was secured before judgment fell on Jericho.

2. *The sin of homosexuality*. The Bible explicitly warns that homosexuals will not inherit the kingdom of God (1 Corinthians 6:9-10). The Scriptures consistently condemn homosexual practices (for example, Leviticus 18:22; Romans 1:26). God loves all persons, including homosexuals, but He hates homosexuality. The Bible condemns all types of fornication, which would include homosexuality (Matthew 15:19; Mark 7:21; Acts 15:20,29; Galatians 5:19-21; 1 Thessalonians 4:3; Hebrews 13:4). The good news is that the apostle Paul speaks of the possibility of complete liberation from homosexual sin (1 Corinthians 6:9-11).

Digging Deeper with Cross-References

Angels used in judgment—Numbers 22:22; Judges 5:23; 2 Samuel 24:16; 2 Kings 19:35; 1 Chronicles 21:15; 2 Chronicles 32:21; Psalms 35:5; 78:49; Isaiah 37:36; Acts 12:23

Interceding for others—Genesis 20:7,17; Exodus 10:18; Numbers 11:2; Deuteronomy 9:20,26; 1 Samuel 7:5; 2 Samuel 24:17; 1 Kings 13:6; 1 Chronicles 21:17; 2 Chronicles 30:18; Job 42:10; Psalm 106:23; Jeremiah 18:20; Ezekiel 9:8; Daniel 9:16; Zechariah 1:12; 7:2; Luke 7:3; Acts 8:15; Romans 15:30; Ephesians 1:16; 1 Timothy 2:1; 2 Timothy 1:18

Life Lessons

1. *With God all things are possible*. Even though Abraham and Sarah were too old to have a baby (from a human perspective), the Lord said to Abraham, "Is anything

too hard for the Lord?" (Genesis 18:14). We must not forget that God can bring about anything He desires. Job affirmed to God, "I know that You can do all things; no plan of Yours can be thwarted" (Job 42:2 nasb). God asserted, "My purpose will stand, and I will do all that I please" (Isaiah 46:10 niv). God assures us, "Surely, as I have planned, so it will be, and as I have purposed, so it will happen" (Isaiah 14:24).

2. *Sexual purity*. Scripture is clear that a sexual relationship is only for the confines of a marriage between a male and a female (1 Corinthians 7:2). The apostles urged all Christians to abstain from fornication (Acts 15:20). Paul said that the body is not for fornication and that a man should flee it (1 Corinthians 6:13,18). Adultery is condemned in Scripture (Exodus 20:14). Jesus pronounced adultery wrong even in its basic motives (Matthew 5:27-28). Paul called adultery an evil work of the flesh (Galatians 5:19). Sex within marriage, however, is good (see Genesis 2:24; Matthew 19:5).

Questions for Reflection and Discussion

1. Do you ever feel as if God is waiting too long to answer your prayers? What have you learned in this lesson that helps you gain perspective?
2. Are you a believer in intercessory prayer? How is Abraham a good model for us in this regard?
3. Do you ever struggle with sexual purity? Has this lesson motivated you to make any new resolutions?

Day 15

Abraham Encounters King Abimelech

Genesis 20

Scripture Reading and Insights

Begin by reading Genesis 20 in your favorite Bible. As you read, trust God to open your eyes so you can discover wondrous things from His Word (Psalm 119:18).

In yesterday's reading, we learned about God's visit to Abraham, Abraham's intercession for Lot's survival, and the destruction of Sodom. Now let's examine the details of Abraham's sojourn at Gerar and his encounter with Abimelech. With your Bible still accessible, consider the following insights on the biblical text.

Genesis 20:1-7

Negeb (20:1): The desert region south of Palestine.

Between Kadesh and Shur (20:1): Kadesh is an area southeast of the Dead Sea. Shur is in the northwest portion of the Sinai Peninsula.

Gerar (20:1): A Philistine city between Palestine and Egypt.

"She is my sister" (20:2): Abraham lied about his wife to Egypt's Pharaoh 25 years earlier (12:10-20). Sarah was getting up in years (90 years old at this time), but she had maintained her attractive appearance. Abraham therefore feared that if Abimelech wanted Sarah for himself, he would think nothing of disposing of him as her husband. He thus decided to stretch the truth by telling Abimelech that Sarah was his sister. (She was actually his half sister, as we see in verse 12.) Isaac would

later engage in the same kind of deception (26:1-11), having learned well from his father. Deception would plague Abraham's family throughout the rest of Genesis. See Digging Deeper with Cross-References.

Abimelech...took Sarah (20:2): Abimelech wanted Sarah for his harem.

God came to Abimelech in a dream (20:3): God frequently communicated His will to people through dreams in biblical times (see 28:12; 31:10-11; 37:5-9; 40:5; 41:1; Numbers 12:6; Judges 7:13; 1 Kings 3:5; Daniel 2:3; 4:5; 7:1). This is the first of three occasions in the Bible where God appears in a dream to non-Jews to warn them against carrying out their intentions (see Genesis 31:24; Numbers 22:12).

"Behold, you are a dead man" (20:3): As God had done previously, He took prompt steps to save Sarah. God was not about to allow the woman who would soon give birth to the child of promise (Isaac) be sexually violated by a heathen king. Abraham was afraid to tell the truth to Abimelech, but God is never afraid to tell the truth to anyone. He got Abimelech's immediate attention.

"Will you kill an innocent people?" (20:4-5): Abimelech desperately argued for his integrity and innocence. However, as he was about to discover, ignorance does not excuse guilt (see Leviticus 4:13-14).

"Yes, I know" (20:6): God's knowledge is infinite (Psalms 33:13-15; 139:11-12; 147:5; Proverbs 15:3; Isaiah 40:14; 46:10; Acts 15:18; 1 John 3:20; Hebrews 4:13). Because God is all-knowing, He searches the human heart and examines motives and intentions of the heart. In Jeremiah 17:10 God said, "I the Lord search the heart and test the mind." The Lord is fully aware of the "the purposes of the heart" (1 Corinthians 4:5). The Lord "searches mind and heart" (Revelation 2:23). God therefore knew Abimelech's heart on this matter.

"It was I who kept you from sinning against me" (20:6): Notice that adultery is primarily viewed as a sin against God even though people are injured in the process. After David committed adultery with Bathsheba, he confessed to God and said, "Against you, you only, have I sinned and done what is evil in your sight" (Psalm 51:4).

The fact that God kept Abimelech from sinning is an evidence of God's sovereign and providential control of all things. Job affirmed to

God, "I know that you can do all things, and that no purpose of yours can be thwarted" (Job 42:2). God asserts, "My counsel shall stand, and I will accomplish all my purpose" (Isaiah 46:10). God assures us, "As I have planned, so shall it be, and as I have purposed, so shall it stand" (Isaiah 14:24). Proverbs 16:9 tells us, "The heart of man plans his way, but the LORD establishes his steps." Proverbs 19:21 says, "Many are the plans in the mind of a man, but it is the purpose of the LORD that will stand." God sovereignly and providentially kept Abimelech from sinning against Him.

"Return the man's wife" (20:7): God has promised judgment ("Behold, you are a dead man"—verse 3), but He will spare those who repent. The Ninevites were warned that after 40 days God would judge and destroy them (Jonah 3:4). They all repented, and God withheld His judgment. God explains His policy in Jeremiah 18:7-8: "If at any time I declare concerning a nation or a kingdom, that I will pluck up and break down and destroy it, and if that nation, concerning which I have spoken, turns from its evil, I will relent of the disaster that I intended to do to it." God was giving Abimelech the opportunity to repent and return Sarah to Abraham, which would avert God's judgment. This is a manifestation of God's grace.

"He is a prophet" (20:7): Notice the irony here. Abraham is a liar, but he is still a prophet (one who tells the truth about God).

The word "prophet"—from the Hebrew word *nabi*—refers to a spokesman for God who either (1) declares God's message regarding a contemporary situation to humankind, or (2) foretells God's actions based on divine revelation. The predictive role is often stressed, but the Bible equally emphasizes the teaching function. Both aspects require communication from God to the prophet (see 2 Samuel 7:27; Jeremiah 23:18).

Of course, the Abrahamic covenant involves predictive prophecy, for it details what God would do with the countless descendants of Abraham. In this sense, prophecy may be considered God's revelation regarding history in advance. Recall God's words in Isaiah 46:9-11:

> I am God, and there is no other; I am God, and there is none like me, declaring the end from the beginning and

> from ancient times things not yet done, saying, "My counsel shall stand, and I will accomplish all my purpose"...I have spoken, and I will bring it to pass; I have purposed, and I will do it.

"If you do not return her" (20:7): God graciously opened the door for Abimelech to save his life by returning Sarah to Abraham. If he failed to act, however, he was a dead man.

Genesis 20:8-13

Abimelech...called all his servants (20:8): Abimelech was not in this alone. Those under his rule were affected as well. They were understandably afraid.

"What have you done to us?" (20:9): Being interrogated and rebuked by a heathen king must have been humiliating for Abraham.

"A great sin" (20:9): The sin of adultery was a capital offense in Bible times (Exodus 20:14). This was considered a great sin throughout the entire ancient Near East.

"No fear of God" (20:11): The fear of God involves a holy reverence for God that leads to obedience to Him. Solomon tells us that "the fear of the Lord is the beginning of knowledge" (Proverbs 1:7). Exodus 20:20 reveals that people who fear the Lord turn from sin. Job was unique in his time because he "feared God and turned away from evil" (Job 1:1,8). When people do not fear the Lord, they think they can get away with anything. This is what Abraham feared in the case of Abimelech and his people. If Abimelech and his people had no fear of God, Abraham feared they might take his life in order to obtain Sarah.

"They will kill me because of my wife" (20:11): One begins to wonder why Abraham could trust the omnipotent God to fulfill His covenant promises but not trust Him to protect Abraham's life. Abraham had no need to engage in such fraud.

"She is indeed my sister" (20:12): Sarah was Abraham's half sister, so he actually engaged in half a lie.

"This is the kindness you must do me" (20:13): Sarah submitted to Abraham and thus participated in his lie.

Genesis 20:14-18

Returned Sarah his wife to him (20:14): Fearing for his life, Abimelech promptly returned Sarah to Abraham.

"Dwell where it pleases you" (20:15): Despite Abraham's mistreatment of Abimelech, Abimelech made amends with Abraham by allowing him to dwell wherever he wanted.

"Thousand pieces of silver...sign of your innocence" (20:16): Abimelech gave Abraham a thousand shekels. The term "shekel" was used to describe pieces of silver and gold of varying sizes. Some shekels were heavy, and some were light. One cannot help but notice that in this situation, Abimelech acted more forthrightly and honestly than Abraham did.

Abraham prayed...God healed Abimelech, and also healed his wife and female slaves (20:17-18): Abraham's intercession before God not only saved Abimelech's life but also healed Abimelech's household of infertility. Scripture consistently testifies that God sovereignly opens and closes wombs (see Genesis 25:21; 29:31; 30:2,17,22-23; 1 Samuel 1:19-20; Psalms 113:9; 127:3; Luke 1:13).

Major Themes

1. *God is an aggressor in revealing Himself.* God has always been the aggressor in making Himself known. He has always taken the first initiative in revealing Himself to people. He does this through revelation (Hebrews 1:1-2). We see this even in today's reading in Genesis, where God gave Abimelech a startling revelation in the form of a dream. Much later, in New Testament times, the ultimate revelation of God came in the person of Jesus Christ (John 1:18; Hebrews 1:2; Revelation 1:1). For us today, God's special revelation comes to us in the pages of the Bible (see 2 Timothy 3:16; 2 Peter 1:21).
2. *An innocent wrong is still a wrong.* As Abimelech discovered, even though he was unaware that he was committing a wrong with Sarah, he was in fact guilty, and God held him

accountable. Because Abimelech was unaware of Sarah's true status as Abraham's wife, God made a way for him to avoid judgment so long as he returned Sarah to Abraham immediately. Otherwise, if he kept Sarah for himself, he was truly a dead man. The principle seems to be this—when you become aware that you have broken a divine law, respond immediately to make it right. James 4:17 warns, "Whoever knows the right thing to do and fails to do it, for him it is sin."

Digging Deeper with Cross-References

Dishonesty and deception in Genesis—Genesis 12:13; 20:2; 26:1-11; 27:19; 30:34-36; 31:35; 37:18-35; 39:7-20

God's justice is consistent—Genesis 18:25; Exodus 34:7; Numbers 14:18; Deuteronomy 32:4; Job 4:7; 34:12; Psalms 9:8; 67:4; 89:14; 98:9; Isaiah 28:17

Life Lessons

1. *We all stumble.* All human beings are imperfect—including Christians. Abraham was imperfect (Genesis 20:2). Ecclesiastes 7:20 asserts, "Surely there is not a righteous man on earth who does good and never sins." The apostle Paul said, "I do not understand my own actions. For I do not do what I want, but I do the very thing I hate…I know that nothing good dwells in me, that is, in my flesh" (Romans 7:15,18). James 3:2 states, "We all stumble in many ways." Here, then, is something to remember—when people you know stumble, consider cutting them some slack. They're sinners, just like you and me!
2. *Be quick to repent.* Abimelech was quick to repent before God, thus averting certain judgment. You and I can learn a lesson here. A failure to repent of sin always brings God's discipline. David took almost a full year to repent of his

sin with Bathsheba. God had to discipline him severely. When he finally did repent, he beseeched God, "Let the bones that you have broken rejoice" (Psalm 51:8; see also Psalm 32:3-4; Hebrews 12:5-11). First Corinthians 11:31 thus urges, "If we judged ourselves truly, we would not be judged."

Questions for Reflection and Discussion

1. Based on what you've learned so far in Genesis, what is your assessment of the policy of telling half-truths?
2. Does the fear of the Lord motivate you to avoid sin?
3. What do you learn from this passage about the importance of being quick to repent?

Day 16

Isaac Is Born and Offered in Sacrifice

Genesis 21–22

Scripture Reading and Insights

Begin by reading Genesis 21–22 in your favorite Bible. As you read, trust God to open your eyes so you can discover wondrous things from His Word (Psalm 119:18).

In the previous lesson, we examined Abraham's sojourn at Gerar and his encounter with Abimelech. In this chapter, we cover much ground as Isaac enters the world, Abraham sends Hagar and Ishmael away, Abimelech makes a treaty with Abraham, and Abraham nearly sacrifices Isaac. With your Bible still accessible, consider the following insights on the biblical text.

Genesis 21:1-7

The Lord did to Sarah as he had promised (21:1): After decades of promises from God, Sarah's infertility ended. She conceived and gave birth to the child of promise. Joy replaced the laughter of derision.

Isaac (21:3): Means "he laughs."

Circumcised (21:4): A sign of the covenant that indicated something like this: "If I do not honor the covenant, may the Lord cut me off as I have cut off the foreskin."

A hundred years old (21:5): A lot of time passed before God's promise came to fruition. During many years of waiting, Abraham had some false hopes and false moves. But now God fulfills the promise He made so long ago.

"God has made laughter for me" (21:6): Earlier Sarah had laughed in unbelief (18:12). Now her laughter was genuine, stemming from inner joy.

Genesis 21:8-21

Weaned (21:8): Hebrew children were normally weaned two or three years after birth.

Great feast (21:8): This was an occasion to be celebrated.

Son of Hagar...laughing (21:9): Apparently Hagar's son, who was 17, was laughing in ridicule and mockery at the feast celebrating Isaac's passage from infancy to childhood. Perhaps Ishmael became so negative because when Isaac appeared on the scene, all of Ishmael's hopes of an inheritance vanished.

"Cast out this slave woman with her son" (21:10): Sarah had finally had enough. She demanded that Hagar and her mocking son be sent away. Sarah was so infuriated that she didn't even use their names. Sarah may have felt that with Ishmael's vanished hopes of an inheritance, he was now a threat to Isaac, who was to receive the inheritance.

Displeasing to Abraham (21:11): This request went against the social customs of the day. The archaeological discovery of the Nuzi tablets reveals that expelling or sending away the son of a female servant was prohibited. Moreover, such an act would have offended Abraham's sensibilities. Abraham loved the boy, his own flesh and blood.

God said to Abraham, "Be not displeased" (21:12): God gave the okay to send Hagar and her son away.

"Through Isaac shall your offspring be named" (21:12): Isaac alone would be the covenant child of promise (17:19; 22:18; Romans 9:6-8; Hebrews 11:17-19).

"I will make a nation of the son of the slave woman also" (21:13): Earlier, when Hagar was fleeing to Egypt, God assured her, "I will surely multiply your offspring" (16:10). He also said she would be the mother of a multitude. Later, when God reaffirmed his covenant with Abraham, He included the promise of a line through Ishmael (Genesis 17:20). We find a genealogy of Ishmael in Genesis 25:13-16.

God heard the voice of the boy (21:17): Ishmael had earlier used his voice to mock Isaac's ceremony. Now he was crying out because of his great thirst in the desert. The Angel of God heard his voice.

The angel of God called to Hagar (21:17): The Angel of God is the same as the Angel of the Lord (or Angel of *Yahweh*). This was a theophany, an appearance of God. Some believe it was a Christophany, an appearance of the preincarnate Christ. This episode clearly illustrates that even though Sarah had no mercy or compassion on Hagar or Ishmael, God did.

"Fear not...I will make him into a great nation" (21:17-18): God reaffirmed to Hagar what He had told her earlier.

God opened her eyes, and she saw a well of water (21:19): God providentially helped her see a well so she and Ishmael could quench their thirst. God soothed their despair, sustained them with needed water, and reaffirmed a promise for the future. Hope was restored.

God was with the boy, and he grew up (21:20): God continued to watch over and providentially bless Ishmael so that the promises made regarding his line would be fulfilled.

Wilderness of Paran (21:21): In what is today the Arabian Peninsula.

Genesis 21:22-34

"Swear to me here by God...I will swear" (21:23-24): This terminology was common when people made covenants.

Made a covenant (21:27): Abraham and Abimelech made a treaty stipulating that they would not deal with each other falsely. Abimelech may have wanted this covenant because of his possible knowledge of Abraham's untrustworthiness with other national leaders. Note that Abimelech actually had a stronger army than Abraham. But Abimelech wisely saw that God was with Abraham in all that he did. For that reason, Abimelech wanted Abraham as an ally and not an enemy.

"Seven ewe lambs... a witness" (21:30): The seven ewe lambs functioned as a sign of the covenant, much as circumcision was a sign of the Abrahamic covenant (17:11) and the rainbow was a sign of the Noahic covenant (9:12).

Tamarisk tree (21:33): The tree also commemorated the covenant just enacted.

Beersheba (21:33): Means "well of the oath," commemorating the covenant oath just enacted.

Called...on the name of the Lord, the Everlasting God (21:33): God's creatures depend on the Creator, so calling on Him is appropriate (see, for example, Genesis 4:26; 12:8; 13:4; 26:25).

Genesis 22:1-24

God tested Abraham (22:1): God tested Abraham. He did not tempt Abraham, for God does not tempt anyone (James 1:13). The purpose of the test was to confirm his commitment and faith (see Exodus 20:20). This test would demonstrate that Abraham loved God more than he loved his now 20-year-old child of promise. One must not miss the fact that Abraham had earlier committed to obey God as part of his covenant obligations (17:9). When commanded to sacrifice Isaac, Abraham chose to obey even though for more than 20 years Abraham had gotten to know and deeply love his son. The test is all the more intense for Abraham, knowing that he had already sent away the other possible covenant candidate (Ishmael). Abraham could potentially end up with no children.

Abraham rose early in the morning (22:3): Abraham was prompt in his obedience to God. There was no hesitation in his actions.

On the third day (22:4): The journey from Beersheba to Moriah was 48 miles.

"I and the boy will go over there and worship and come again to you" (22:5): Abraham here expresses faith that somehow, he and his son would return, despite the fact that God had instructed him to sacrifice his son. Hebrews 11:17-19 reveals that Abraham believed that perhaps God would simply resurrect Isaac from the dead.

"Where is the lamb?"... "God will provide" (22:7-8): Abraham did not know what provision God would make, but he knew that one way or another, God would provide.

The angel of the Lord called to him... "Abraham, Abraham!...Do not lay your hand on the boy" (22:11-12): The repetition of Abraham's name communicates urgency. The context of Genesis 22 makes it clear that God (the Angel of the Lord, or Angel of *Yahweh*) never intended this

2. *Principles of answered prayer*. God answered Abraham's prayer about Ishmael (Genesis 17:20). Scripture provides a number of principles for effective praying:

    - All our prayers are subject to the sovereign will of God (1 John 5:14).
    - Prayer should be continual (1 Thessalonians 5:17).
    - Sin hinders answered prayer (Psalm 66:18).
    - Living righteously is a great benefit to prayer being answered (Proverbs 15:29).
    - We should pray in faith (Mark 11:22-24).
    - We should pray in Jesus's name (John 14:13-14).

Questions for Reflection and Discussion

1. Walking before God, being blameless...are these realistic goals for you? What do you think that kind of life looks like? Do you want to make any midcourse corrections in your life?
2. What do you learn from the names of God that gives you confidence that He is worthy of your trust and that He'll take care of you?
3. Are you a daily pray-er? Why not keep a prayer journal to track your prayers and God's answers?

command to be executed. God restrained Abraham's hand just in the nick of time. Scholars agree that God was only testing Abraham's faith. The test served to show that Abraham loved God more than he loved his own son. God said, "Now I know that you fear God, seeing you have not withheld your son, your only son, from me" (verse 12). It is important to note that later in the process of progressive revelation, God would reveal that child sacrifice was actually an abomination to Him (Leviticus 18:21; 20:1-5; Deuteronomy 18:10; 2 Kings 16:2-3; Isaiah 57:5; Jeremiah 32:35).

A ram (22:13): The ram functioned as a substitute to be sacrificed in place of Isaac. Christ Himself would ultimately be the Lamb of God who would die as a substitute on our behalf (see John 1:29).

The Lord will provide (22:14): This was an appropriate name for the place. After all, God provided a ram to be a substitute in place of Isaac on the altar of burnt offering.

"By myself I have sworn" (22:16): The strongest possible oath from God.

"Because you have done this" (22:16): God once again reaffirms some of the blessings of the Abrahamic covenant. Abraham would have countless offspring, and the nations of the earth would be blessed through his line.

"Possess the gate of his enemies" (22:17): God's enemies in Canaan would be dispossessed so the land could be given to Abraham's descendants.

Milcah also has borne children to your brother Nahor (22:20-24): A family genealogy of Abraham's brother. Most of the names in Nahor's family genealogy are ancestors of cities and tribes around Israel. They are among those who will be blessed through Abraham's offspring.

Major Themes

1. *God is everlasting and eternal.* God is called the Everlasting God in Genesis 21:33. He is the King eternal (1 Timothy 1:17 NASB), who alone is immortal (6:16). He is the Alpha and Omega (Revelation 1:8), the first and the last (see

Isaiah 44:6; 48:12). God exists from eternity (Isaiah 43:13 NASB) and from everlasting to everlasting (Psalm 90:2). It is important to note that simply because God is beyond time does not mean that He cannot act within time. From a biblical perspective, God acts within the realm of time but from the realm of eternity. God is eternal, but He does temporal things.

2. *Isaac—a type of Christ.* A type is someone (or something) that prophetically foreshadows or prefigures someone (or something) else. Some Old Testament persons or things foreshadow New Testament persons or things simply because God planned it that way. Isaac may be considered a type of Christ. Isaac's birth was anticipated in the promises of God long before it occurred, as was Christ's birth. Both were beloved by their fathers. Isaac on the sacrificial altar on Mount Moriah foreshadows the death of Christ. The story in Genesis 24 of a bride being secured for Isaac foreshadows the securing of the bride of Christ (the church) for Christ.

Digging Deeper with Cross-References

God's providence—Genesis 1:30; 45:5; Ruth 1:6; Job 38:41; Psalms 23:1; 65:9; 121:3; 147:9; Matthew 5:45; 6:8,26; Luke 12:24

Spiritual tests—Exodus 15:25; 20:20; Deuteronomy 8:2,16; 13:3; Judges 2:22; 7:4; 2 Chronicles 32:31; Psalms 7:9; 11:5; 17:3; 26:2; 66:10; John 6:5-6; Hebrews 11:17; James 1:2-3

Life Lessons

1. *Faith tested.* Abraham's faith was tested when God commanded him to sacrifice his own son. You and I can also experience tests of our faith. James 1:2-3 tells

us, "Count it all joy, my brothers, when you meet trials of various kinds, for you know that the testing of your faith produces steadfastness." The apostle Peter uses similar language in 1 Peter 1:6-7.

> In this you rejoice, though now for a little while, if necessary, you have been grieved by various trials, so that the tested genuineness of your faith—more precious than gold that perishes though it is tested by fire—may be found to result in praise and glory and honor at the revelation of Jesus Christ.

2. *"Fear not."* God said this to Hagar, and He tells us the same thing (Matthew 10:31; Luke 12:7). Our sovereign God remains on the throne, bringing about His eternal purposes, even when the world around us seems tumultuous (see Job 42:2; Psalms 66:7; 93:1; Proverbs 16:9; 19:21; 21:30; Ecclesiastes 7:13; Isaiah 14:24; 40:15,17; 46:10; Lamentations 3:37; 1 Timothy 6:15). Ultimately, no Christian is a victim of his or her circumstances, for God is in control of all our circumstances. Remember that God has the uncanny ability of bringing good out of our bad circumstances (Romans 8:28). He is a Master at it!

Questions for Reflection and Discussion

1. How is your day-to-day living enhanced by the knowledge that God is a relentless promise keeper?
2. What is the most difficult test of faith you have experienced? What did you learn in that experience?
3. What is the most precious thing you have had to surrender to the Lord? What have you learned in this chapter that helps you?

Day 17

Sarah Dies and Is Buried

Genesis 23

Scripture Reading and Insights

Begin by reading Genesis 23 in your favorite Bible. As you read, allow the Word of God to bring revival to your soul (Psalm 119:25,93,107).

In yesterday's reading, we focused attention on Isaac's birth, Hagar and Ishmael's departure, Abimelech's treaty with Abraham, and Abraham's sacrifice of Isaac. Now we zero in on Sarah's death and Abraham's purchase of Sarah's tomb. With your Bible still accessible, consider the following insights on the biblical text.

Genesis 23:1-9

Sarah died (23:2): Sarah died at the age of 127. The promises of land and of many descendants predominate throughout Genesis, but another common theme that cannot be missed is the hard reality of death. Once Adam and Eve sinned in the garden of Eden, death became a regular feature on the earth. The fact that all die is a reminder that all are fallen in sin and the penalty of sin is death (Romans 6:23).

Kiriath-arba (that is, Hebron) (23:2): Literally, "the town of Arba." Arba was a prominent man in the Hebron area.

To mourn for Sarah and to weep for her (23:2): One must feel for Abraham in this. Sarah's longevity was a blessing, but husbands and wives who are together for such a long time truly feel the weight of overwhelming grief when one of them dies. Abraham mourned and wept for his loss.

Hittites (23:3): These were the "sons of Heth" (descendants of Ham and Canaan—10:15) who were in control of the Hebron area at that time. For many years liberal critics questioned the existence of the Hittites because no archaeological digs had uncovered anything about them. Critics claimed the Hittites were mythological. Today the critics are silenced. Archaeologists have uncovered abundant evidence for the existence of the Hittites during the time of Abraham.

"Sojourner and foreigner" (23:4): This phrase has two levels of meaning. On one hand, Abraham left Ur in pursuit of the Promised Land as instructed by God. He would be considered a foreigner and a stranger in the new lands he encountered. He was certainly a sojourner and foreigner among the Hittites. A foreigner in the midst of a new land could become a resident of the community, but his legal rights would be restricted. In some communities, foreigners were not permitted to make land purchases. Abraham was given permission to buy land because of his stellar reputation as a man of God.

There is also a deeper meaning of the phrase "sojourner and foreigner." Just as Abraham was a sojourner and foreigner among the Hittites, he was also a sojourner and foreigner who was passing through earthly life en route to the better country of heaven. "He was looking forward to the city that has foundations, whose designer and builder is God" (Hebrews 11:10; see also 1 Chronicles 29:15; Psalm 39:12). With a similar idea in mind, Peter much later urges sanctification among believers: "Beloved, I urge you as sojourners and exiles to abstain from the passions of the flesh, which wage war against your soul" (1 Peter 2:11).

"Give me property" (23:4): When Abraham said "Give me property," his intended meaning was "sell me property." In Bedouin bargaining, a person will freely give you property (such as land) if you freely give him something in return, such as shekels of silver.

Notice that the property Abraham wanted to buy was in Canaan. In ancient times, people were typically buried in their ancestral homeland.

Such is not the case here. Canaan was the land of promise, so Sarah would be buried there.

"My lord" (23:6): By calling Abraham "lord," the Hittites may have been showing respect. But they also could have been flattering Abraham with a view to making a good financial deal with him.

"Prince of God" (23:6): Abraham's reputation preceded him. People in neighboring communities knew that Abraham was not just a man of God but a prince of God.

"Bury your dead in the choicest of our tombs" (23:6): Because Abraham was a prince of God, the Hittites were willing to offer him the best among their sepulchers.

Abraham rose and bowed (23:7): A sign of respect.

"Ephron the son of Zohar" (23:8): Business was often carried out at the city gates, so Ephron was likely there.

"Cave of Machpelah" (23:9): Abraham's desire was to purchase only a cave for the purpose of burial.

"Full price" (23:9): Abraham offered to pay full price for the cave.

Genesis 23:10-16

Ephron the Hittite answered... "I give you the field" (23:10-11): Ephron offered to give the entire field with its cave to Abraham. Ephron may have done this out of generosity, but another motive is possible. Ephron may have offered Abraham the field along with the cave instead of just the cave in order to reduce his tax liability. It is also likely, as noted previously, that Ephron's ultimate goal was to move this conversation to a sale of property using Bedouin bargaining techniques ("give" in return for "give").

Abraham bowed down (23:12): Another show of respect.

"I give the price of the field" (23:13): Abraham wanted to pay full price for the field along with the cave.

"Four hundred shekels of silver" (23:15): Shekels—which varied in size, from light to heavy—were commonly used in business transactions. In the present case, each shekel probably amounted to less than half an ounce.

"What is that between you and me?" (23:15): Four hundred shekels

was probably an exorbitant price for this plot of land. (Generations later, Jeremiah paid just 17 shekels for a field at Anathoth—Jeremiah 32:9.) In his Bedouin bargaining, Ephron knew he had a captive audience, for Abraham needed the property quickly. Ephron may have been preying on a man in grief by selling the property for an extremely high price. Some Bible expositors note that Ephron's politeness was typical of the bargaining process.

Abraham weighed out for Ephron the silver (23:16): Abraham did not want to be indebted to anyone. God is the sole source of his blessings. He offered to pay full price for the cave. So he weighed out 400 shekels of silver—a wildly escalated price.

Genesis 23:17-20

The field with the cave...and all the trees (23:17): As was common with all business transactions that took place at city gates, a detailed description of the purchased property was provided in front of many witnesses. The witnesses guaranteed that no one would be able to challenge the transfer of property later. Abraham would be purchasing the entire field, which included the cave as well as trees on the field. Everyone present could attest to the sale.

The field...was made over to Abraham (23:17-18): The legal transfer of property took place. It is interesting to observe that much of Genesis speaks of the land God was giving to Abraham and his descendants in Canaan. Abraham now purchases a small plot of land in Canaan to bury his wife. One might say that Abraham was staking his claim in the Promised Land. Canaan was his new homeland.

It is also interesting to observe that the property transfer that took place at the city gate was still considered binding many years later when Abraham's grandson Jacob was on his deathbed. Jacob instructed his sons, "I am to be gathered to my people; bury me with my fathers in the cave that is in the field of Ephron the Hittite, in the cave that is in the field at Machpelah, to the east of Mamre" (49:29-30). In fact, Abraham, Isaac, Rebekah, Leah, and Jacob were all buried in that cave.

Gate of his city (23:18): Lots of activity took place at the gates of a city. Judges settled legal disputes, and official government business was enacted. Also, a great deal of commerce took place at the gates. Vendors set up shop, selling fruit, vegetables, pottery, clothing, and various other goods. In the present case, people near the gates were witnesses of the business transaction that took place between Abraham and the Hittites.

Abraham buried Sarah his wife (23:19): Abraham promptly buried his beloved Sarah.

East of Mamre (that is, Hebron) (23:19): The burial cave was east of Mamre, in Hebron. Earlier, Abraham had lived in Mamre. This is where Abraham had earlier provided hospitality to some visiting angels.

Major Themes

1. *Burial practices in Bible times.* Funerals in biblical times were performed quickly. This is for the practical reason that the hot climate would rapidly cause decay and odor. Traditionally, when a person died, he or she would immediately be bathed and then wrapped in strips of linen. Sometimes a gummy combination of spices was applied to the wrappings. It was then carried by stretcher to the place of burial, whether in the ground or in a cave. In some cases, entire families might be buried in a large cave. Eventually, in some areas, because of a lack of available cave space, bones would often later be removed from a cave and then stored in a wooden or stone chest.
2. *Money in Bible times.* In Old Testament times, merchandise was often bought and sold without the use of money. People used the bartering system, exchanging food, clothing items, livestock, grain, oil, wine, and various kinds of building materials. This system worked well for a long time. Eventually, the use of raw metal came into prominence for bartering purposes. Both silver and gold were used in major transactions (see, for example, 2 Samuel 24:24; 1 Kings 9:13-14). Copper, too, was used for bartering for less expensive items.

Digging Deeper with Cross-References

Longevity in Genesis—Genesis 5; 7:6; 9:29; 11:11; 21:5; 23:1; 25:7,17; 35:28; 47:9,28; 50:22

Sympathy of others—2 Kings 4:27; 20:12; 1 Chronicles 19:2; Job 2:11; 42:11; Proverbs 25:20; Isaiah 39:1; Matthew 18:31; Luke 10:35; John 11:19,31,35; Galatians 6:1-2

Caves in Genesis—Genesis 19:30; 23:9,19; 25:9; 49:29-30; 50:13

Life Lessons

1. *We don't know when death will strike.* Sarah, Abraham's wife, died in Hebron (Genesis 23:2). None of us know when we will die. The Old Testament patriarch Isaac once said, "Behold, I am old; I do not know the day of my death" (Genesis 27:2). Ecclesiastes 9:12 affirms, "Man does not know his time." In Proverbs 27:1 we are urged, "Do not boast about tomorrow, for you do not know what a day may bring." The psalmist prayed, "O Lord, make me know my end and what is the measure of my days; let me know how fleeting I am!" (Psalm 39:4).
2. *Grief over the loss of loved ones.* Abraham grieved over the death of Sarah (Genesis 23:2). Christians are not immune to the pain of grief. Christ has taken the sting out of death (1 Corinthians 15:55), but the loss of a family member or friend is nevertheless extremely painful. The apostle Paul considered death an enemy yet to be conquered (1 Corinthians 15:26). We have this great comfort—we will experience an eternal reunion with Christian loved ones (1 Thessalonians 4:13-17). For this reason, the apostle Paul said that even though we grieve, we do not "grieve as others do who have no hope" (1 Thessalonians 4:13). When faced with the death of a loved one, it is good to anchor ourselves on Psalm 34:18: "The Lord is near to the brokenhearted and saves the crushed in spirit" (see also

Psalms 46:1; 62:2; John 6:51; 11:25; 2 Corinthians 1:4-7; Hebrews 4:16).

Questions for Reflection and Discussion

1. Do you consider yourself a "sojourner and foreigner" passing through your time on earth on your way to the "better country" of heaven? If yes, how does that effect the way you live?
2. Would you say you maintain an eternal perspective—a perspective that recognizes that life on earth is short and that the way we live makes a difference?
3. Do you think you have a good reputation among others? If you could stand to improve in this area, what steps might you take?

Day 18

Isaac and Rebekah

Genesis 24

Scripture Reading and Insights

Begin by reading Genesis 24 in your favorite Bible. As you read, allow the Word of God to bring revival to your soul (Psalm 119:25,93,107).

In the previous lesson, we examined the death of Sarah and Abraham's purchase of her tomb. In today's reading we focus attention on the choice of a bride for Isaac. With your Bible still accessible, consider the following insights on the biblical text.

Genesis 24:1-14

His servant, the oldest of his household (24:2): This is Eliezer of Damascus, first introduced to us in Genesis 15:2. As chief steward of the household, he would have received Abraham's inheritance had Abraham and Sarah not given birth to a child. Even though Eliezer lost a possible inheritance when Isaac was born, he continued to faithfully serve Abraham and Isaac. Abraham and Isaac trusted him fully.

"Put your hand under my thigh" (24:2): This sounds rather odd to modern people. But in Old Testament times, the gesture of touching in an intimate place (near the organ of procreation) indicated a very solemn pledge or oath.

"Swear by the Lord" (24:3): The pledge was so solemn, it included the Lord's name.

"Wife for my son" (24:3): Because Abraham was getting so old, he wanted to take steps to ensure the continuation of the line of promise and the fulfillment of the covenant God made with him. He didn't want to die before ensuring the next generation in this line of promise. So he had Eliezer swear to find a wife for Isaac from among his own people.

In Bible times, parents often arranged their children's marriages. Typically, a boy's parents would select their son's bride, and the bride would become a part of the boy's clan. The bride was chosen because of her compatibility with the boy and his entire family. This would help ensure a successful marriage and family relationship. God later commanded the Israelites not to marry someone from a different nation who worshipped other gods (see Exodus 34:10-17; Deuteronomy 7:3-4; see also 2 Corinthians 6:14). Abraham did not want the line of promise to be contaminated by paganism.

"To my country" (24:4): The journey back to Mesopotamia would be more than 500 miles.

"Do not take my son back there" (24:6): Isaac was the son of promise. A 500-mile trip could involve danger. Abraham would not allow Isaac to be put at risk by such a long trip.

"He will send his angel before you" (24:7): Hebrews 1:14 tells us that angels are "ministering spirits sent out to serve for the sake of those who are to inherit salvation." The word "ministering" in Hebrews 1:14 comes from a Greek word meaning "serving." Angels are spirit-servants who render aid to the heirs of salvation to further God's purposes on earth. This service can include protection (Psalm 91:11), guidance (Genesis 19:17), encouragement (Judges 6:12), deliverance (Acts 12:7), supply (Psalm 105:40), and empowerment (Luke 22:43). In the present case, the angel would likely guide and protect the caravan, ensuring the fulfillment of God's will in this matter.

City of Nahor (24:10): A location near Haran, where Abraham's brother Nahor dwelt.

Time of evening (24:11): When the midday heat had cooled a bit.

"O LORD, God of my master Abraham" (24:12): Eliezer is clearly a devout man. He prays in this verse for God's blessing, he worships

when God answers prayers (verse 26), and he recognizes God's providential guidance (verse 27). No wonder that Abraham trusts him.

"I will water your camels" (24:14): Watering camels was beyond the social call of duty. More typically women would offer water just to travelers, not their animals. Eliezer's prayerful request would therefore sift a servant-hearted woman from the more common women.

Genesis 24:15-33

Drew for all his camels (24:20): Rebekah drew water not just for a camel, but for all ten of Eliezer's camels. That is no small task, considering that each camel could drink multiple gallons of water. Yet Rebekah made provisions without complaint. Rebekah was hard working (24:15), attractive (24:16), and courteous (24:18).

Shekels (24:22): A shekel was about half an ounce.

"Tell me whose daughter you are" (24:23): Rebekah responded by providing a very brief genealogy that indicated that she was Isaac's cousin.

Laban (24:29-31): Laban, the son of Bethuel, was Rebekah's brother. Apparently his welcome was motivated by all the wealth accompanying Eliezer. His response foreshadows the avaricious character that would surface later (see 29:21-27; 30:27-36; 31:1-13).

"I will not eat" (24:33): This was not just a social visit. Abraham had assigned Eliezer a task, and until that task was accomplished, Eliezer would not be content with mere socializing over a meal. Eliezer explained that his master was Abraham, that he was on a mission on behalf of Abraham, and that Abraham was a man of great wealth. He then revealed he was seeking a wife for Abraham's son, Isaac. He described God's revelation that Rebekah was the woman of choice. He wanted everyone to understand that Rebekah was God's choice, not merely his choice.

Genesis 24:34-60

"Turn to the right hand or to the left" (24:49): If the family was not open to the idea of Rebekah being Isaac's wife, he needed to know so he could make his exit and continue with his mission on Abraham's behalf.

"The thing has come from the Lord" (24:50): Both Laban and his

father, Bethuel, recognized God's hand of providence in selecting Rebekah.

Silver...gold...garments (24:53): Eliezer then gave Rebekah and her family a dowry, openly demonstrating Isaac's financial state. The dowry sealed the betrothal to Isaac.

"Send me away to my master" (24:54): Eliezer sought to be dismissed so he could immediately make his way back to Abraham with the good news.

"Let the young woman remain with us a while" (24:55): Rebekah would be moving more than 500 miles away. In days where travel was by foot and by animal, it was slow going. Her family wanted more time with her before she left. Eliezer responded that this was a work of God and that they needed to make haste. He had traveled about two weeks to get there. It would be a two-week trip back. That's a month away from Abraham, who was anxious to hear any news.

"Do not delay me" (24:56): Abraham was an old man, and time was of the essence. Eliezer sought to avert all delays and get back to Abraham immediately.

"Will you go with this man?" (24:58): Rebekah no doubt saw the providential hand of God in all this as well. She did not hesitate to leave with Eliezer. God had chosen. She obeyed, thereby proving herself worthy to be Isaac's wife and continue the line of promise.

They sent away Rebekah...and her nurse (24:59): The nurse's name was Deborah (see 35:8).

"May you become thousands of ten thousands" (24:60): This prayer for Rebekah to have countless descendants went right along with God's covenant promises to Abraham that he would have countless descendants. The prayer for her son to "possess the gate" of his enemies likewise points to a time when the Jews would inherit the land of Canaan and defeat their enemies.

Genesis 24:61-67

Beer-lahai-roi (24:62): This location is unknown.

Isaac went out to meditate (24:63): The Hebrew term for "meditation" has rich nuances of meaning. In different contexts, "meditate" can mean to utter, imagine, speak, roar, mutter, meditate, and muse. For example, the word is used in Isaiah 31:4 to express the roar of a lion. It is used in Isaiah 38:14 in reference to the sound of the mourning of doves. In both cases, the idea seems to be that outward expression is an outgrowth of strong inner emotions and thoughts. The term often carries the basic idea of murmuring. It portrays a person who is very deep in thought, mumbling with his lips as though talking to himself.

Took her veil and covered herself (24:65): In Old Testament times, a betrothed woman veiled her face until the day of the wedding. Some Bible expositors believe the veil was a means of indicating an unmarried woman. Others believe the veil was a gesture of modesty and respect.

Brought her into the tent of Sarah his mother (24:67): A gesture indicating his welcome of her into his family.

She became his wife, and he loved her (24:67): Under God's providential guiding, Isaac received the perfect wife. This brought him great comfort while he continued to grieve the loss of his mother. Isaac was 40 years old when he married Rebekah (verse 20), and Abraham was 140 (21:5).

Major Themes

1. *God's providence.* God often works behind the scenes in events on earth in order to accomplish His will. For example, He providentially worked in Joseph's life (even when his brothers sold him into slavery) to bring him to Egypt, exalt him in Egypt, and use him to rescue people from a famine (Genesis 50:20). God's providential actions ensured that Jonah reached Nineveh (by being swallowed and later vomited up by a big fish) so he could deliver God's message to the Ninevites (Jonah 1–2). Likewise, God providentially led Abraham's servant to find Rebekah as a wife for Isaac (Genesis 24:44).
2. *Finding a good wife.* Scripture speaks often about finding a good wife. Proverbs tells us that "he who finds a wife finds a good thing and obtains favor from the Lord" (18:22),

that "a prudent wife is from the Lord" (19:14), and that "an excellent wife is the crown of her husband" (12:4). The perfect picture of a godly wife is found in Proverbs 31:10-31. A godly wife's conduct can have a profound effect on her husband (1 Peter 3:1-5).

Digging Deeper with Cross-References

Seeking God's guidance—Judges 1:1; 13:8,12; 1 Samuel 23:4; 30:8; 2 Samuel 2:1; 5:19,23; 21:1; 1 Kings 22:5; 1 Chronicles 14:10; Psalms 5:8; 25:5; 27:11; 31:3; 43:3; 143:10; Acts 1:24; 1 Thessalonians 3:11

Confidence in God's response—Genesis 24:7,40; 48:21; 50:24; Numbers 14:8; Judges 11:24; 1 Samuel 14:10; 17:37; 2 Samuel 22:19; 2 Chronicles 13:12,18; 14:11; 16:8; Nehemiah 2:20; Psalms 3:6; 20:7; 23:4; 27:3; 46:2; 56:4; 118:6; Proverbs 3:26; Isaiah 12:2; Jeremiah 20:11; Daniel 3:17; Zechariah 12:5; Romans 8:31; 2 Corinthians 3:4; 4:14; Philippians 1:6; 2 Timothy 4:18; Hebrews 11:19; 13:6

Life Lessons

1. *Prayer and God's sovereignty*. It is clear from our passage that God sovereignly and providentially handpicked Rebekah for Isaac. But even though God is sovereign, human beings cannot forfeit praying to God to bring about certain things. God sovereignly handpicked Rebekah, but notice that Abraham's servant first prayed that God would grant him success in finding the right wife (Genesis 24:12-14). God is sovereign over all things (Ephesians 1:18-23), and He has sovereignly ordained not only the ends but also the means to those ends. In other words, God has sovereignly ordained not only to bring certain things about but also to accomplish certain things as a result of the individual prayers of His people. Therefore we should most definitely

pray for specific needs (see Philippians 4:6; see also James 4:2).

2. *Praising God—the right response.* When Abraham's representative encountered and spoke with Rebekah, he recognized God's providential work on his behalf and offered worship and praise to God (Genesis 24:26). Worship and praise belong together. Scripture reveals that praise to God should always be on our lips (Psalm 34:1). We should praise God in the depths of our heart (Psalm 103:1-5,20-22) and continually "offer to God a sacrifice of praise" (Hebrews 13:15 NIV). One means of praising God is through spiritual songs (Psalm 69:30; see also Psalms 33:3; 40:3; Isaiah 12:5-6; 27:2; 30:29; 42:10-11; 44:23).

Questions for Reflection and Discussion

1. Do you make a strong effort (like Eliezer) to be a person of your word?
2. What is your attitude toward the providence of God? Are you confident that He is working behind the scenes to bring about His will in your life?
3. Does this lesson motivate you to pray more?

Day 19

Abraham Dies but Has Many Descendants

Genesis 25

Scripture Reading and Insights

Begin by reading Genesis 25 in your favorite Bible. As you read, never forget that God urges you to quickly obey His Word in all things (Psalm 119:60).

In yesterday's reading, we focused on the choice of a bride for Isaac. Now we shift attention to Abraham's death, Ishmael's sons, and Isaac and Esau's bargaining regarding the birthright. With your Bible still accessible, consider the following insights on the biblical text.

Genesis 25:1-18

Keturah (25:1): Keturah was actually Abraham's concubine (1 Chronicles 1:32). She was called Abraham's wife, but as a concubine she was actually a lower wife than Sarah had been—a secondary wife. The reference to "the sons of his concubines" (verse 6) would therefore include the sons of Keturah. Abraham was 140 years old at this time.

She bore him (25:2): In keeping with God's promise to Abraham that he would be the father of many nations, a number of Arab tribes emerged from the descendants of the children of Keturah.

Abraham gave all he had to Isaac (25:5): Abraham's act of conferring his estate upon Isaac revealed to all present that Isaac was his rightful legal heir.

To the sons of his concubines (25:6): Concubines were considered secondary wives in biblical times. Abraham gave gifts to the children of his concubines—probably flocks and herds, which were common measures of wealth in ancient times. He thereby demonstrated his love and care for them.

Sent them away (25:6): By sending the sons of his concubines away, he circumvented any possible threat to Isaac from a jealous half brother.

175 years (25:7): Abraham lived for 100 years in the land of promise (compare with Genesis 12:4).

Breathed his last (25:8): A physiological description of death.

Died in a good old age (25:8): God had earlier promised Abraham, "You shall be buried in a good old age" (Genesis 15:15).

Gathered to his people (25:8): This apparently refers to reuniting with other believers in the afterlife following the moment of death (see Matthew 8:11; Luke 16:22-23). See Major Themes.

Isaac and Ishmael his sons buried him (25:9): It is noteworthy that Abraham's death was important enough for his two sons to overlook their differences and join together in burying him. Notice that Isaac is mentioned first even though Ishmael was born before Isaac. Isaac was Abraham's son of promise and had priority.

In the cave of Machpelah (25:9): This is the cave Abraham purchased from Ephron the son of Zohar to bury Sarah following her death. He paid 400 shekels of silver for it. Abraham, Isaac, Rebekah, Leah, and Jacob were all buried in that cave.

Beer-lahai-roi (25:11): Isaac settled at Beer-lahai-roi, a term meaning "well of the Living One who sees me." Hagar named the well because God saw her there in her distress and ministered to her needs.

Generations of Ishmael (25:12): God had earlier promised Hagar, "I will surely multiply your offspring so that they cannot be numbered for multitude" (16:10). He also promised Abraham, "As for Ishmael...He shall father twelve princes, and I will make him into a great nation" (17:20-21). The promise of 12 princes was now fulfilled, for they are listed in Genesis 25:12-18. These princes and their many descendants settled in central and north central Arabia. Even today, Arabs claim Ishmael as their ancestor.

Ishmael...breathed his last and died, and was gathered to his people

(25:17): Following his death, he reunited with other believers in the afterlife. See Major Themes.

Havilah (25:18): Located in central Arabia.

Shur (25:18): A desert located in the northwest portion of the Sinai Peninsula, between Beersheba and Egypt (Genesis 16:7; 20:1; 25:18; Exodus 15:22).

Genesis 25:19-28

Generations of Isaac (25:19): The family genealogy of Isaac.

Paddan-aram (25:20): Means "plain of Aram." This is an area east of Palestine.

Isaac prayed to the LORD for his wife (25:21): By now, Isaac and Rebekah had been married for 20 years, and they'd yet to conceive and bear a child. Scripture consistently demonstrates that God sovereignly opens and closes wombs (see Genesis 29:31; 30:2,17,22-23; 1 Samuel 1:19-20; Psalms 113:9; 127:3; Luke 1:13). Knowing this, Isaac interceded on behalf of Rebekah, asking God to open her womb. This was of obvious importance because the line of promise was to be carried on through Isaac and Rebekah. Notice that Isaac did not follow Abraham's example of trying to bring about the line of promise through human means (such as bearing a child with Hagar). Isaac apparently had learned from his father's mistake and now turned to the Lord in faith. Isaac's children could be seen only as direct gifts from God.

Barren (25:21): Rebekah was infertile. But God was soon to intervene in answer to Isaac's prayer.

Rebekah his wife conceived (25:21): Rebekah became pregnant soon enough, with not just one child, but two.

The children struggled together within her (25:22): Rebekah was suffering a difficult pregnancy. She asked, "Why is this happening to me?" This caused her to inquire of the Lord in prayer. (Notice that she was following her husband Isaac's example in prayer to God.)

"Two nations are in your womb" (25:23): God answered Rebekah's prayer and told her that the two children in her womb would give rise to two nations.

"Shall be divided" (25:23): The two nations that would arise from

two children in Rebekah's womb—the Edomites, who would descend from Esau, and the Israelites, who would descend from Jacob—would not get along with each other. The struggle of the twins within the womb was a preview of things yet to come.

"The one shall be stronger than the other" (25:23): In the conflicts that would emerge between Jacob's descendants (the Israelites) and Esau's descendants (the Edomites), the Israelites would achieve supremacy.

"The older shall serve the younger" (25:23): In biblical times the firstborn son was always in the privileged position. He received the birthright and the larger inheritance that accompanied it. The firstborn in the family enjoyed positional preeminence and supremacy (see Exodus 22:29; Numbers 8:14-17; Deuteronomy 21:17). However, in the case of Rebekah's twins, things would be reversed. The older son (that is, the firstborn) would actually serve the younger son. We will see later in this chapter that this reversal came about because Esau sold his birthright to Jacob in exchange for some food, and because Jacob tricked Isaac into giving him Esau's inheritance when Isaac was a very old man and could not see well.

Twins (25:24): Rebekah gave birth to twins.

The first came out red... like a hairy cloak, so they called his name Esau (25:25): Esau means "red." He was so named because he came out of Rebekah's womb red. Esau's hair was like the fur coat of an animal.

His brother came out with his hand holding Esau's heel... Jacob (25:26): Jacob's name means "supplanter" or "trickster" or "heel catcher." The name is indicative of his future character. Jacob would be revealed to be a constant schemer, always trying to gain advantage over others.

Esau was a skillful hunter (25:27): Esau was an outdoorsman who loved to hunt. He cared more for physical things than spiritual things.

Jacob was a quiet man (25:27): Jacob was more reserved, had a quiet temperament, and preferred a gentler lifestyle.

Isaac loved Esau... but Rebekah loved Jacob (25:28): Isaac and Rebekah clearly engaged in favoritism.

Genesis 25:29-34

"Let me eat" (25:30): Esau was ruled by his physical appetites.

His name was called Edom (25:30): Recall that Esau "came out red" (verse 25). Now he wanted to eat red stew—a lentil stew (see verse 34). Edom means "red."

"Sell me your birthright now" (25:31): The birthright guaranteed a double portion of the inheritance (see Deuteronomy 21:17).

"Swear to me now" (25:33): Swearing an oath was necessary to make the transfer of the birthright legally binding.

Sold his birthright (25:33): Jacob's name means "he supplants," and indeed, Jacob was a supplanter, for he talked his hungry and exhausted brother into giving him his birthright, including the greater inheritance that accompanies it, in exchange for a mere bowl of food.

Esau was the acknowledged hunter in the family. However, a case could be made that Jacob was the real predator. He was in the hunt for the birthright and the inheritance.

Esau despised his birthright (25:34): Esau seemed to have little regard for his birthright. He did not value it the way most firstborn sons did.

Major Themes

1. *"Gathered to his people."* Abraham's death is described as his being "gathered to his people" (Genesis 25:8). This was a common way of referring to death in biblical times. For example, when the Lord spoke to Moses about the impending death of Aaron, He said, "Let Aaron be gathered to his people, for he shall not enter the land that I have given to the people of Israel…Aaron shall be gathered to his people and shall die there" (Numbers 20:23-26). The phrase "gathered to his people" refers to a reuniting with other believers in the afterlife, for Old Testament believers are portrayed as being alive and in God's presence (Luke 20:38).
2. *Birthright in Bible times.* The term "birthright" refers to the special privileges belonging to the firstborn son in the family. He not only became the head of the family but also received a double portion of the inheritance

(Deuteronomy 21:15-17). However, such birthrights could be forfeited or transferred to others. Reuben, for example, was deprived of his birthright because of his shameful conduct (Genesis 49:4; 1 Chronicles 5:1). Jacob talked his hungry and exhausted brother into transferring his birthright to him, along with the greater inheritance that accompanies it, in exchange for a mere bowl of food. Esau acted foolishly and was later angry about it.

Digging Deeper with Cross-References

The death of the righteous—Genesis 25:8; 49:33; 50:26; Numbers 23:10; Deuteronomy 34:5; Joshua 24:29,33; 1 Samuel 25:1; 2 Kings 13:20; Psalm 23:4; Proverbs 14:32; Luke 2:29; 16:22; Romans 14:8; 2 Corinthians 5:1; Philippians 1:21; Hebrews 11:13; Revelation 14:13

God answers the prayers of His people—Psalms 50:15; 91:15; 99:6; 118:5; 138:3; Isaiah 30:19; 58:9; 65:24; Daniel 9:21-23; 10:12; Jeremiah 29:12; Matthew 7:7

Life Lessons

1. *Sibling rivalry.* Jacob and Esau provided a classic example of sibling rivalry (Genesis 25:21-26; 27; 33). So did Cain and Abel (see 4:4-9) and Joseph and his estranged brothers (Genesis 37). In the New Testament we find that Jesus Himself was rejected by His half brothers (John 7:5). The older brother's attitude toward his prodigal brother seemed to involve some kind of rivalry (Luke 15:11-32). Of course, God desires that there be no estrangement in families. As Psalm 133:1 puts it, "How good and pleasant it is when brothers dwell in unity." Romans 12:18 instructs, "If possible, so far as it depends on you, live peaceably with all." Paul also urges us to walk "with all humility and gentleness, with patience, bearing with one another in love,

eager to maintain the unity of the Spirit in the bond of peace" (Ephesians 4:2-3).

2. *God foreknows all—trust Him with your future.* Because God knows the future, He could tell Rebekah that the twins in her womb would give rise to two nations. God has absolute knowledge of the future. God transcends time—He is above the whole course of time—so He can see the past, present, and future as a single act. God sees things on earth from the vantage point of eternity, so the past, present, and future are all encompassed in a single ever-present now to Him. You and I may not know what the future holds for us, but we do know the One who knows every single detail. To trust Him with our future therefore makes good sense (Psalm 37:5; Proverbs 3:5-6).

Questions for Reflection and Discussion

1. Do you ever struggle with physical appetites controlling you more than the things of the Spirit?
2. When making decisions for the future, it is often helpful to first take the long look. (That is, where do you see yourself five years from now? Ten years from now?) How did Jacob take the long look? How did Esau fail to take the long look?
3. Are you truly trusting God with your future?

Day 20

Isaac Encounters Abimelech

Genesis 26

Scripture Reading and Insights

Begin by reading Genesis 26 in your favorite Bible. As you read, never forget that God urges you to quickly obey His Word in all things (Psalm 119:60).

In yesterday's reading, we focused on Abraham's death, Ishmael's sons, and Jacob and Esau's bargaining for the birthright. In today's reading, we focus attention on Isaac's sojourn among the Philistines. With your Bible still accessible, consider the following insights on the biblical text.

Genesis 26:1-5

Famine in the land (26:1): Famine is a recurring theme in the book of Genesis (see 12:10; 41–43; 45; 47). Threats to the food supply were common—even in Palestine, the land of milk and honey (Exodus 13:5). During a famine, people had no choice but to go to another location where there was a food supply.

Gerar (26:1): A Philistine city on the southern border of Palestine (10:19; 20:1-2).

Abimelech king of the Philistines (26:1): The term Abimelech was apparently a kingly title (such as Pharaoh) instead of a personal name. This was likely a different king from the one who interacted with

Abraham 97 years earlier. Perhaps this Abimelech was a son or grandson of the previous Abimelech.

The Philistines were inhabitants of Philistia, directly southwest of Canaan. This pagan nation later stood against the people of God. They believed in pagan gods, including Dagon, Ashtoreth, and Beelzebub (see Judges 16:23; 1 Samuel 5:1-7; 2 Kings 1:2). At this early juncture, however, the Philistines were friendly with Isaac.

And the Lord appeared to him and said (26:2): Here we have yet another reaffirmation of the Abrahamic covenant, this time to Isaac. God reiterates His promises relating to land, seed, and blessing.

"I will be with you" (26:3): God often affirmed that He would be with His people to protect them from danger (Genesis 31:3; Joshua 1:5; Isaiah 41:10; Jeremiah 1:8,19; Matthew 28:20; Acts 18:10).

"Because Abraham obeyed my voice" (26:5): Abraham is commended for his obedience to God. We here witness an ongoing blessing of the descendants of Abraham because of his obedience even though he is no longer on earth (see Major Themes). This is the implication for Isaac: "Just as Abraham was fully obedient, so you also must be fully obedient."

But let's not forget that the Abrahamic covenant is an unconditional covenant that does not depend on people's behavior for its fulfillment. God Himself would sovereignly fulfill the promises of the covenant.

"My charge, my commandments, my statutes, and my laws" (26:5): Similar terms are used throughout the book of Deuteronomy to describe Israel's covenant obligations to God.

Genesis 26:6-16

"She is my sister" (26:7): Here we witness a "like father, like son" deception. Abraham and Isaac seem to share many parallels. They both obeyed God's covenant stipulations, and they both experienced a famine. Each had a beautiful wife, and each lied about his wife. Each was rebuked by an Abimelech, and each Abimelech was concerned about adultery. See Life Lessons.

"How then could you say, 'She is my sister?'" (26:9): Abimelech caught on to Isaac and Rebekah's true relationship when he saw them outside his window, apparently treating each other as only a married couple would. (The phrase "Isaac laughing with Rebekah" could easily be translated "Isaac sporting with Rebekah" or "Isaac caressing Rebekah.") He was understandably offended and therefore questioned Isaac. Abimelech recognized that he and his people could easily have become guilty of a heinous sin.

"Lest I die because of her" (26:9): Isaac gave the same excuse his father did.

Abimelech warned (26:11): Abimelech announced that anyone who harmed Isaac or Rebekah would be executed. Some Bible expositors suggest that Abimelech did this according to God's providential leading, bringing much-needed protection to the couple so the line of promise would not be endangered.

Isaac sowed...and reaped...a hundredfold (26:12): Isaac was very prosperous as he farmed the land. The reason for his prosperity is clear. "The LORD blessed him, and the man became rich." See Major Themes.

The Philistines envied him (26:14): The Philistines were jealous about Isaac's rapid accumulation of wealth.

The Philistines...stopped and filled...all the wells (26:15): Water was an extremely important commodity in desert territories. Without water, no one could survive the dry heat. In view of this, plugging up someone's well was a heinous act. When the Philistines did this to all the wells Abraham's workers had dug, that was cause for war. This may have been done as a means of thwarting Isaac's rapid buildup of wealth. Instead of retaliating, however, Isaac simply had his workers dig new wells.

"Go away from us" (26:16): Abimelech now seems to see Isaac and his descendants as a threat.

"You are much mightier than we" (26:16): Isaac's family line grew in number and in strength—an obvious indication that God was in the process of fulfilling His covenant promises before their very eyes. Things were happening just as God promised they would happen.

Genesis 26:17-22

Isaac departed from there (26:17): Isaac moved to the Gerar Valley, which was about ten miles from the city.

Dug again the wells of water (26:18): Isaac reopened the wells previously dug by Abraham.

The herdsmen of Gerar quarreled (26:20): Isaac experienced more opposition. He got the distinct feeling he was not welcome, but he avoided fighting.

Called the name of the well Esek (26:20): Literally means "contention." Contention and disputes over water wells were common in desert territories in ancient times. Isaac gives this and other wells names that reflect the dispute.

Sitnah (26:21): Literally means "enmity."

Rehoboth (26:22): Rehoboth means "room enough" or "plenty of room." There's room for everyone to have a well. Finally—a well without contention!

Genesis 26:23-35

Beersheba (26:23): This is where Isaac's father, Abraham, had dug a well and later had made a covenant with a previous Abimelech (21:31-32).

The Lord appeared to him... "Fear not" (26:24): By now, Isaac may have started worrying about the conflicts he had just faced regarding wells. Enemies could easily become angered and invade. God thus appeared to him and said, "Fear not" and then reaffirmed key elements of the Abrahamic covenant. God was assuring Isaac that the line of promise was safe.

He built an altar there (26:25): Isaac responded in faith as Abraham had done—by building an altar to the Lord.

Abimelech went to him (26:26): This was not just a social visit. Abimelech had important business to discuss.

"The Lord has been with you" (26:28): God had clearly blessed Isaac, so Isaac had become both wealthy and powerful. Here we find another parallel between Abraham and Isaac. Just as the earlier Abimelech

acknowledged that God was with Abraham (21:22), so now the later Abimelech acknowledges that God is with Isaac. The wells provided concrete evidence that the Lord was with Isaac. Finding water in the wilderness was considered a strong sign of God's supernatural blessing. The Philistines may have thought that by filling up a few wells, they would ruin Isaac. But God's obvious blessing thwarted those plans.

"Let there be a sworn pact between us" (26:28): This was a wise move for Abimelech. He sought a covenant that would guarantee peaceful relations between the two. Abimelech knew he'd be on the losing end of a conflict between them. Peace was much preferable.

He made them a feast (26:30): A celebratory meal was commonly part of the ratification of a covenant. The meal was intended to signify the bond of friendship.

Shibah (26:33): Means "oath," commemorating the oath just taken with Abimelech.

They made life bitter for Isaac and Rebekah (26:35): When Abraham sent out his servant in search for a wife for Isaac, he instructed him, "You will not take a wife for my son from the daughters of the Canaanites" (24:3). He did not want his son to marry a pagan who worshipped false deities. Isaac and Rebekah were no doubt greatly saddened that their son Esau had taken pagan Hittite wives.

Major Themes

1. *Ongoing blessing because of Abraham's faithfulness.* In Scripture we often find God continuing to bless His people because of the faithfulness of Abraham. For example, even though Abraham was already dead, God said to Isaac, "In your offspring all the nations of the earth shall be blessed, because Abraham obeyed my voice and kept my charge, my commandments, my statutes, and my laws" (Genesis 26:4-5). God later appeared to Isaac and said, "Fear not, for I am with you and will bless you and multiply your offspring for my servant Abraham's sake" (verse 24).

2. *The Lord can make one rich.* Genesis 26:12-13 says of Isaac, "The Lord blessed him, and the man became rich, and gained more and more until he became very wealthy." Scripture consistently teaches that God is the one who makes a person rich. "The Lord makes poor and makes rich; he brings low and he exalts" (1 Samuel 2:7). Deuteronomy 8:18 states, "You shall remember the Lord your God, for it is he who gives you power to get wealth." Of course, whether we are rich or poor, we should be content (see Philippians 4:12).

Digging Deeper with Cross-References

Fear of other human beings—Genesis 12:12; 26:7; 31:31; 32:7; 34:30; Exodus 14:10; Numbers 13:31; Judges 6:27; 1 Samuel 7:7; 15:24; 23:3; Ezra 3:3; Job 31:34; Psalm 31:13; Proverbs 29:25; Isaiah 51:12; Jeremiah 1:8; 38:19; 42:11; Matthew 2:22; 14:5

Trouble in the family—Genesis 16:5; 26:35; 27:41,46; 37:4; Numbers 12:1; 2 Samuel 6:16; 12:11; Esther 1:12; Matthew 5:31

Life Lessons

1. *A parent's influence.* It is sobering to ponder the influence a parent can have on a child. Isaac followed his father Abraham's negative example in deception (Genesis 26:6-11). Ahaziah "was evil in the sight of the Lord and walked in the way of his father and in the way of his mother" (1 Kings 22:52). Jeremiah 9:14 speaks of those who "have gone after the Baals, as their fathers taught them." By contrast, there are many examples in Scripture of parents being good models for their children. "The Lord was with Jehoshaphat, because he walked in the earlier ways of his father David" (2 Chronicles 17:3). Uzziah "did

what was right in the eyes of the Lord, according to all that his father Amaziah had done" (2 Chronicles 26:4; see also 2 Timothy 1:5). Our children are watching what we do and how we act. Never forget that the way you live your life is the primary message your child receives. Your convictions are caught more than taught.

2. *The nature of envy*. The Philistines envied Isaac (Genesis 26:14). Jesus taught that negative emotions emerge from the human heart. "What comes out of a person is what defiles him. For from within, out of the heart of man, come evil thoughts, sexual immorality, theft, murder, adultery, coveting, wickedness, deceit, sensuality, envy, slander, pride, foolishness" (Mark 7:20-22). James indicates that such negative emotions are earthly and unspiritual. "If you have bitter jealousy and selfish ambition in your hearts…This is not the wisdom that comes down from above, but is earthly, unspiritual, demonic" (James 3:14-16; see also Galatians 5:19-21). The better policy is to love.

Questions for Reflection and Discussion

1. Just as God told Isaac, "I will be with you," so God tells us, "I will never leave you nor forsake you" (Hebrews 13:5). What does that mean to you personally?
2. Do you want to make any changes in your life in view of the spiritual principle that obedience brings blessing?
3. Do you ever experience envy or jealousy? Would you like to make any resolutions in this regard?

Day 21

Jacob Gets Blessed by Deception

Genesis 27

Scripture Reading and Insights

Begin by reading Genesis 27 in your favorite Bible. As you read, ask God to help you understand His Word (Psalm 119:73).

In the previous lesson, we focused on Isaac's sojourn among the Philistines. In today's lesson, we witness Jacob's deception to obtain Isaac's blessing. With your Bible still accessible, consider the following insights on the biblical text.

Genesis 27:1-13

Isaac was old and his eyes were dim (27:1): Isaac is now 137 years old. It was not uncommon in biblical days for elderly people to become blind or develop poor vision. Because he felt his death may be near, Isaac wanted to bless Esau before passing from this life.

"Prepare for me delicious food" (27:4): This was apparently a ceremonial meal to accompany the formal blessing of Esau. See Major Themes.

"Bless you before I die" (27:4): Isaac was apparently attempting to tamper with God's sovereign plan. God had earlier told Rebekah, "Two nations are in your womb, and two peoples from within you shall be divided; the one shall be stronger than the other, the older shall serve the younger" (Genesis 25:23). Esau was to serve Jacob and not vice versa. If Isaac did in fact bestow the blessing on Esau, this would have necessitated Jacob serving Esau.

Rebekah was listening (27:5): Rebekah was eavesdropping for Jacob's sake. Notice the favoritism in this family—Isaac wanted the best for Esau while Rebekah protected Jacob's interests (see Genesis 25:28). Rebekah also remembered God's words to her and was therefore willing to do anything to secure the blessing for Jacob so that he would indeed rule over Esau, as instructed by God.

"Obey my voice" (27:8): Rebekah knew that she was being deceitful, yet she called on Jacob to obey.

"So that he may bless you before he dies" (27:10): Rebekah wanted Jacob to receive Isaac's blessing while Esau was away. Don't miss the parallel here. Earlier in Genesis we saw Esau lose his birthright after returning home from a hunt. Now we are about to see him lose Isaac's blessing as he sets out on another hunt.

"Esau is a hairy man" (27:11): Jacob objected that his physical attributes were entirely different from Esau's. He feared not passing Isaac's inspection.

"Bring a curse upon myself" (27:12): Jacob was initially resistant to the plan. It might backfire, thereby causing Isaac to curse Jacob instead of blessing him. Rebekah disarmed Jacob's objection by accepting full responsibility for all that would transpire. Jacob then went along with Rebekah's scheme. Notice that Jacob never said anything about feeling guilty over the deception. He just didn't want to get caught.

Genesis 27:14-29

His mother prepared delicious food (27:14): Rebekah's good cooking was part of the conspiracy to bring blessing to Jacob.

The best garments of Esau (27:15): Even though Isaac was old and handicapped, Rebekah knew he would still try to make sure he was blessing the right son. Jacob's use of Esau's clothing would help lower Isaac's defenses.

The skins of the young goats (27:16): Another part of the deception was to make Jacob seem as hairy as Esau.

"I am Esau your firstborn" (27:19): An outright lie from Jacob.

"How is it that you have found it so quickly?" (27:20): Isaac is initially suspicious.

"Please come near, that I may feel you" (27:21): Isaac's vision is no help, but his sense of touch was still intact. He wanted to touch his son.

"The voice is Jacob's...the hands of Esau" (27:22): The conflicting facts were disconcerting to Isaac. His son felt hairy, but he didn't sound like Esau.

He blessed him (27:23): Jacob pulled off the deception and received the blessing. Unfortunately for him, he would soon pay a heavy price for his deception.

"Are you really my son Esau?" (27:24): Isaac was still having some doubts.

"I am" (27:24): Notice how one lie leads to another. Jacob first lied by telling his father he was Esau. He lied again when asked how he was able to work so fast. As Isaac attempted to verify identity by touch and smell, Jacob let the deception stand when Isaac touched the goatskins and smelled Esau's clothing.

Kissed him (27:27): This was a kiss of deception (compare with Matthew 26:49).

Blessed him (27:27): The blessing Isaac pronounced on Jacob—thinking all along it was Esau—included fruitful crops and dominion over nations and his own brothers. Further, those who cursed him were to be cursed, just as those who blessed him were to be blessed. This language is highly reminiscent of God's covenant with Abraham (see 12:2-3).

Genesis 27:30-46

"Arise...eat...bless me" (27:31): Unaware of what had transpired, Esau approached his father with the meal he had prepared and sought his father's blessing.

Trembled very violently (27:33): Isaac was utterly shocked with the sudden realization that he had blessed Jacob instead of Esau. At that moment, his mind probably flashed back to God's earlier words to Rebekah: "The older shall serve the younger" (25:23). Those words were now set in concrete. Just as God said, Esau would serve Jacob.

"He shall be blessed" (27:33): Isaac's blessing on Jacob was irreversible.

Once given, it could not be taken back. In modern vernacular, Isaac's blessing was legally binding.

Esau...cried out with an exceedingly great and bitter cry (27:34): The sudden awareness of what had happened was catastrophic for Esau. He had just lost a blessing that would have changed the entire course of his life. This was not just a disappointment for a day—it had life-long consequences.

"Your brother came deceitfully" (27:35): Isaac recognized he had been deceived by Jacob. Earlier in his life, Isaac himself had engaged in deception (Genesis 26).

"Is he not rightly named Jacob?" (27:36): Jacob's name means "supplanter" or "trickster."

"He took away my birthright...he has taken away my blessing" (27:36): This verse contains a Hebrew play on words. The word "birthright" is the Hebrew word *bekorah*. The word "blessing" is the Hebrew word *berakah*. So Esau said, "He took away my *bekorah*, and behold, now he has taken away my *berakah*."

"I have made him lord over you" (27:37): From now on, Jacob would be the preeminent son.

"Bless me, even me also, O my father" (27:38): In desperation Esau seeks any kind of blessing from his father. Anything is better than nothing.

Esau lifted up his voice and wept (27:38): Esau couldn't believe what had happened. He fully recognized that Isaac's blessing on Jacob was irreversible. Hebrews 12:17 tells us, "When he desired to inherit the blessing, he was rejected...though he sought it with tears."

Isaac his father answered and said to him (27:39): Whatever Isaac could say to Esau could not undo the blessing already given to Jacob. Isaac's words to Esau are essentially a reiteration of his words to Jacob but stated negatively. Jacob was told that he would be lord over his brothers, and Esau was now told that he would serve his brother. Isaac's words also indicated that the land Esau would dwell in would be less fertile. Esau thus would not enjoy the earth's riches as would Jacob, to whom Esau would now be subservient. His life would now be much harder.

"You shall break his yoke from your neck" (27:40): Despite the fact that Esau was told he would serve Jacob, Esau's descendants (the Edomites) fought often with Jacob's descendants (the Israelites) and even broke away from Israelite domination on occasion (see 2 Kings 8:20; 2 Chronicles 21:8-10; 28:16-17).

Esau hated Jacob (27:41): Esau was full of resentment and bitterness.

"Days of mourning for my father" (27:41): This refers to mourning following death. Esau may have believed his father would die soon.

"I will kill my brother Jacob" (27:41): Esau sought to murder Jacob, but not while his father was yet alive. Such an act would grievously injure Isaac. Isaac lived more than four decades longer.

The words of Esau...were told to Rebekah (27:42): Rebekah discovered Esau's plans and needed to act quickly.

"Flee to Laban" (27:43): As instructed by his mother, Jacob would now have to flee for his life and take refuge with Laban, Rebekah's brother.

"Stay with him a while" (27:44): The "while" turned out to be 20 years.

"Why should I be bereft of you both in one day?" (27:45): Rebekah grasped that things could easily get out of control and she could lose both of her sons. If Esau murdered Jacob, it would then be the task of the "next of kin" in the family to bring vengeance by executing Esau (see Exodus 21:12; Leviticus 24:17; Numbers 35:19,21,27,33). Rebekah sought to avoid this outcome.

Rebekah said to Isaac, "I loathe my life" (27:46): Jacob obviously wasn't the only deceiver in the family. Rebekah had masterminded Jacob's deception of Isaac in order to obtain the blessing. Rebekah is now dishonest again. She told Isaac how disgusted she was with her two Hittite daughters-in-law, Judith and Basemath (Esau's wives). She insisted that Jacob leave to go find a wife from among her own people and not the Hittites. Jacob was thus able to leave with his father's blessing.

Major Themes

1. *The father's blessing.* The blessing of a father on a son is a primary emphasis throughout the book of Genesis. The patriarchs Abraham, Isaac, and Jacob all gave formal blessings to their children. Jacob also gave blessings to his grandchildren. In Old Testament times, receiving a father's blessing was considered an honor. Conversely, to lose a father's blessing was considered a curse. A father's blessing typically included encouragement, the specifics of the son's inheritance, and some prophetic words regarding the son's future (see, for example, Genesis 27:28-29,39-40).
2. *Eating and blessing.* Isaac's blessing on his son was accompanied by a ceremonial meal. Religious occasions were often celebrated by eating and drinking—especially when a covenant was enacted. Isaac's formal blessing of his son was apparently of such import in the family that Isaac requested a special meal as part of the blessing ceremony (Genesis 27:4). This being so, the meal should not be viewed as a merely incidental but rather an integral part of the conveyance of the blessing.

Digging Deeper with Cross-References

Disguises—Genesis 27:16; 38:14; 1 Samuel 28:8; 1 Kings 14:2,6; 20:38; 22:30; 2 Chronicles 18:29; 35:22

Lying—Genesis 3:4; 4:9; 18:15; 27:24; 37:20,32; 39:17; Psalm 58:3; Isaiah 59:3; Jeremiah 29:23; Matthew 26:74; John 8:44

Life Lessons

1. *Cheating.* Jacob's name means "he supplants," and indeed, Jacob was a supplanter, for he took hold of his brother Esau's birthright (Genesis 25:29-34), his father's blessing

and inheritance (27:1-29), and his father-in-law's flocks (more on this in chapter 29–30). The Lord hates cheating (Proverbs 11:1) and instructs that we are not to cheat anyone (Leviticus 19:13). Dishonesty is an abomination to God (Proverbs 20:23). Conversely, the Lord delights in honesty (Proverbs 11:1).

2. *Honoring parents.* Jacob deceived his father, Isaac (27:18-29). In so doing, he failed to show honor to him. Scripture instructs that we ought to show honor to our parents. In Exodus 20:12 God says, "Honor your father and your mother, that your days may be long in the land that the Lord your God is giving you" (see also Deuteronomy 5:16; 27:16). He says, "Every one of you shall revere his mother and his father" (Leviticus 19:3; see also 20:9). This theme continues throughout the New Testament (see Matthew 15:4; 19:19; Mark 7:10; 10:19; Luke 18:20; Ephesians 6:2).

Questions for Reflection and Discussion

1. How important is it to you personally that you honor and respect your parents? Are you a parent?
2. What do you learn from this lesson about parental influence over children?
3. Can you think of a time in your own life where one lie led to another lie? Has your view of truth-telling strengthened as a result of this lesson?

DAY 22

Jacob Has a Dream

Genesis 28

Scripture Reading and Insights

Begin by reading Genesis 28 in your favorite Bible. As you read, ask God to help you understand His Word (Psalm 119:73).

In yesterday's reading, we zeroed in on Jacob's deception to obtain Isaac's blessing. Now let's focus some attention on Jacob's vision at Bethel. With your Bible still accessible, consider the following insights on the biblical text.

Genesis 28:1-5

"You must not take a wife from the Canaanite women" (28:1): Isaac is stern. Do not marry a Canaanite woman. Such a marriage could lead only to spiritual contamination and compromise. The promised line of covenant blessings must be kept pure with no defilement.

"Paddan-aram" (28:2): A city in northwest Mesopotamia, east of Palestine, where both Isaac and Jacob took their wives (25:20; 28:2-7; 31:18).

"Laban" (28:2): The son of Bethuel, brother of Rebekah, and father of Leah and Rachel (Genesis 24:29).

"God Almighty" (28:3): This is the Hebrew term *El Shaddai*. *El* in Hebrew refers to "Mighty God." *Shaddai* derives from a root word that refers to a mother's breast. This name, then, indicates not only that God is a Mighty God, but that He is full of compassion, grace, and mercy.

"Bless you and make you fruitful" (28:3): Isaac had experienced quite a turnaround. He had previously put all his hopes in Esau as the person through whom the covenant blessings were to be fulfilled. He now concedes that Jacob is God's choice. He thus speaks openly of the covenantal promises that would be fulfilled in Jacob and his descendants.

"The land... God gave to Abraham" (28:4): In his words of blessing to Jacob, Isaac speaks of the land promises given to Abraham (15:18-21) and affirms that Jacob's descendants would be blessed and take possession of it. God had originally promised Abraham, "To your descendants I give this land, from the Wadi of Egypt to the great river, the Euphrates—the land of the Kenites, Kenizzites, Kadmonites, Hittites, Perizzites, Rephaites, Amorites, Canaanites, Girgashites and Jebusites" (15:18-21 NIV). The land promises were then passed down through Isaac's line: "To you and your descendants I will give all these lands and will confirm the oath I swore to your father Abraham. I will make your descendants as numerous as the stars in the sky and will give them all these lands, and through your offspring all nations on earth will be blessed" (Genesis 26:3-4 NIV). The land promises then passed from Isaac to Jacob.

Isaac sent Jacob away (28:5): Esau was an outdoorsman, but Jacob was more of a home boy. He liked the comforts of home. The act of leaving home for another land no doubt caused Jacob some stress.

Genesis 28:6-9

Esau... took as his wife... Mahalath the daughter of Ishmael (28:9): After finding out that Isaac did not favor Canaanite women, Esau married Mahalath—the daughter of Ishmael—in an effort to win Isaac's favor. Perhaps by marrying into Ishmael's family, he reasoned, he could make up for past mistakes. And perhaps Isaac might even bless him after all. Of course, through it all, Esau failed to put away his pagan wives. As well, he failed to understand that the covenantal blessings were given to Jacob by divine design.

Genesis 28:10-22

Beersheba (28:10): The name of a well dug by Abraham (21:31).

Haran (28:10): A Mesopotamian city (11:31-32).

Taking one of the stones... he put it under his head (28:11): People who traveled often slept on the ground and used a large stone as a support for the head, like a hard pillow.

He dreamed (28:12): This is the third occasion in Genesis in which God communicates to someone through a dream (see also 15:12; 20:3). This is the first time God speaks directly to Jacob in the book of Genesis. God's appearance to Jacob in a dream was apparently divinely engineered to assure Jacob of both protection on his journey and the promises related to the Abrahamic covenant. Jacob would have needed this reassurance because he and his descendants were to possess the Promised Land, not to leave it. God brought strong assurance that Jacob would be coming back to the land.

A ladder (28:12): Not a vertical latter with rungs, but more of a stairway, such as one might see on the side of an ancient ziggurat. This explains how angels could be ascending and descending on it at the same time.

Angels of God were ascending and descending (28:12): This likely represents heaven's busy oversight of the things of the earth—especially as related to the fulfilling of the Abrahamic covenant. The dream emphasized to Jacob that he was never really alone. God's celestial workers are with him all the way even though he might not actually see them. And God Himself was with him wherever he went.

"The God of Abraham your father and the God of Isaac" (28:13): Before reaffirming the Abrahamic covenant with Jacob, God identified Himself as the God who dealt with both Abraham and Isaac—He Himself was the covenant maker. Jacob would soon gain stronger convictions than ever that the God of Abraham and Isaac was also the God of Jacob.

"The land...your offspring...all the families of the earth be blessed" (28:13-14): God reaffirmed the key elements of the Abrahamic covenant with Jacob—the land promises (17:8), his posterity of innumerable descendants (13:16; 22:17), and universal blessing through him (see 12:2-3; 15:5,18; 17:3-8; 22:15-18; 35:11-12).

"I am with you and will keep you wherever you go" (28:15): This idea of being with God's people wherever they go is extremely common

in Scripture (see 26:24; 31:3). In the New Testament, God's people are promised, "I will never leave you nor forsake you" (Hebrews 13:5). There is an obvious contrast here between the one true God and the gods of ancient paganism. The gods of ancient paganism were considered to be local deities who could be with you only when you remained in the territory. Once outside the territory, you were on your own. The one true God, by contrast, is with His people wherever they go.

"Will bring you back to this land" (28:15): Jacob's trek to Laban's territory was only temporary. Unlike Abraham, who forever left his land of Ur in pursuit of a new land, Jacob would be returning to the land he now leaves. God's land promises were still intact, and nothing could stand in the way of their fulfillment.

"Surely the Lord is in this place" (28:16-17): Jacob responded worshipfully to this vision of God. If there was any question up to this time about Jacob's commitment to God, it ends here with his response to the vision. This seems to be a milestone event in his spiritual life.

He was afraid (28:17): Jacob experienced reverential awe for God following his awakening from the dream.

Jacob took the stone...and set it up for a pillar (28:18): Setting up pillars was common in ancient times. They often marked significant sites. They were considered to be memorials. Such memorial stones reminded visitors of divine visitations (see Joshua 4:6). This particular site was significant, as Jacob declared in verse 16: "Surely the Lord is in this place."

Poured oil (28:18): Oil was typically used in ceremonies of dedication and/or consecration (see Exodus 30:25-29). Oil was poured on the pillar to consecrate the site where God spoke to Jacob and reaffirmed the Abrahamic covenant.

Bethel (28:19): A term meaning "house of God." Bethel is a city located six miles north of Jerusalem and fifty miles north of Beersheba. Bethel would later became a holy site for Israel (Judges 20:18-27; 1 Samuel 7:16; 10:3; 1 Kings 12:26–13:10; 2 Kings 2:2-3).

Luz (28:19): An ancient city near the site of Bethel (35:6).

Jacob made a vow... "the Lord shall be my God" (28:20-21): Jacob was now getting serious about God. He affirmed that if God will do what He said He'd do—taking care of him and providing for him—then "the LORD shall be my God."

Give a full tenth (28:22): People often gave a tenth (or a tithe) in biblical times to a supreme personage—whether Pharaoh, a king, or God Himself. In most cases, tithing to God was a way the people of God acknowledged that God owned all things and was sovereign over them.

This stone...shall be God's house (28:22): Some Bible expositors believe Jacob's stone memorial may be a metaphorical reference to the future stone temple of Israel, which will be built to house God's presence among His people.

Major Themes

1. *Dreams in Bible times*. God often communicated with people in Old Testament times through dreams. He communicated this way to Abimelech (Genesis 20:3-7), Jacob (28:12; 31:10), Laban (31:24), Joseph (37:9-11), Pharaoh's chief butler and baker (40:5), and Pharaoh himself (41:1-8). Such revelatory dreams continued in New Testament times—such as Joseph's dream about Mary's pregnancy by the Holy Spirit (Matthew 1:20; see also 2:12-13,19). Today, the Bible is God's primary means of revelation to us (2 Timothy 3:15-17).
2. *God—a relentless promise keeper*. Generation after generation the evidence mounts that God is a relentless promise keeper. As noted previously in the chapter, God reaffirmed the covenant promises He had earlier given to Abraham (Genesis 28:13-14). Now fast-forward to New Testament times. Jesus descended from the physical line of Abraham, through whom all the families of the earth would be blessed (see Matthew 1:1-2). This gives us boldness in believing that all the other promises in the Bible about our divine Savior are just as reliable. We have good reason to anchor ourselves on the promises of God.

Digging Deeper with Cross-References

God's protective providence—Genesis 28:15,20; Exodus 23:20; Numbers 6:24; Deuteronomy 1:31; 1 Samuel 2:9; Psalms 12:7; 17:8; 19:13; 25:20; 31:20; 32:7; 34:20; 37:17; 41:12; 91:11; 116:8; 121:4; 127:1; 140:4; 141:9; Proverbs 2:8; 3:26; Isaiah 26:3; 27:3; 42:6; 63:9; Matthew 2:13; Luke 4:10; John 6:39; 17:11,15; 18:9; 2 Thessalonians 3:3; 2 Timothy 1:12; 1 Peter 1:5; 4:19; Jude 24; Revelation 3:10

Bethel in Genesis—Genesis 12:8; 13:3; 28:19; 31:13; 35:1,6,15

Life Lessons

1. *Tithing*. In Genesis 28:22, Jacob promised God, "Of all that you give me I will give a full tenth to you." This was an early form of tithing. The Hebrew word translated "tithe" literally means "a tenth." David affirmed, "The earth is the LORD's, and all it contains, the world, and those who dwell in it" (Psalm 24:1 NASB), and the tithe was a means whereby the people of God acknowledged that God owned all things and was sovereign over them. God commanded His people to bring a tithe of the land and its produce (Leviticus 27:30; Deuteronomy 14:22), the animals (Leviticus 27:32), and new wine, oil, and honey (2 Chronicles 31:5).

   The New Testament emphasis is on grace-giving as opposed to a 10 percent tithe. We are to freely give as we have been freely given to. And we are to give as we are able (2 Corinthians 8:12). For some, this will mean less than 10 percent. But for others whom God has materially blessed, this will mean much more than 10 percent. To have a right attitude toward giving to the church, we must first give ourselves to the Lord (see 2 Corinthians 8:5).

2. *Angels are among us*. According to Genesis 28:12, Jacob dreamed of a ladder, and "the angels of God were ascending and descending on it." In other books of the

Bible, we learn much about God's angels. Hebrews 1:14 tells us that angels are spirit-servants who render aid to the heirs of salvation in the outworking of God's purposes on earth. Angelic aid can take many forms. Angels can be involved in protection (Psalm 91:11), guidance (Genesis 19:17), encouragement (Judges 6:12), deliverance (Acts 12:7), supply (Psalm 105:40), and empowerment (Luke 22:43). In the present case, God's angels seem to be involved in protecting and guiding Jacob as the son of promise.

Questions for Reflection and Discussion

1. Do you make efforts to guard yourself against spiritual contamination from things of this world?
2. What does it mean to you personally that God is *El Shaddai*?
3. What does it mean to you personally that God has promised to never leave you nor forsake you (Hebrews 13:5)?

Day 23

Jacob Gets Married and Has Children

Genesis 29

Scripture Reading and Insights

Begin by reading Genesis 29 in your favorite Bible. As you read, remember that God's Word is the true source of hope (Psalm 119:81).

In the previous reading, we learned much about Jacob's vision at Bethel. Now let's find out about Jacob's marriages and Laban's deception. With your Bible still accessible, consider the following insights on the biblical text.

Genesis 29:1-14

Jacob went on his journey (29:1): Jacob had a purpose for this journey. God had appeared to Jacob and reaffirmed the key elements of the Abrahamic covenant with him—including the seed promises. Jacob was to have innumerable descendants. Before that could happen, he needed a wife.

People of the east (29:1): God had previously instructed Jacob, "I am with you and will keep you wherever you go" (28:15). The fact that God was with Jacob accounts for the fact that he providentially encountered people who knew Laban. God's providential hand was also evident in Jacob's easy meeting of Rachel. All this took place near Haran, a Mesopotamian city (Genesis 11:31-32). This is east in the sense of being east of Canaan.

A well in the field (29:2): It is significant that Jacob would meet

Rachel at a well. Elsewhere in Genesis we find that good things often happen at wells (see, for example, 16:13-14; 21:19; 24:11-20).

The stone on the well's mouth was large (29:2): The primary purpose of the large stone was to protect the water supply from both evaporation and contamination.

"Laban the son of Nahor" (29:5): In biblical times, people often used the term "son of" to refer to any male descendant—including a son or a grandson. Laban was actually the grandson of Nahor (24:15,29).

"Water the sheep and go" (29:7): Apparently Jacob liked what he saw in Rachel and was inviting these men to exit the scene so he could be alone with her.

Rachel...was a shepherdess (29:9): That Rachel was a shepherdess shows that she was a strong woman capable of the task. The sons in a family normally assumed this task. Laban had sons, but they may have been too young at the time to care for the herds. Or Laban may have had so many herds that the entire family had to help care for them.

Jacob kissed Rachel (29:11): It might seem odd at first reading that Jacob immediately kissed Rachel. One must keep in mind, however, that Jacob and Rachel were cousins, and such a greeting among cousins was common. The kiss was a custom, not an indiscretion.

Jacob told Rachel that he was her father's kinsman (29:12): Rebekah had left almost 100 years earlier. Understandably, Jacob was welcome.

"You are my bone and my flesh" (29:14): Bible expositors have different views as to what this may mean. Some believe the term to indicate that they were blood relatives. Others take it to mean that Laban was welcoming Jacob as a son, much like an adoption.

Stayed with him a month (29:14): In biblical times, people who traveled necessarily had to depend on the generosity of others. People commonly took travelers and strangers into their homes for up to three days. After that, if the visitor stayed longer, it was expected that he would "earn his keep."

Genesis 29:15-30

The older was Leah...the younger was Rachel (29:16): These sisters were born into a shepherding family. Their names are therefore quite appropriate, meaning "cow" (Leah) and "ewe lamb" (Rachel).

Eyes were weak (29:17): This does not necessarily mean that Leah had poor vision. It may mean that in terms of appearance, Leah's eyes were a weak feature—perhaps pale. Perhaps she had no sparkle in her eyes. This was in contrast to Rachel, who was "beautiful in form and appearance." Wives of other patriarchs were considered beautiful (12:11; 24:15-16).

Jacob served seven years for Rachel (29:20): Jacob's work for Laban was a kind of dowry given in exchange for marrying Rachel.

Laban... took his daughter Leah and brought her to Jacob (29:22-23): Jacob had worked seven years in order to marry Rachel. When Jacob had completed his commitment, Laban held a feast. In the evening, Laban brought Leah to Jacob. Jacob did not know it was Leah. There are several reasons for this. First, it was getting dark outside, and it was therefore more difficult to see faces. Further, it was customary in biblical times for brides to be veiled when they were delivered to their husbands. Still further, Jacob had just participated in a feast, where there was likely a good amount of drinking. His senses would have been impaired. In any event, Jacob had marital relations with Leah. (The phrase "he went in to her" is a euphemism for sexual intercourse.)

Female servant (29:24): In biblical days, fathers often gave a female servant to their daughters as a wedding gift.

"What is this you have done to me?" (29:25): Jacob was offended. He had worked seven years in order to marry Rachel, and yet Laban had brought Leah when it was dark. Jacob wasn't aware of what happened until the next morning.

"It is not so done in our country" (29:26): Laban was every bit as much a deceiver as Jacob had been (see 27:1-29). Jacob had deceived both his father and his brother, and now—in a twist of irony—is himself deceived by his mother's brother. Laban knew full well that Jacob worked seven years for Rachel. Now, having already given Leah to Jacob, Laban wanted Jacob to work seven more years to obtain Rachel. After all, it was not customary in Laban's land to give the younger sister in marriage before the older sister.

Perhaps now Jacob is beginning to experience what it is like to be on the receiving end of such deception. Galatians 6:7 warns, "Do not be deceived: God is not mocked, for whatever one sows, that will he also reap."

One must not miss the irony here. Laban had given Leah to Jacob instead of Rachel because it was not customary to marry off the younger daughter before the older daughter. One wonders if this made Jacob think back to how he had deceptively sought the blessing of the firstborn, and now he was deceptively given the firstborn daughter in marriage. He had pretended to be the older brother, and now the older sister was pretending to be the younger sister.

We also see some interesting parallels between Isaac being deceived and Jacob being deceived. Jacob enjoyed a feast before being deceived (29:22), just as Isaac had a delicious stew before being deceived (27:25). Jacob in the evening darkness was unable to recognize Leah (29:24-25), just as Isaac in the darkness of his vision was unable to recognize Jacob (27:1). Just as Jacob was fooled by the wedding veil over Leah's face, so Isaac was fooled by Esau's clothing that veiled Jacob's body (27:15).

"Complete the week, and we will give you the other also" (29:27): Laban agreed to give Rachel to Jacob in exchange for another seven years of work. However, the marriage took place prior to the seven years of work, not after. Laban indicated he could marry Rachel after the week-long wedding celebration for Leah.

Genesis 29:31-35

Leah was hated (29:31): Leah was hated by her husband despite the fact that she bore him four sons. Meanwhile, Rachel—whom Jacob loved—was unable to bear children. A rivalry developed between them.

Reuben (29:32): Leah gave names to her sons in keeping with her difficult situation. The Lord saw that Leah was hated, so He opened her womb. Once she bore a son, she named him Reuben, meaning "See, a son." She thought that perhaps once Jacob saw that she had a son, he would love her.

Simeon (29:33): Leah said, "The LORD has heard that I am hated," and she believed that was why He gave her another son. She named him Simeon, which sounds like a Hebrew word for "heard."

Levi (29:34): Leah gave birth to a third son. She reasoned, "Now this time my husband will be attached to me." She therefore named her son Levi, which sounds like the Hebrew word for "attached."

Judah (29:35): She bore a fourth son and said, "This time I will praise the Lord." She therefore named her son Judah, which sounds like the Hebrew word for "praise."

Two of these sons are particularly important as related to two institutions that would play a prominent role in Israel—the priesthood came from Levi, and the royal line was from Judah.

The rivalry between these two sisters continues with their sons as well as the tribes that came from them. Some of the most intense conflicts seem to develop within families.

Major Themes

1. *Shepherding in Bible times*. In Bible times, shepherds were simultaneously leaders of the sheep and companions to the sheep. They were typically strong people, capable of defending flocks against wild beasts (1 Samuel 17:34-37; Matthew 10:16; Acts 20:29). Shepherds were gentle with the sheep, knowing their condition (Proverbs 27:23), carrying them (Isaiah 40:11), adapting to their needs (Genesis 33:13-14), and cherishing each and every one of them as their own children (2 Samuel 12:3). Laban's sons were evidently too young to be shepherds at this time, or perhaps they were busy caring for other animals.
2. *Seven years*. The time frame of seven years comes up often in Scripture. Jacob offered to work seven years for Laban in exchange for marrying Rachel (Genesis 29:18). Later, there was seven years of "great plenty" throughout Egypt followed by seven years of famine (Genesis 41:29,54). Another seven-year famine took place during the time of Elisha (2 Kings 8:1). Ezekiel 39:9 reveals that in the future,

there will be an "Ezekiel invasion" of Muslim nations into Israel. God will destroy the invading forces, after which the Israelites will burn the invaders' weapons for seven years.

Digging Deeper with Cross-References

Polygamy—Genesis 4:19; 16:3; 26:34; 28:9; 31:50; 36:2; Exodus 21:10; Deuteronomy 21:15; Judges 8:30; 1 Samuel 1:2; 25:43; 27:3; 2 Samuel 5:13; 1 Kings 11:3; 1 Chronicles 2:26; 4:5; 7:4; 14:3; 2 Chronicles 13:21; 24:3; Daniel 5:2

Feasts in Genesis—Genesis 19:3; 21:8; 26:30; 29:22; 40:20; 43:16

Life Lessons

1. *Beware of the craftiness of others.* The book of Genesis says much about craftiness. Laban was quite crafty in dealing with Jacob (Genesis 29:27). The serpent was crafty in tempting Eve in the garden (Genesis 3:1). Jacob was crafty in obtaining Esau's birthright (Genesis 25:31) and Isaac's blessing (Genesis 27:16,35). Joseph's brothers were crafty in dipping Joseph's robe in blood, thereby indicating to their father that Joseph had been killed (Genesis 37:31). There are two applications for us: (1) Never be crafty in dealing with others. God stands against such deceptive methods (Proverbs 11:1; 20:10,23). (2) Beware of the craftiness of others. One of the best ways to do this is to saturate your mind with the book of Proverbs, which greatly increases one's level of discernment in dealing with people.
2. *Children are gifts from the Lord.* The Lord opened Leah's womb so that she was able to have children (Genesis 29:31-32). When Eve conceived Cain, she said, "I have gotten a man with the help of the Lord" (Genesis 4:1). When she conceived Seth, she said, "God has appointed for

me another offspring" (Genesis 4:25). When Jacob was reunited with his son Joseph in Egypt, Joseph introduced his sons to him, saying, "They are my sons, whom God has given me here" (Genesis 48:9). When Ruth married Boaz, "the Lord gave her conception, and she bore a son" (Ruth 4:13). In 1 Samuel 2:21 we read that "the Lord visited Hannah, and she conceived and bore three sons and two daughters." We read in Psalm 127:3, "Behold, children are a heritage from the Lord, the fruit of the womb a reward." If you have children, such verses should help you see them in a new light.

Questions for Reflection and Discussion

1. Does the teaching that "whatever one sows, that will he also reap" motivate you to make any changes in your life?
2. Have you ever experienced a rivalry with a sibling or someone else? What have you learned about the folly of rivalries?
3. Are there any crafty people in your life at present? What have you learned in this chapter that might help you deal with them?

Day 24

Infertile Rachel Bears a Son

Genesis 30:1-24

Scripture Reading and Insights

Begin by reading Genesis 30:1-24 in your favorite Bible. As you read, remember that God's Word is the true source of hope (Psalm 119:81).

In yesterday's reading, we were introduced to Jacob's marriages and Laban's deception. Now let's find out more about Jacob's family. With your Bible still accessible, consider the following insights on the biblical text.

Genesis 30:1-8

Envied her sister (30:1): In ancient times, a barren wife carried a stigma. "Not pregnant" meant "not blessed by God." "Pregnant," by contrast, meant "blessed by God." Because Leah bore children to Jacob and Rachel did not, Rachel was jealous.

"Give me children, or I shall die" (30:1): In biblical times children were considered a gift from God (Psalm 127:3). The inability to have children was, by contrast, considered a disgrace (Luke 1:24-25; see also Genesis 16:1-2). In a way, the inability of a woman to bear a child was like a social death.

Baby boys were especially coveted among the ancient Jews. This is so for several reasons. First, a boy would be needed to carry on the family name. Further, a boy would eventually be able to assist the father in the family trade, thereby contributing to the family income. Still further, a boy would be better able to care for his parents in old age.

"Am I in the place of God?" (30:2): Jacob was essentially saying, "Only God has the power to open the womb, so why are you saying this to me? Do you think I can do what only God can do?" There is a little irony here. Jacob had for years tried to bring divine blessing into his life by human efforts. But here he concedes that no one can bless the womb but God (see Genesis 25:21; 29:31; 30:17,22-23; 1 Samuel 1:19-20; Psalms 113:9; 127:3; Luke 1:13). Jacob recognizes that only God can open the womb, but we do not find Jacob praying for Rachel as Isaac had prayed for Rebekah (25:21).

"Bilhah...she may give birth on my behalf" (30:3): Bilhah was Rachel's handmaiden. Rachel instructed Jacob to "go in to her"—that is, have marital relations with her as a kind of proxy child-bearer or surrogate mother. She was to give birth on Rachel's behalf. The phrase "on my behalf" is literally "on my knees." In the Bible, the knee was viewed as symbolic of a parent's care (Job 3:12). The delivery of a handmaiden's baby on the knees of the primary wife symbolized the adoption of that child by the primary wife.

The Nuzi tablets, discovered east of the Tigris River, include legal tablets indicating that an infertile wife had the prerogative of giving her maidservant to her husband in order to provide him an heir. All children born to a surrogate wife were regarded as belonging to the head wife of the husband.

Bilhah as a wife (30:4): Bilhah was a secondary wife, a concubine wife.

"God has judged me" (30:6): That is, God has rendered a favorable verdict in Rachel's predicament and provided a son through the surrogate mother.

Dan (30:6): Because God judged in favor of Rachel, she named her son Dan, which means "He judged" or "He brought justice" or "He vindicated."

Bilhah conceived again (30:7): Rachel rejoiced that another son had been provided her through the surrogate mother, Bilhah. Rachel thus said, "With mighty wrestlings I have wrestled with my sister and have prevailed" (verse 8). She therefore named the son Naphtali, which sounds like the Hebrew word for "wrestling."

It is important not to miss the fact that the names Rachel chooses for the children born through Bilhah are reflective of her competitive struggle with Leah—"justice" (Dan) and "wrestled" (Naphtali).

Genesis 30:9-21

Leah...took her servant Zilpah (30:9): When Leah stopped bearing children, she continued the child-bearing competition with Rachel by giving her handmaiden Zilpah to Jacob as a surrogate mother. She bore a son. For this reason, Leah said, "Good fortune has come" (verse 11). She therefore named the child Gad, which sounds like the Hebrew word for "good fortune."

Zilpah...a second son (30:12): When Zilpah bore a second son as a surrogate mother, Leah exclaimed, "Happy am I" (verse 13). She therefore named the child Asher, which sounds like the Hebrew word for "happy."

Reuben...found mandrakes (30:14): Reuben, Leah's son, went out to the field and found some mandrakes. In Bible times, this orange-colored fruit was believed to be an aphrodisiac. It was also superstitiously thought to make a woman fertile, able to bear children. Interestingly, the Hebrew words for mandrake and love come from the same root word. Mandrakes were considered "love fruits."

"Give me some of your son's mandrakes" (30:14): Rachel desperately wanted to become pregnant. She reasoned that if she could secure some mandrakes, she might succeed. Rachel had gotten tired of waiting for God to make her fruitful, so she thought eating this fruit might change things. She was attempting to "open the womb" by human means, whereas in truth only God has the power to do so.

"Taken away my husband" (30:15): Leah—ever maintaining the competitive spirit with Rachel—charged that Rachel had already taken away her husband and now has the gall to want her mandrakes. Rachel then bargained with Leah by giving her permission to "lie with" Jacob that night in exchange for mandrakes. Leah took Rachel up on this opportunity.

Leah...bore Jacob a fifth son (30:17): After her son was born, she said, "God has given me my wages because I gave my servant to my husband" (verse 18). She therefore named the son Issachar, which sounds like the Hebrew word for "wages."

Leah conceived again (30:19): When she bore a sixth son to Jacob, she affirmed, "Now my husband will honor me, because I have borne him six sons" (verse 20). The son was appropriately named Zebulun, which sounds like the Hebrew word for "honor."

Dinah (30:21): After having six sons, Leah finally gave birth to a daughter.

Genesis 30:22-24

God remembered Rachel (30:22): When the Bible says "God remembered," it doesn't mean He had forgotten or that something suddenly popped into His mind. Rather, the phrase always indicates that God is concerned and is about to act on behalf of the one He remembers. In this case, God remembered Rachel by opening her womb.

Conceived and bore a son (30:23): Rachel was filled with joy at bearing a son to Jacob and exclaimed, "God has taken away my reproach." No longer did she have to bear the shame of being childless. The word "reproach" carries the idea, "cutting taunt or painful ridicule." Given the resentment that seemed to exist between the two sisters, Leah may have taunted Rachel over her inability to bear children, so Rachel would have lived under reproach. Rachel named the child Joseph, and then said, "May the LORD add to me another son" (verse 24). Joseph means "may He add" and sounds like the Hebrew word for "taken away." Rachel would indeed bear another son (Genesis 35:16-19).

Notice that Rachel here uses two terms in speaking of Deity. When Rachel said, "God has taken away my reproach," the term for God is *Elohim*. This name means "Strong One," and it indicates fullness of power (Genesis 1:1). It pictures God as the powerful and sovereign Governor of the universe, ruling over the affairs of humanity. This mighty God took away Rachel's reproach.

Rachel then says, "May the LORD add to me another son." The term Lord here is *Yahweh*. This name means that God is eternally self-existent (see Exodus 3:14-15). He never came into being at a point in time. He has always existed. This name is also reflective of the idea that

God faithfully keeps covenant promises. He delivers on all that He has promised, including the promises regarding Jacob's descendants.

Major Themes

1. *Interpersonal conflict.* Interpersonal conflict was common in families who lived in Bible times. In Genesis 30, the conflict is between two sisters. John MacArthur explains the conflict this way:

   > The competition between the two sisters/wives is demonstrated in using their maids as surrogate mothers (vv. 3,7,9,12), in declaring God had judged the case in favor of the plaintiff (v. 6), in bartering for time with the husband (vv. 14-16), in accusing one of stealing her husband's favor (v. 15), and in the name given to one son—"wrestled with my sister" (Naphtali, v. 8). The race for children was also accompanied by prayers to the Lord or by acknowledgment of his providence (vv. 6,17,20,22; also 29:32,33,35)."[3]

   The two sisters obviously had a bitter and intense rivalry.

2. *One husband for one wife.* From what we have learned in Genesis thus far, it seems that a husband with more than one wife is a recipe for interpersonal conflict. No wonder monogamy has been God's ideal for the human race all along. From the very beginning God set the pattern by creating a monogamous marriage relationship with one man and one woman—Adam and Eve (Genesis 1:27; 2:21-25). This God-established example of one woman for one man was the general practice of the human race (Genesis 4:1) until interrupted by sin (Genesis 4:23). The Law of Moses clearly commands, "You shall not multiply wives" (Deuteronomy 17:17). Our Lord affirmed God's original intention by creating one "male and [one] female" and joined them in marriage (Matthew 19:4). The New Testament stresses that "each man should have his own

wife, and each woman her own husband" (1 Corinthians 7:2).

Digging Deeper with Cross-References

God remembered—Genesis 8:1; 19:29; 30:22; 1 Samuel 1:19; Psalms 98:3; 136:23; Isaiah 49:15-16; Jeremiah 2:2; Hebrews 6:10

Conception in Genesis—Genesis 4:1,17,25; 16:4; 21:2; 25:21; 29:32; 30:5,17,23; 38:3,18 (This is important as related to God's command to Adam and Eve in Genesis 1:28: "Be fruitful and multiply and fill the earth.")

Life Lessons

1. *Mighty wrestlings.* Such wrestling between two sisters represents a sad chapter in biblical history. We can easily fall prey to this same type of behavior. I have come to believe that personal offense is one of the devil's most effective tools for causing conflict among Christians. We tend not to forgive those who render offense against us. Scripture, however, teaches that because God has forgiven us, we should also forgive others. Peter once came up to Jesus and asked, "Lord, how often will my brother sin against me, and I forgive him? As many as seven times?" Jesus said to him, "I do not say to you seven times, but seventy-seven times" (Matthew 18:21-22). The backdrop to this is that the Pharisees taught that righteousness demanded that a person be forgiven two times. The Jewish rabbis taught that if one wanted to be magnanimous one should forgive up to three times. When Peter asked Jesus about forgiving someone seven times, he no doubt thought he was being quite generous. Jesus went far beyond what Peter had in mind by saying we should

forgive 77 times—or, in other words, there should be no limitations on our forgiveness (see Matthew 18:23-35).

2. *Range of emotions.* In our passage we witness a range of emotions—from envy and resentment to happiness. We've all experienced these emotions. I particularly like the way Solomon helps us to deal with emotions in the book of Proverbs. For example, those who make a habit of living in righteousness typically have a life characterized by joy and gladness (Proverbs 10:28; 29:6). Those who promote peace have joy in their lives (Proverbs 12:20). A key to contentment is maintaining a continual reverence for God (Proverbs 19:23). Jealousy can virtually consume a person and, if unchecked, entice him or her to lose control (Proverbs 6:34-35; 27:4). Insofar as emotions are concerned, wisdom urges one to maintain self-control (Proverbs 29:11).

Questions for Reflection and Discussion

1. Have you ever noticed envy or jealousy among members of your immediate or extended family? What insights have you gained from this lesson on this ugly issue?
2. What evidence do you find in this chapter that supports Jesus's New Testament teaching that "all things are possible with God" (Mark 10:27)?
3. What consequences might arise when we violate God's ideal for marriage (one man for one woman)?

Day 25

Jacob Bargains with Laban and Separates from Him

Genesis 30:25–31:55

Scripture Reading and Insights

Begin by reading Genesis 30:25–31:55 in your favorite Bible. As you read, remember that great spiritual wisdom comes from studying God's Word (Psalm 119:98-104).

In the previous lesson, we learned more about Jacob's family. In today's reading, we pause to consider Jacob's flight from Laban. With your Bible still accessible, consider the following insights on the biblical text.

Genesis 30:25-43

"Send me away" (30:25): Jacob considered his stay with Laban to be temporary. His ultimate desire was to return to the land God promised to him and his ancestors.

"Give me my wives and my children" (30:26): Earlier Rachel had requested of Jacob, "Give me children" (30:1). Jacob now says to Laban, "Give me my wives and my children."

"I have learned by divination" (30:27): People used divination in ancient times to discover information about other people, the future, or the will of the gods. All forms of divination are forbidden by God. See Major Themes.

"Name your wages" (30:28): Laban's statement was profit driven. He

knew his wealth had increased greatly as a result of Jacob working for him. He wanted that to continue well into the future. He didn't want to lose a good thing.

"What shall I give you?" (30:31): Laban wanted Jacob to stay. Jacob agreed to stay for a time but wanted to avoid becoming further indebted to Laban. Jacob told Laban that all he wanted for wages was to keep the yet-unborn animals that would be off-colored or spotted.

"Let it be as you have said" (30:34): The profit-driven Laban went along with what Jacob said. He then arranged for all the animals that were off-colored or spotted to be separated off and put in the care of his own sons. These animals were moved a distance of three days' journey away from the remaining flocks, which would be under Jacob's care. This was to ensure that Jacob would not end up with a large flock.

Laban was not counting on the fact that the animals that remained with Jacob—animals that were not off-colored or spotted—carried latent genes within them that enabled them to produce off-colored or spotted offspring. Jacob was aware of this, for he had tended animals for many years.

Set the sticks...in the troughs (30:38): The ancients believed that sticks with peeled white streaks in them could influence the kind of animal that would be born. The idea was that the white streaks in the sticks would influence the animals to produce likewise streaked (or spotted) offspring. Of course, God alone bestows fertility. Jacob followed the procedure of using peeled sticks, but he knew that God prospered his breeding efforts and gave him great wealth (31:11-13).

They bred when they came to drink (30:38): It is possible that the peeled sticks released a stimulant into the water that moved animals toward sexual activity—that is, put them in heat.

Stronger of the flock (30:41): Jacob knew that strong animals breed strong offspring. Whenever the stronger of the flock were near the troughs, he "lay the sticks in the troughs before the eyes of the flock." He wanted the stronger of the flocks to give birth to many off-colored or speckled animals.

Feebler of the flock (30:42): Conversely, Jacob knew that feeble animals breed feeble offspring. He therefore would not lay the sticks in the troughs when the feebler of the flock were near it.

The man increased greatly (30:43): Jacob became very wealthy, in keeping with the blessing given him by Isaac: "May God give you of the dew of heaven and of the fatness of the earth and plenty of grain and wine" (27:28).

Genesis 31:1-16

The sons of Laban were saying (31:1): Trouble was brewing. Laban's sons became resentful that Jacob was gaining such wealth from that which belonged to their father. They knew that as Jacob's wealth grew, their own inheritance shrank. Jacob soon fell from Laban's favor.

The LORD said to Jacob, "Return to the land" (31:3): The Lord instructed Jacob to depart from Laban and return to Canaan, the Promised Land.

Called Rachel and Leah into the field (31:4): Jacob called a private meeting with his wives to confidentially inform them of his plans.

"Your father has cheated me and changed my wages ten times" (31:7): Laban had repeatedly cheated Jacob. The number ten could be literal, or it may be a numerical expression indicating completeness. If this latter view is correct, it would indicate that Laban had consistently cheated Jacob his entire time there.

The angel of God (31:11): This is the Angel of the Lord, or Angel of *Yahweh*. As we have seen, this angel is a manifestation of God (see Genesis 31:13; Exodus 3:6)—probably the preincarnate Christ.

Rachel and Leah answered (31:14): Rachel and Leah saw that their inheritance was now in question. They were regarded as foreigners with no claim to the family fortune. Laban had continually exploited them. They therefore told Jacob, "Whatever God has said to you, do" (verse 16).

Genesis 31:17-35

So Jacob arose (31:17): Jacob would now make a hasty departure. He put his family members on camels and drove his animals straight toward Canaan.

Rachel stole her father's household gods (31:19): These were figurines of deities who were thought to bring protection and blessing. Whoever possessed the household idols customarily had legal ownership of the estate. See Major Themes.

Jacob tricked Laban (31:20): Jacob decided to slip away without informing Laban of his plans. If Jacob had said anything, Laban would likely have sought to intervene and stop them from leaving.

He fled (31:21): Recall that Jacob had earlier fled from Esau (27:42-43).

Crossed the Euphrates (31:21): Also called "the river" (Exodus 23:31 NKJV) or "the great river" (Deuteronomy 1:7 NKJV), the Euphrates is the longest river of Western Asia—almost 1800 miles long.

Hill country of Gilead (31:21): A good grazing area.

Laban...pursued him for seven days (31:22-23): This was an extended pursuit of hundreds of miles.

"Driven away my daughters like captives" (31:26): Laban was apparently under the delusion that Jacob forced his daughters to leave with him. In reality, they were in full agreement with Jacob (see verses 14-16).

"With mirth and songs, with tambourine and lyre" (31:27): Laban claims he would have much preferred to have a proper send-off—a going-away party.

"Be careful not to say...either good or bad" (31:29): God warned Laban not to use any arguments at all to motivate Jacob to return to Haran. Just as God had watched over Abraham and Isaac (12:17-20; 20:3-7; 26:8-11), so now He watches over Jacob.

"Why did you steal my gods?" (31:30): To Laban, these gods were not just figurines used for decor. Laban was entrenched in pagan religion, and he was convinced that his future blessing in life hinged on these household gods. Moreover, in view of the ancient idea that he who possessed the household gods also had a right to the estate, Laban did not want Jacob to have those gods and make claim to his estate.

"I was afraid" (31:31): Jacob did not want to lose his wives, who were to play a key role in the seed promises of the Abrahamic covenant.

Rachel had taken the household gods (31:34): One sin often leads to another. Rachel not only stole the household gods from Laban but also hid them so her father would not discover them. She lied to him in the process. Jacob was also unaware of what she had done, so she was also being dishonest with him.

"The way of women is upon me" (31:35): A woman's menstrual period.

Genesis 31:36-55

"My kinsmen and your kinsmen" (31:37): Jacob wanted his name cleared of the charge of stealing the household gods. He challenged Laban to put the matter before all who were present on both sides of the family.

"I bore the loss of it myself" (31:39): Jacob had gone above and beyond the call of duty when working for Laban. It was customary in ancient times that shepherds not be held responsible for losses to wild animals.

"If... God... had not been on my side" (31:42): Jacob described the way Laban had mistreated him for years. Laban's treatment of Jacob had been unfair. Jacob knew that if God had not been on his side, he would have come away empty-handed.

"The Fear of Isaac" (31:42): The God whom Isaac held in great reverence.

"All that you see is mine" (31:43): Laban claimed that everything was his—his daughters, the children, and the animals. But he now asks what he can do for his daughters and their children.

"Let us make a covenant" (31:44): Not having found the household gods, Laban was now feeling vulnerable. He was the aggressor in wanting a protective covenant in which they mutually agreed not to attack each other. Like other such covenants, there was a witness (God), a visible testament (the stones), a meal (to ratify the covenant), and oaths in the name of God.

Took stones and made a heap (31:46): The heap of stones marked clear boundaries between the territories of Jacob and Laban. *Jegar-sahadutha* (verse 47) means "heap of witnesses" in the Aramain dialect. *Galeed* (verses 47-48) means the same thing in Hebrew. *Mizpah* (verse 49) means "watchpost," representing an appeal to God to watch over them.

"The Lord watch between you and me... God is witness between you and me" (31:49-50): Jacob and Laban could not trust each other, so God would be the true Judge who ensures that the right will be done.

Laban departed and returned home (31:55): Laban would never see Jacob's family again.

Major Themes

1. *Divination.* Laban said to Jacob, "I have learned by divination that the Lord has blessed me because of you" (30:27). People of pagan nations often engaged in various forms of divination to discover information about other people, the future, or the will of the gods. People would conjure spells (Deuteronomy 18:11), practice sorcery (Exodus 22:18; Deuteronomy 18:10), interpret omens (Genesis 30:27; 44:5), or interpret the stars (Daniel 1:20; 2:2,10,27; 4:7; 5:7,11,15). The Bible condemns *all* forms of occultism (Exodus 22:18; Leviticus 19:26,31; 20:27; 1 Samuel 28:3; Acts 19:19).
2. *Household gods.* In ancient times, the person in possession of a family's household gods was considered the legitimate heir of the family fortune. The gods were also thought to bring protection and blessing as well as ensure the fertility of women in the household. These household gods were actually small figurines of female deities between two and three inches long with accentuated sexual features. Rachel may have stolen them because she thought they would render her a fertile mother.

Digging Deeper with Cross-References

Dishonest gain—Leviticus 6:4; Psalms 37:16; 62:10; Proverbs 10:2; 13:11; 15:6; 16:8; 20:14; 21:6; 22:16; Jeremiah 17:11; 22:13; Ezekiel 22:13; Micah 6:10; Matthew 27:3; 1 Corinthians 5:11; James 5:4

Stealing—Exodus 20:15; Leviticus 19:11; Hosea 4:2; Matthew 6:19-20; Ephesians 4:28

Life Lessons

1. *Be a person of your word.* Laban did not seem to be a person of his word. Jesus tells us that all Christians should be truthful with no duplicity. In Matthew 5:37, Jesus said, "Let what you say be simply 'Yes' or 'No.'" The problem Jesus was addressing was that oaths became so common that people started to assume that when you did not take an oath, perhaps you were not being truthful. To counter such an idea, Jesus tells His followers that they should have no duplicity in their words, that their yes should be yes and their no should be no.
2. *God is your defender*. An underlying theme in our passage today is that God is the protector of His faithful people. This is a common theme throughout all of Scripture. In 2 Chronicles 16:9 we are told, "The eyes of the Lord run to and fro throughout the whole earth, to give strong support to those whose heart is blameless." Psalm 34:7 tells us, "The angel of the Lord encamps around those who fear him, and delivers them." Rejoice that God is watching over you!

Questions for Reflection and Discussion

1. Divination has made a big comeback in our day. Can you think of any ways false religion has penetrated the Christian church today?
2. Have you ever committed one sin that led to committing another?
3. When you're treated unfairly, do you trust in God as your Defender?

Day 26

Jacob Reconciles with Esau

Genesis 32–33

Scripture Reading and Insights

Begin by reading Genesis 32–33 in your favorite Bible. As you read, remember that great spiritual wisdom comes from studying God's Word (Psalm 119:98-104).

In the previous lesson, we considered Jacob's flight from Laban. We now see Jacob attempt to appease Esau and then wrestle with God. With your Bible still accessible, consider the following insights on the biblical text.

Genesis 32:1-21

The angels of God (32:1): Jacob traveled in fear at the prospect of encountering Esau, so he must have felt great comfort when he encountered God's angels. Angels are ministering spirits that God created to serve His purposes (Hebrews 1:14). As spirit beings, they are typically invisible, but in the present case they manifested themselves visibly to Jacob (compare with Hebrews 13:2). The last time Jacob had seen angels, he was at Bethel, on his way to Paddan-aram (Genesis 28:11-15). Now he's on his way back to Canaan.

God had earlier promised Jacob, "Behold, I am with you and will keep you wherever you go" (28:15). The angels work for God. They were watching out for Jacob because God assigned them to.

"This is God's camp!" So he called…that place Mahanaim (32:2):

Mahanaim literally means "two camps" or "double camp." Jacob was apparently referring to the angels and his own entourage. The company of angels and Jacob's own company were now in the same place, east of the Jordan River in Gilead.

Seir...Edom (32:3): Seir is a mountainous region occupied by the Edomites, along the southern portion of the Dead Sea (Genesis 32:3; 33:14,16). Edom is the land inhabited by Esau and his descendants (Genesis 36:16; Numbers 20:14-21).

Jacob sent messengers before him to Esau (32:3): Jacob sent peace-making envoys ahead of him. He is fearful but hopeful of a reconciliation with Esau.

"Your servant Jacob" (32:4): By identifying himself this way to Esau, he was showing humility.

"Find favor in your sight" (32:5): Years earlier Jacob had earned Esau's disfavor by obtaining Esau's birthright and his blessing. Jacob remembered how Esau desired to kill him following the death of Isaac (27:41-42). Jacob was hoping the years had softened Esau's intent so that a reconciliation was possible.

"Esau...is coming to meet you" (32:6): Jacob's peace-making envoy returned with the news that Esau was coming to meet him—accompanied by 400 men. Upon hearing this news, Jacob was "greatly afraid and distressed" (verse 7). Jacob surmised that perhaps Esau sought revenge instead of reconciliation.

Divided the people...into two camps (32:7): Anticipating an attack from Esau, Jacob divided his entourage into two camps of people and animals. Jacob reasoned that if Esau destroyed the one camp, the other might survive.

"O God of my father Abraham" (32:9): Jacob remembered the covenant promises that God had made to him. Those promises included the idea that he would have innumerable descendants. Jacob promptly prays for God's intervention and deliverance. Jacob had been a selfish cheater in earlier days, but now we now witness a humbler man praying, confessing his own unworthiness before God.

"The mothers with the children" (32:11): For all Jacob knew, Esau might kill not just him but his family as well.

"Offspring...cannot be numbered" (32:12): Jacob in his prayer for deliverance from Esau reminded God of the covenant promise that his descendants would be so massive that they could not be numbered (28:14).

Took a present for his brother Esau (32:13-16): Jacob arranged for his servants to take a large number of animals and stagger their traveling so Esau would receive wave after wave of gifts. Jacob hoped this would soften Esau's heart while he was en route toward Jacob.

"My lord Esau" (32:18): Isaac had earlier said to Esau regarding Jacob, "Behold, I have made him lord over you" (27:37). But here Jacob refers to Esau as "my lord." This is a different Jacob than the one of earlier years.

Genesis 32:22-32

Jabbok (32:22): A 65-mile-long stream on the east of Jordan.

A man wrestled with him (32:24): Even though the person is called a man, he was apparently not an ordinary man. Hosea 12:4 tells us that Jacob "strove with the angel and prevailed; he wept and sought his favor." Apparently Jacob wrestled with the Angel of the Lord (or Angel of *Yahweh*), most likely a preincarnate appearance of Christ (compare with verses 28 and 30, where the man is identified as God).

Bible expositors are careful to point out that God Himself is omnipotent or all-powerful (see 1 Kings 8:39; Jeremiah 17:9-10,16). So God, for His own purposes, evidently allowed Himself as the Angel of the Lord to be overcome by Jacob (much as a daddy today wrestles with his five-year-old son). Note that by touching Jacob's hip socket, the divine Angel revealed that if He chose to, he could easily disable Jacob.

"I will not let you go unless you bless me" (32:26): Jacob was relentlessly persistent for a blessing. In a way, this was a milestone event. Through the years Jacob had been trying to force blessing by human means. Here he seems to recognize that blessing must come from God. He therefore refuses to give up until he receives it.

"Your name shall no longer be called Jacob, but Israel" (32:28): No longer would the patriarch be called Jacob (meaning "supplanter" or "deceiver"). His new name would be Israel (which means "he strives

with God" or perhaps "God fights"). The name change occurred because Jacob had "striven with God and with men, and…prevailed."

From here, the nation of Jacob's descendants would derive their name—Israel. This is an appropriate place for God to make this change because Jacob is about to reenter the Promised Land.

"Please tell me your name" (32:29): Now that Jacob has received a new name, he wants to the know the divine Angel's name. The divine Angel declines to divulge this information. But he did bless Jacob, as requested.

We should not miss the fact that the divine Angel had, in fact, already revealed His name to Jacob. He informed Jacob that his new name would be Israel, and the *el* part of this word means "God." (Israel means "strives with God.")

Peniel (32:30): Jacob named the place Peniel, which means "the face of God." He chose this name because, as Jacob put it, "I have seen God face to face, and yet my life has been delivered." In Old Testament days, people believed that no one could see God and live (see Exodus 33:23; Judges 13:22).

Do not eat the sinew (32:32): The prohibition served as an ongoing reminder of Jacob's (Israel's) encounter with God.

Genesis 33:1-20

Esau was coming (33:1-3): The dreaded moment had arrived. Esau and his company of 400 men were within eyesight of Jacob. He sent his family out in three groups, and he led the way to greet his long-estranged brother. Jacob bowed to the ground seven times—a sign of great respect.

Rachel and Joseph last of all (33:2): Jacob lines up his family in order of least loved to most loved. He put his favorites in the back, safest from possible attack.

Esau ran to meet him and embraced him (33:4): In one of the most touching scenes in all of Scripture, the long-estranged brothers embraced and kissed and wept. Twenty-one years of estrangement were now over. Old resentments were gone, replaced with renewed affection.

Women and children (33:5): Jacob introduced his family to Esau, and they too bowed before Esau, showing respect.

"What do you mean by all this company?" (33:8): Esau initially declined all the generous gifts Jacob had brought. But Jacob—full of joy that Esau had accepted him—insisted that Esau receive the gifts. Esau accepted.

"I have seen your face, which is like seeing the face of God" (33:10): Instead of encountering a man raging with vengeance, Jacob encountered a man full of forgiveness. God had obviously been transforming Esau's heart over the years. Jacob likened the dramatic change in Esau to seeing the face of God.

"Let me leave with you some of the people" (33:15): Esau wanted to loan Jacob some of his men to make the remaining trip easier and safer. Traveling entourages were always vulnerable to attackers. The 400 were apparently intended to be a military escort for his brother. Jacob declined. He wanted to leave well enough alone. Besides, Jacob now trusted God as his protector.

Esau returned that day on his way to Seir (33:16): Esau went back to the mountainous region along the southern portion of the Dead Sea.

Jacob journeyed to Succoth (33:17): Jacob traveled (for unknown reasons) not to Seir, but to Succoth, east of Shechem and north of Jerusalem.

Jacob came safely to the city of Shechem (33:18): This city is in the central part of Canaan. Jacob had earlier vowed in Bethel to return to Canaan (28:20-22). That vow was now fulfilled.

He bought...the piece of land on which he had pitched his tent (33:19): Abraham had purchased some property in the Promised Land (23:17-18), and now Jacob does as well.

Erected an altar (33:20): The word "altar" literally means "place of sacrifice." He called the altar *El-Elohe-Israel*, meaning "God, the God of Israel" or "a Mighty God is the God of Israel." This was an affirmation of the one true God who had been with him all these years.

Major Themes

1. *A magnificent gift of animals.* The gifts Jacob gave Esau were extravagant: "Two hundred female goats and twenty male goats, two hundred ewes and twenty rams, thirty milking camels and their calves, forty cows and ten bulls, twenty female donkeys and ten male donkeys" (Genesis 32:14-16). Today, in our consumerist society, we tend to think that the gift of animals is no big deal. But to the ancients, who were not part of a consumerist society (with food stores and the like), animals represented great wealth.
2. *Brothers reconciled.* Jacob had good reason to fear Esau's arrival. Recall that Jacob's name means "he supplants" (a word meaning "to take the place of another"). Jacob talked a hungry and exhausted brother—Esau, Isaac's firstborn son—into giving him his birthright, along with the greater inheritance that accompanies it, in exchange for a mere bowl of food (Genesis 25:29-34). Jacob then tricked Isaac into giving him Esau's inheritance when Isaac was a very old man and could not see well (27:1-29). Instead of Esau seeking vengeance against Jacob, however, our text tells us they embraced and wept. They had been separated for some 21 years. Jacob likely thought that Esau's anger had been simmering all that time. In reality, their hearts had changed. Bad memories were a thing of the distant past. The brothers were reconciled. "Behold, how good and pleasant it is when brothers dwell in unity" (Psalm 133:1).

Digging Deeper with Cross-References

Reconciliation—Genesis 33:4; 45:15; Joshua 22:33; Job 42:8; Matthew 5:24; 18:15

Favor in the eyes of others—Genesis 33:10; 39:4,21; Exodus 3:21; 11:3; 12:36; Numbers 32:5; Ruth 2:10,13; 1 Samuel

2:26; 16:22; 20:3; 2 Samuel 14:22; Esther 2:9,15; Proverbs 3:4; 22:1; Daniel 1:9

Life Lessons

1. *Letting go of bitterness.* Jacob cheated Esau out of his birthright and his inheritance. Esau could have chosen to hold on to bitterness. But when we are bitter at the person we're angry with, we only hurt ourselves. Esau let go of it. When we feel cheated in life, the best thing to do is to forgive those who have wronged us (Matthew 6:12,14; 18:21-22; Luke 6:37; Ephesians 4:32) and turn the situation over to God (Philippians 4:6-7).
2. *Persistence in wanting God's blessing.* Jacob was persistent in wrestling all night with the Angel of the Lord just to get blessed. Persistence is emphasized in the New Testament as well. In Matthew 7:7-8 Jesus said, "Ask, and it will be given to you; seek, and you will find; knock, and it will be opened to you. For everyone who asks receives, and the one who seeks finds, and to the one who knocks, it will be opened." In these verses the words "ask," "seek," and "knock" are in the present tense, which indicates continuous activity. We are to keep on asking, keep on seeking, and keep on knocking. If we do so, we will obtain our desired result, assuming our request is in keeping with God's will for our lives.

Questions for Reflection and Discussion

1. Do you make a conscious effort to "strive for peace with everyone" (Hebrews 12:14)?
2. Do any of your relationships need reconciliation?
3. Are you persistent in waiting for God's blessing?

Day 27

Jacob's Latter Years

Genesis 34–36

Scripture Reading and Insights

Begin by reading Genesis 34–36 in your favorite Bible. As you read, remember that reading Scripture can strengthen your faith in God (Romans 10:17).

In yesterday's reading, we considered Jacob's wrestling match with God and his reunion with Esau. Now let's find out about the rape of Dinah and her brothers' retaliation, Jacob's return to Bethel, and Esau's descendants. With your Bible still accessible, consider the following insights on the biblical text.

Genesis 34

Dinah...went out to see the women (34:1): Dinah wanted a glance at how other women lived in the nearby city. Being alone, however, she was easy prey for Shechem. Dinah was probably just 14 or 15 at this time and was naive in making such a trip alone.

Saw her...seized her...lay with her...humiliated her (34:2): Shechem raped Dinah. He saw her, forcibly seized her against her will, raped her, and humiliated her. He later claimed he loved her and wanted to marry her, but this does not lessen the heinous nature of his crime against her.

Jacob held his peace (34:5): There would be a definite response to this crime. First, however, all the facts must be uncovered so a proper judgment can be made. Once his sons returned from overseeing the livestock in the field, he would counsel with them.

The sons of Jacob...were indignant and very angry (34:7): The response of Jacob's sons confirms the heinous nature of Shechem's act.

Outrageous thing...must not be done (34:7): This was an unthinkable act to the people of Israel, especially because it involved a teenager.

"Shechem longs for your daughter" (34:8): Shechem's father, Hamor, sought to negotiate his son's marriage to Dinah. Parents commonly negotiated the marriage of their children in ancient times.

"Give your daughters...take our daughters" (34:9): The idea is, "Let's all become one. Let's merge our peoples." Hamor had his eyes on the wealth that the Lord had bestowed on Jacob's family. As Hamor spoke, Jacob likely pondered inwardly that he certainly had no intent of defiling the purity of the covenant line of promise by intermarrying with this people.

"Dwell and trade" (34:10): Hamor's appeal was that merging their people would be a win-win—an economic plus for everyone. Jacob knew, however, that he needed no such human associations to gain or maintain wealth. God Himself had promised to prosper him.

Shechem also said... "Let me find favor in your eyes" (34:11): An amazingly brazen request in view of what has just happened to young Dinah.

"Bride price" (34:12): Shechem offered to pay whatever was necessary as a bride price. Instead, he would soon pay for his heinous sin against Dinah.

Sons of Jacob answered...deceitfully (34:13): Vengeance was on the minds of Jacob's sons. They feigned interest in the idea of Dinah marrying Shechem (and further intermarriages after that) but told them it would be impossible unless all the men of their city were circumcised. Otherwise it would be a disgrace to the people of Israel. (Notice that Jacob's sons were being deceitful, just as Jacob himself had been so many times—27:24.)

The young man did not delay (34:19): Shechem wasted no time in getting circumcised.

Gate of the city (34:20): The place where all official business of the city took place.

"Only on this condition" (34:22): Hamor and Shechem explained to the people at the city gate the benefits of becoming one with Jacob's clan. They also explained the condition of circumcision.

"Livestock...property...beasts" (34:23): The people at the gate were informed that Israel's livestock, property, and beasts would become theirs. Here's the idea: "We'll all be richer if we only suffer the pain of circumcision. So let's do it."

Every male was circumcised (34:24): Things were going according to the plan of Jacob's sons.

When they were sore (34:25): Recently circumcised men make lousy warriors. Until the wound heals, they are incapacitated. Two of Jacob's sons, Simeon and Levi, went into the city as vigilantes and killed all the males. Dinah was rescued from Shechem's house. Because of this act, Simeon and Levi would later be passed over in Jacob's blessings (49:5-7).

Sons of Jacob (34:27): Simeon and Levi murdered the men of the city, and Jacob's other sons soon joined in to continue the assault on the city.

Plundered the city (34:27): Jacob's sons seized the material goods of the city. Women and children were also captured.

"You have brought trouble on me" (34:30): Jacob's sons went far beyond the boundaries of justice. Only one male was guilty, and yet all the males were murdered. Their crime far exceeded Shechem's. Jacob now felt vulnerable from other peoples in the territory.

"Making me stink" (34:30): Jacob mused that this episode injured his reputation.

"Perizzites" (34:30): An early Canaanite tribe that occupied the fertile regions south and southwest of Carmel (Exodus 23:23).

"If they gather themselves against me" (34:30): If neighboring communities launched an attack against Jacob and his people, they might not survive. Then again, God did promise, "Behold, I am with you and will keep you wherever you go" (28:15).

Genesis 35:1-15

"Bethel" (35:1): A term meaning "house of God," in reference to a city north of Jerusalem. This is the locale where God reaffirmed the Abrahamic covenant to him (verses 13-15).

"Make an altar there" (35:1): For the purpose of worship and dedication.

"Put away the foreign gods" (35:2): Heading back to Bethel required that everyone spiritually clean up their act. Idols would not be permitted (see 31:19).

"Purify yourselves and change your garments" (35:2): The act of bathing and changing garments was an outward symbolic expression that indicated a rejection of idolatry and a renewed consecration to the Lord.

Rings (35:4): Used in pagan countries as a charm or amulet.

Hid them under the terebinth tree (35:4): Jacob took all the idolatrous items and buried them under a tree.

A terror from God (35:5): Jacob had feared that neighboring communities might launch an attack against him and his people (34:30). God, however, induced a "terror" among these peoples so that they were afraid of Israel.

Built an altar and called the place El-bethel (35:7): *El-bethel* means "God of Bethel."

Deborah...died, and she was buried (35:8): The biblical text is unclear as to when Deborah joined Jacob. It may be that she joined him after the death of Rebekah. This old and experienced nurse would have greatly benefited Jacob's young family. Because female nurses in biblical times had little means of self-support, the families they had served commonly cared for them in old age. The place of burial was called *Allon-bacuth*, which means "oak of weeping."

"No longer...Jacob, but Israel" (35:10): God appeared to Jacob and again told him that he would no longer be called Jacob, but Israel. This was a reaffirmation of God's earlier instruction about his name change (see 32:28).

"I am God Almighty" (35:11): *El Shaddai*—a "mighty God" who is full of mercy.

"Nations...and kings shall come from your own body" (35:11): Royalty would be among his descendants (including David, Solomon, and the King of kings—Jesus Christ).

"The land...I will give to you" (35:12): The same land promise given to Abraham and his descendants is reaffirmed (Genesis 17:8).

"Offspring" (35:12): Jacob's offspring and descendants would be beneficiaries of all the blessings of the Abrahamic covenant.

God went up (35:13): God had appeared as a theophany to Jacob, and then He "went up."

Jacob set up a pillar (35:14): Probably as a memorial or witness to the reaffirmation of the Abrahamic covenant.

Drink offering (35:14): Drink offerings involved an offering of a liquid that was intended to bring pleasure to God. They were often given on the Sabbath, new moon, and annual festivals.

Genesis 35:16-29

Ephrath (35:16): An early name for Bethlehem.

Soul was departing (35:18): Rachel was dying due to hard labor. At death the soul, or spirit, departs from the body. The spirits of believers go into God's presence in heaven (see 2 Corinthians 5:8; Philippians 1:23).

Ben-oni (35:18): The dying Rachel named her son *Ben-oni*, meaning "son of my sorrow."

Benjamin (35:18): Jacob named the son Benjamin, meaning "son of the right hand."

Jacob set up a pillar over her tomb (35:20): The pillar served as a memorial for Rachel.

Tower of Eder (35:21): A shepherd's watchtower for keeping an eye on the sheep.

Reuben went and lay with Bilhah (35:22): Reuben's sexual relations with Bilhah defiled his father's marriage bed. This would cost Reuben his birthright.

Sons of Jacob were twelve (35:22): In fulfillment of God's covenant promises, multiple nations and offspring would come from his descendants.

Mamre...Hebron (35:27): The place where Abraham dwelt and provided hospitality to some visiting angels (23:17-19; 35:27). Jacob now visited his father Isaac there in old age. This was also the location of the patriarchal burial plot for Abraham, Jacob, and Leah (see 23:17; 25:9; 35:27; 49:29-31; 50:13).

Breathed his last...gathered to his people (35:29): Isaac died physically, but his spirit was gathered to his people in heaven.

Esau and Jacob buried him (35:29): The two sons reunite for Isaac's funeral, just as Isaac and Ishmael had earlier come together to bury Abraham (25:9). They buried Isaac in the cave of Machpelah (23:9,15,19).

Genesis 36

Generations of Esau (36:1): The genealogy of Esau. The descendants of Esau (Edom) eventually became bitter enemies of the descendants of Jacob (Israel).

Their possessions were too great (36:7): Jacob and Esau had so many animals that grazing conditions became too crowded. Esau decided to permanently relocate to Edom.

Country of Seir (36:8): The mountainous region occupied by the Edomites, along the southern portion of the Dead Sea. God said, "I have given Mount Seir to Esau as a possession" (Deuteronomy 2:5; Joshua 24:4).

Father of the Edomites (36:9): Edom was located southeast and southwest of the Dead Sea and was largely a semidesert, not very conducive to agriculture.

Major Themes

1. *The penalty for rape in Bible times*. Because of the heinousness of this sin, Old Testament law prescribed the death penalty for rape. Deuteronomy 22:25-27 tells us, "If in the open country a man meets a young woman who is

betrothed, and the man seizes her and lies with her, then only the man who lay with her shall die. But you shall do nothing to the young woman." But if the woman was within the city and did not cry out for help—apparently consenting to the man's advances—then both were to be stoned to death (verses 23-24).

2. *Altars in Bible times*. The Hebrew noun for "altar," *mizbeah*, means "place of sacrifice." Altars played a prominent role in Genesis. For example, altars were built by Noah (Genesis 8:20), Abraham (Genesis 12:7), Isaac (Genesis 26:25), and Jacob (Genesis 33:20). In later times, altars were built by Moses (Exodus 17:15), Saul (1 Samuel 14:35), David (2 Samuel 24:15-25), and Solomon (2 Chronicles 4:1). They were used for various religious purposes—including offering animals as burnt offerings as sacrifices to God.

Digging Deeper with Cross-References

Meetings at city gates—Genesis 19:1; 23:10,18; 34:20; Deuteronomy 21:19; 22:15; 25:7; Joshua 20:4; Ruth 4:1,11; 2 Samuel 15:2; 19:8

Treachery—Genesis 34:25; 1 Samuel 19:11; 2 Samuel 11:15; Esther 3:8; Jeremiah 9:8; Matthew 26:16,23

Life Lessons

1. *Seek God, not good luck*. Jacob urged the people in his household, "Put away the foreign gods that are among you" (Genesis 35:2). People in ancient times often possessed household gods as good-luck charms. Jacob didn't believe in luck. He believed in a sovereign God who providentially worked in His people's lives. He therefore wanted to get rid of all household gods. Besides, the use of foreign gods is a form of idolatry—something that is off-limits to God's

people (1 Corinthians 5:11; 10:7,14; 2 Corinthians 6:16; Galatians 5:20; Colossians 3:5; 1 John 5:21).

2. *The effects of sin can remain long after the sin.* Reuben may have thought he had gotten away with his sin of engaging in relations with Bilhah, Jacob's concubine (Genesis 35:22). Much later, when Jacob was on his deathbed, Reuben's birthright was withheld as a result of this sin. We learn an important lesson here. The consequences for a wrongful act can come back to haunt us long after we commit the act.

Questions for Reflection and Discussion

1. Idolatry can take many forms in our lives. Are there any secret idols in your life?
2. Do you have an assurance that the moment you die, your spirit will depart the body and go to be with the Lord in heaven (2 Corinthians 5:6-8; Philippians 1:21-23)?
3. Does the reality that the effects of sin can surface long after the sin motivate you to righteousness?

Day 28

Joseph Is Sold into Slavery

Genesis 37

Scripture Reading and Insights

Begin by reading Genesis 37 in your favorite Bible. As you read, remember that reading Scripture can strengthen your faith in God (Romans 10:17).

In the previous lesson, we learned about the rape of Dinah and the revenge of Simeon and Levi, Jacob's return to Bethel, and Esau's descendants. Now let's zero in on Joseph's lofty dreams and his being sold into slavery by his brothers. With your Bible still accessible, consider the following insights on the biblical text.

Genesis 37:1-11

Generations of Jacob (37:2): Genealogy of Jacob.

Joseph (37:2): Joseph's name means "May God give increase." He was now 17 years old, younger than all his brothers except Benjamin.

Brought a bad report (37:2): Joseph had bad things to say about his four half brothers born through Jacob's two handmaids, but only good things to say about himself.

Israel loved Joseph more (37:3): Jacob (Israel) succumbed to favoritism, and there was no hiding it. Joseph was Jacob's favorite not only because he was born to him in his old age but also because he was the firstborn son of his favorite wife, Rachel.

Robe of many colors (37:3): Such a unique and special robe would have pinpointed Joseph as the favorite son. The honor of the first-born meant that Joseph was destined to receive the largest part of the inheritance.

Hated him (37:4): Jacob loved Joseph, but his brothers hated him. Their hateful response proved they were not worthy of a position of leadership in the family. They were too emotionally high-strung.

Joseph had a dream (37:5): God communicated in a number of ways in patriarchal times, including visions, dreams, audible voices, and theophanies (appearances of God). In the present case, God communicated to Joseph in a dream. His self-exalting dream fanned into flame the negative feelings his brothers already felt toward him.

"Hear this dream that I have dreamed" (37:6): Joseph may have been truthful in sharing the dream with his brothers, but it was unwise for him to do so. As a 17-year-old, he hadn't yet developed the necessary humility to govern his words and actions.

"Your sheaves... bowed down to my sheaf" (37:7-8): This prediction would be fulfilled when Joseph was exalted in Egypt (42:6; 43:26; 44:14). Joseph would later be called "prince among his brothers" (Deuteronomy 33:16).

Dreamed another dream (37:9): Joseph dreamed another divinely inspired dream that revealed his future exaltation. In this dream, the sun (his father), the moon (his mother), and 11 stars (his 11 brothers) would bow before him. Unlike the previous dream, this dream included Joseph's mother and father bowing before him.

As a form of divine revelation in Old Testament times, dreams were considered especially important if they occurred twice. That Joseph had two dreams indicating his future exaltation indicates it is a sure thing from God's perspective.

His father rebuked him (37:10): At Joseph's young age, the family couldn't imagine why the entire family would bow before him.

"Your mother" (37:10): Rachel was dead by this time. Leah was probably functioning in the role of his mother.

His brothers were jealous (37:11): An understandable resentment after hearing the two dreams.

Kept the saying in mind (37:11): Even though Jacob rebuked Joseph after hearing the dream, he kept Joseph's words in his mind. At this time, he had virtually no concept that Joseph would one day rise to great power in Egypt. But that didn't stop Jacob from wondering what Joseph's dreams might have meant. One must not forget that Jacob himself had a dream in which God promised to protect and prosper him (28:12,15). Jacob knew firsthand that God could speak through dreams, so he did not dare dismiss what Joseph said.

Genesis 37:12-28

From the Valley of Hebron... to Shechem (37:14): Shechem was about 50 miles north of Hebron.

Dothan (37:17): A grassy pasture about 15 miles north of Shechem. Merchants en route to Egypt would likely have passed through or near this area.

Conspired against him to kill him (37:18): Some of Joseph's brothers sought to kill him and then hide their crime by throwing him into a pit. This was the fruit of jealousy and envy. Clearly, the brothers never believed Joseph's dreams were from God. If anything, they wanted to take steps to ensure that the dreams never came to fruition.

"Here comes this dreamer" (37:19): Literally, "Here comes the master of dreams." This was obviously a sarcastic statement.

Reuben... rescued him... saying, "Let us not take his life" (37:21): Reuben was the firstborn and therefore carried the most responsibility. He suggested throwing Joseph into a pit so he could come back later to rescue him and restore him to their father.

They stripped him of his robe... and threw him into a pit (37:23-24): Though forcefully confined, at least Joseph was still alive.

Caravan of Ishmaelites (37:25): These were descendants of Ishmael. They were also known as Midianites (see verse 28). The Ishmaelites were descendants of Abraham through Hagar (16:5), whereas the Midianites were descendants of Abraham through Keturah (25:1-2). They intermingled into a single group. The caravan of Ishmaelite/Midianite traders was en route to Egypt, no doubt to engage in business activities.

Judah said... "Let us sell him to the Ishmaelites" (37:26-27): Judah suggested that instead of killing Joseph, they could take a personal profit by selling him as a slave to the Ishmaelite traders. Slave trade was common in this area in ancient times. Later Mosaic law would institute the death penalty for such an act (Exodus 21:16).

Twenty shekels of silver (37:28): The term "shekel" described a standard weight utilized in all business transactions. A shekel was less than half an ounce. Twenty shekels of silver (about eight ounces of silver) was the going price for a young slave in Old Testament times.

The account of Joseph gives us an important insight. Joseph was a righteous (though not always wise) young man, and he still fell into great suffering. Good people do suffer. Of course, God providentially worked in Joseph's circumstances so that he eventually would rise to great power in Egypt. During the time of trial itself, however, Joseph was unaware that this was what God was doing. This calls for the need for faith during difficult circumstances because God might ultimately be bringing about a greater good (see 50:20).

Genesis 37:29-36

Reuben... tore his clothes (37:29): Tearing clothes is an expression of grief. He was apparently not around when his brothers sold him to the Ishmaelite traders. Now that the dastardly act had been done, he went along with his brothers in the concocted story that they had found Joseph's bloodied robe.

Bible expositors note that Reuben's influence as firstborn had waned due to his sin of sleeping with Bilhah, thereby defiling his father's marriage bed (35:22; 49:3-4). Simeon and Levi had forfeited their position by killing the men of Shechem (34:25-26; 49:5-7), so leadership passed to Judah (43:3-10; 44:14-34; 46:28; 49:8-12).

They took Joseph's robe... and dipped the robe in the blood (37:31): The brothers manufactured evidence to support their story that Joseph was apparently dead. They dipped his robe in goat's blood.

Notice that just as Jacob in earlier years had used a goat in his deception of Isaac for the firstborn's blessing (27:5-17), so now Jacob's sons use a goat to deceive him. What goes around comes around!

"It is my son's robe" (37:33): Jacob, full of grief, recognized the robe

as Joseph's and concluded he had been eaten by wild animals, a story that Jacob's other sons let stand. Notice that just as Jacob himself had deceived his father earlier, so now his sons are deceiving him.

Tore his garments and put sackcloth on (37:34): These were expressions of severe grief. A sackcloth was a burlap-like cloth that people wore during times of mourning.

"I shall go down to Sheol to my son, mourning" (37:35): Sheol is a general term that can mean either the grave or the abode of the dead (see Numbers 16:30,33; Psalm 16:10). If the former is meant, Jacob was saying he would go to his grave still in mourning. If the latter is meant, Jacob was saying that he would join Joseph in the afterlife.

Potiphar, an officer of Pharaoh (37:36): An Egyptian high-ranking court official in Pharaoh's government. His name carries the meaning, "the one whom the god Ra has given." (Ra was the highest god in the Egyptian pantheon of deities.)

Major Themes

1. *Slavery in Bible times.* The practice of human slavery was a way of life among the ancients. In fact, every ancient people of which there are historical records practiced slavery. Among the ancient peoples, slaves were considered property without any personal rights. This was not the case among the Israelites. Though slaves were still considered property, they developed definite rights under the Mosaic Law. In many cases, the slave was treated as a member of the family. Indeed, in many cases the slave was better off as a slave (in terms of having food and other provisions) than he was before. The Law provided that no Israelite (including slaves) could be treated harshly (Leviticus 25:39-43), and if a slave was beaten, the Law said he could go free (Exodus 21:26-27).

   Contrary to what some have claimed, the Bible does not condone slavery. From the very beginning, God declared that all humans are created in the image of God (Genesis

1:27; see also Acts 17:29). Despite the fact that slavery was countenanced in the Semitic cultures of the day, the Law of Moses demanded that slaves eventually be set free (Exodus 21:2; Leviticus 25:40). Likewise, servants had to be treated with respect (Exodus 21:20,26). Israel, itself in slavery in Egypt for a prolonged time, was constantly reminded by God of this (Deuteronomy 5:15), and their emancipation became the model for the liberation of all slaves (see Leviticus 25:40).

2. *Joseph—a type of Christ.* A type is someone (or something) that prophetically foreshadows someone (or something) else. Joseph is a more complete type of Christ than any other person in the Old Testament. Both were the objects of special love by their fathers (Genesis 37:3; Matthew 3:17; John 3:35). Both were hated and rejected by their brethren (Genesis 37:4; John 15:24-25). Both were rejected (at least initially) as rulers over their brethren (Genesis 37:8; Matthew 21:37-39; John 15:24-25). Both were stripped of their robes (Genesis 37:23; Matthew 27:35). Both were the targets of conspiracy (Genesis 37:18,24; Matthew 26:3-4; 27:35-37). Both were betrayed and sold for silver (Genesis 37:28; Matthew 26:14-15). Both were condemned even though they were innocent (Genesis 39:11-20; Isaiah 53:9; Matthew 27:19,24). And both were exalted to glory by God (Genesis 45:16-18; Isaiah 65:17-25).

Digging Deeper with Cross-References

Malice toward others—Genesis 27:41; 37:20; Deuteronomy 19:11; 1 Samuel 19:10; Esther 3:6,13; Matthew 14:8

Sheol—Genesis 37:35; 2 Samuel 22:6; Psalms 6:5; 16:10; 18:5; 49:15; 86:13; 89:48; Proverbs 15:24

Parental partiality—Genesis 25:6,28; 37:3; 42:4; 48:22; 1 Chronicles 5:1; 26:10; 2 Chronicles 11:22

Life Lessons

1. *The domino effect.* We witness an example of the domino effect in this passage. I'm referring to the way one sin can easily lead to another. In this case, the ten brothers sinned against their father by selling his beloved Joseph into slavery, and then they deceived Jacob by spilling blood on Joseph's coat and giving it to Jacob, wrongly implying Joseph's death. Sin is like a cancer. Unless checked, it can grow and grow and grow. Better to nip it in the bud.
2. *What goes around comes around.* Jacob had deceived others throughout his life. Now he was the target as some of his sons deceived him into thinking that Joseph was dead. In an ironic way, this points to the importance of Jesus's golden rule: "Whatever you wish that others would do to you, do also to them" (Matthew 7:12).

Questions for Reflection and Discussion

1. What have you learned in this lesson about the folly of speaking highly of yourself in the presence of others?
2. Do you believe that what goes around comes around? (For example, if you deceive others, others will deceive you.)
3. Do you ever struggle with jealousy or envy? Do you want to make a resolution today to put those negative emotions behind you?

Day 29

Judah, Tamar, and Dishonorable Behavior

Genesis 38

Scripture Reading and Insights

Begin by reading Genesis 38 in your favorite Bible. As you read, keep in mind that God desires you not only to hear His Word but also to do it (James 1:22).

In yesterday's reading, we considered Joseph's lofty dreams and his being sold into slavery by his brothers. In today's reading, we consider the biblical account of Judah and Tamar. With your Bible still accessible, consider the following insights on the biblical text.

Genesis 38:1-11

It happened at that time (38:1): Chapter 37 ends with Joseph being sold to Potiphar, a high official in Egypt. Chapter 39 begins by recounting the same incident and then continues the story. Between the two is chapter 38, where we find an episode relating to Judah, Joseph's immoral brother. Some refer to this chapter as the Judah Interlude. It is inserted here because its events occurred while Joseph was enslaved.

Went down from his brothers (38:1): Joseph was forcefully separated from his brothers, but Judah separated from his brothers by personal choice.

Adullamite (38:1): Adullam was a royal city in Canaan, northwest of Hebron by 15 miles (Joshua 12:15; 15:35).

The daughter of a certain Canaanite (38:2): Unlike Isaac and Jacob, who sought wives from among their own people, Judah felt comfortable marrying among the Canaanites.

Went in to her (38:2): A euphemism for sexual intercourse.

Er... Onan... Shelah (38:3-5): The three sons born to Judah and his Canaanite wife.

Chezib (38:5): This city is probably the same as Achzib, about ten miles north of Accho in Phoenicia.

Wife for Er... Tamar (38:6): Tamar was a common name in Old Testament times.

Er... was wicked in the sight of the Lord (38:7): Like father, like son. Judah acted with great immorality and wickedness. His son Er was likewise wicked. The phrase "in the sight of the Lord" is especially important here. The Canaanites may have considered Er's activities acceptable, but our true moral barometer lies in our holy God.

The Lord put him to death (38:7): Because of Er's great wickedness, the Lord put him to death. We are not provided details of his death except that he "died in the land of Canaan" (Numbers 26:19). Premature death can be a form of God's judgment (see Deuteronomy 32:39). See Major Themes.

"Go in to your brother's wife" (38:8): Judah instructed his second son, Onan, to engage in sexual relations with Tamar, wife of Er, to bear her a child. Judah's instructions are based on what is called the levirate marriage. This is an ancient custom in which a surviving brother would marry a deceased brother's wife, raise her children, and thereby guarantee that the deceased brother's family line would continue (Deuteronomy 25:5-10).

Wicked in the sight of the Lord (38:10): Like his brother Er, Onan did that which was wicked in the sight of the Lord. Again, like father, like son.

In the present case, Judah had instructed him to perform the duties of a levirate marriage. Onan, however, took immoral steps to ensure that Tamar would not get pregnant. With Er having died, Onan now wanted the firstborn inheritance for himself. If Tamar—wife of the actual firstborn—had a child, the firstborn inheritance would then go to the child despite the fact that Onan fathered the child. Onan sought to prevent this. The way he went about it was especially detestable to the Lord. For that reason, the Lord took his life.

Judah said to Tamar (38:11): Because Tamar was not pregnant, Judah instructed her to just stay in her father's house for the time being. Then, once his third son, Shelah, matured, perhaps he would perform the duties associated with the levirate marriage.

Genesis 38:12-19

In the course of time (38:12): By now a certain number of years had passed. We are not told how many years, but it was enough years for Shelah to have grown up (verse 14).

The wife of Judah... died (38:12): With the passing of time, not only had Shelah grown up, but Judah's wife (who bore Shelah) died.

Timnah (38:12): Somewhere in the hill country, specific location unknown.

Hirah the Adullamite (38:12): Hirah was an inhabitant of Adullam, about 15 miles northwest of Hebron.

Tamar was told (38:13): Tamar was informed that Judah was headed to Timnah. By this time she was getting desperate. Having apparently been forgotten by Judah and Shelah, she had no prospects of being impregnated. She therefore disguised herself as a prostitute in hopes of entrapping Judah. She removed her widow's garments, veiled herself, and sat at the entrance to Enaim, a city in the lowland of Judah, near Timnah. Knowing Judah's low character, she apparently thought her plan stood a good chance of success.

Shelah was grown up (38:14): Shelah was now a man, old enough to fulfill his duties relating to the levirate marriage. That Shelah had not yet been given to Tamar in marriage was further confirmation that Judah and Shelah had forgotten her.

Prostitute... cult prostitute (38:15,21): In verse 15 Tamar is referred to as a prostitute. In verse 21 she is referred to as a cult prostitute, or temple prostitute. In ancient times, cult prostitutes were made available to people as part of the worship of a false deity. Judah, however, had no interest in worshipping a false deity. He was a fleshly man looking for a good time.

He did not know (38:16): With Tamar veiled, Judah was unaware that the woman he was propositioning was actually his daughter-in-law.

"What will you give me?" (38:16): Tamar was shrewd and was planning for her future. Judah agreed to give her a young goat in exchange for her services. (Animals in ancient times were considered a form of wealth.) Judah temporarily gave her a pledge to ensure that she'd be paid—his signet (a seal used in the signing of documents), which was attached to a cord (worn around the neck), and a staff (verse 18).

Tamar knew Judah was her father-in-law, yet she was clearly open to having sexual relations with him. Some Bible expositors suggest that perhaps Tamar was acting on an ancient Hittite custom that one's father-in-law could perform the duties associated with levirate marriage in the absence of a son to do so. Nevertheless, while with Judah, she never let on that she was his daughter-in-law.

She conceived...went away...put on the garments of her widowhood (38:18-19): Tamar did not linger to receive the payment of a goat. She took the items Judah had given her as a pledge, went back home, and put her mourning garments back on.

Genesis 38:20-30

Judah sent the young goat (38:20): Judah sought to fulfill his end of the bargain. So he had his Adullamite friend seek her out to deliver the goat. He asked around for her whereabouts, but no one had seen her. He had no option but to return the goat to Judah.

"Let her keep the things as her own" (38:23): Judah decided to just let her keep the items he had given her as a pledge. He didn't want to be laughed at by people watching him roam the landscape looking for the prostitute so he could pay her. That wouldn't be good for his reputation.

"Tamar your daughter-in-law has been immoral" (38:24): After three months, it was clear that Tamar had become pregnant. Since she was now unmarried, the natural assumption was that she had been immoral.

"Let her be burned" (38:24): The penalty for this type of immorality

was death (see Leviticus 20:14; 21:9). How unfair that Tamar should be condemned when the man condemning her was just as guilty.

"By the man to whom these belong" (38:25): Tamar's plan of action was now in full swing. She revealed that she was pregnant by the man who owned the items in her hand. The items obviously belonged to Judah.

"She is more righteous than I" (38:26): Judah immediately recognized that Tamar was attending to the inheritance rights of her family line. He also saw that he himself had not been righteous, for he failed to have Shelah fulfill the responsibility of a levirate marriage. Tamar's execution was promptly canceled.

Perez (38:29): Tamar had twins. The first to be born was Perez. Amazingly, we find Tamar and Perez in the genealogy of Jesus Christ (Matthew 1:3). His name means "breach" because he pushed through ahead of his twin brother at birth. The second twin was Zerah (meaning "scarlet"). He was so named because the midwife had tied a scarlet thread to his wrist.

Major Themes

1. *Death as a judgment.* Death can be a form of God's judgment. Such was the case with Er, Judah's firstborn (Genesis 38:6). Earlier, all of humanity—with the exception of Noah and his family—were executed for their unrestrained sin (Genesis 6:7). Saul was later put to death because of his sin against God (1 Chronicles 10:13). Ananias and Sapphira were killed for lying to the Holy Spirit (Acts 5:1-10). Some Corinthians got sick and died as a result of partaking of the Lord's Supper while remaining in a state of sin (1 Corinthians 11:30; see also 1 John 5:16). By contrast, the path of righteousness leads to long life (Proverbs 10:27; Deuteronomy 4:40; 2 Kings 20:1-6; Ephesians 6:2-3).
2. *Provisions for widows.* Though the widow Tamar acted immorally, the passage leads us to reflect on the need to

care for widows. In Bible times, widows had no viable means of monetary support and were no longer living under the protection of a husband. The Bible therefore instructed that widows were to be cared for. Deuteronomy 27:19 tells us, "Cursed be anyone who perverts the justice due to the sojourner, the fatherless, and the widow." James 1:27 tells us, "Religion that is pure and undefiled before God, the Father, is this: to visit orphans and widows in their affliction." In Acts 6:1-15 steps were taken to ensure that widows were not overlooked in the daily distribution of provisions. The principle seems to be this: Take the initiative in watching out for others who can't watch out for themselves.

Digging Deeper with Cross-References

Harlotry—Genesis 38:15,21; Leviticus 19:29; 21:7,14; Deuteronomy 23:18; 1 Kings 3:16; Proverbs 2:16; 9:13; Isaiah 23:15; Ezekiel 23:44

Death by burning—Genesis 38:24; Leviticus 20:14; 21:9; Daniel 3:6,21

Life Lessons

1. *First take the log out of your own eye.* Judah was ready to execute his daughter-in-law, Tamar, for her immorality. Yet he thought nothing of his act of sleeping with a woman he thought was a prostitute. This is the very type of hypocrisy Jesus condemned in the New Testament: "You hypocrite, first take the log out of your own eye, and then you will see clearly to take the speck out of your brother's [or sister's] eye" (Matthew 7:5).
2. *God can bring good out of evil.* Judah, Tamar, and Perez are direct ancestors of Jesus Christ (Matthew 1:1-6). Despite Judah's and Tamar's horrendous sins, they were

nevertheless part of the messianic line. God brought good out of evil even in this dire situation. We should always be watching for God to bring good out of the evil circumstances we sometimes face. Let us not forget Romans 8:28: "We know that for those who love God all things work together for good, for those who are called according to his purpose."

Questions for Reflection and Discussion

1. Have you ever experienced God bringing something good out of a bad circumstance? If so, what did you learn from that experience?
2. We all have some logs in our eyes. That's why it's important to engage in periodic self-examination. Are you are aware of any logs that need to be removed from your own eyes?
3. Are you a member of a church that takes social responsibility seriously? For example, does your church have a program for taking care of widows and others who are less fortunate? Do you want to be involved?

Day 30

Joseph in Potiphar's House

Genesis 39

Scripture Reading and Insights

Begin by reading Genesis 39 in your favorite Bible. As you read, keep in mind that God desires you not only to hear His Word but also to do it (James 1:22).

In yesterday's reading, we considered the biblical account of Judah and Tamar. Now let's find out about Joseph's encounter with Potiphar's wife. With your Bible still accessible, consider the following insights on the biblical text.

Genesis 39:1-6

Egypt (39:1): Egypt is at the northeast corner of Africa and naturally divides into two realms—Upper Egypt, which is the valley of the Nile, and Lower Egypt, which is the plain of the Delta. Because of its close proximity to the Nile, the land is extremely fertile. The ancients worshipped the Nile as a god.

Egyptians were polytheistic (they believed in many gods). Even today, scholars are unsure how many gods the Egyptians worshipped. Most lists name about 80 deities. The ancient Egyptians' dedication to their gods is evident even to casual observers touring modern Egypt. Beautiful temples honoring various gods virtually fill the landscape. In Egyptian religion, the most important god was the sun god, Ra. He was considered the creator, father, and king of the gods. He was the most excellent, most distinguished god in the pantheon. Next in line was the Pharaoh of Egypt, who was considered to be the son of Ra. In the midst of this polytheistic culture, Joseph held firm in his belief in the one true God, and God blessed him for it.

Potiphar (39:1): An Egyptian high-ranking court official in Pharaoh's government. His name carries the meaning, "the one whom the god Ra has given."

The Lord was with Joseph (39:2): Joseph was attacked by his brothers, sold as a slave to Ishmaelite traders, and then resold to an Egyptian official. One might think God was not blessing his life. To the contrary, our text tells us, "the Lord was with Joseph." Clearly, when the Lord is in charge of your life, you are never a victim of circumstances. God had previously promised to be with both Isaac and Jacob (26:3,24,28; 28:15,20; 31:3). Now God was with Joseph every step along the way, providentially overseeing his circumstances to accomplish a greater good. (Compare with Acts 7:9-10. More on this greater good later.)

He became a successful man (39:2): Joseph was successful precisely because the Lord was with him. Joseph had now been in Egypt about 13 years.

His master saw (39:3): Joseph's master, Potiphar, saw "that the Lord was with him and that the Lord caused all that he did to succeed in his hands." Notice that Joseph was not secretive about his faith. His trust in the true God was obvious to this Egyptian official. The official also witnessed the benefits of believing in the one true God, for everything Joseph did succeeded.

Joseph found favor in his sight (39:4): Note the progression: Joseph was obedient to the Lord in all things. God providentially guided Joseph's life. Regardless of the circumstances, God was with Joseph and blessed all that he did. This reality became evident to those around him. As a result, Joseph found favor in the eyes of Potiphar. This reminds us of Proverbs 22:29: "Do you see a man skillful in his work? He will stand before kings; he will not stand before obscure men."

He made him overseer (39:5): Joseph proved himself trustworthy, so he was put in a position of authority, and he thrived. One recalls Jesus's words in Luke 16:10: "One who is faithful in a very little is also faithful in much." Joseph was just such a man.

The LORD blessed the Egyptian's house (39:5): Potiphar received God's blessing because of God's favor on Joseph. In a way, we see a preliminary fulfillment of the Abrahamic covenant here. Recall that God had promised Abraham, "I will bless those who bless you" (12:3). Potiphar had blessed Joseph with trust and a position of authority. God was therefore bringing blessing to Potiphar. Recall that God had earlier blessed Laban because of Jacob (30:27).

He left all that he had in Joseph's charge...he had no concern (39:6): So trustworthy was Joseph that he needed no oversight. Potiphar had no concerns about Joseph overseeing his home. Recall that Laban had earlier entrusted all his flocks into Jacob's care (30:31-34).

Handsome in form (39:6): A fact that would prove troublesome because Potiphar's wife became attracted to him. Perhaps Joseph took after his mother, who herself was "beautiful in form and appearance" (29:17).

Genesis 39:7-18

Cast her eyes...and said, "Lie with me" (39:7): Temptation begins in the mind. Potiphar's wife sees with desire, is tempted in her mind, and then makes her move.

He refused (39:8): Joseph didn't hesitate in his refusal. Joseph reminded her, "My master trusts me, and I won't violate that trust."

"How can I do this great wickedness and sin against God?" (39:9): To do as Potiphar's wife requested would not only violate Potiphar's trust in Joseph but also be a great wickedness and sin against God. Of course, all sin is ultimately against God. Recall that following his sin with Bathsheba, David confessed to God, "Against you, you only, have I sinned and done what is evil in your sight" (Psalm 51:4). Joseph was intent on not letting down either Potiphar or God.

She spoke to Joseph day after day (39:10): Joseph did not experience a one-time temptation. He experienced a daily temptation but never once gave in.

She caught him by his garment, saying, "Lie with me" (39:12): Potiphar's wife is now moving beyond a mere verbal invitation. She now gets physical, grabbing Joseph by his garment. He left his garment behind and fled out of the house. Joseph would not give in. He had learned the lesson that would later be recorded in the New Testament: "Flee from sexual immorality" (1 Corinthians 6:18). "Flee youthful passions and pursue righteousness" (2 Timothy 2:22).

This brings to mind Proverbs 7, where the adulterous woman says to a young man, "Come, let us take our fill of love till morning; let us delight ourselves with love. For my husband is not at home." The young man is thus warned, "Let not your heart turn aside to her ways; do not stray into her paths" (verses 18-19,25). Joseph responded just as he should have.

Notice the irony. Previously Joseph's multicolored robe played a role in his being sold into slavery by his brothers. Now his garment plays a role in getting him into trouble with Potiphar. In both cases Joseph was serving faithfully but ended up in bondage.

She called to the men (39:14): "Hell hath no fury like a woman scorned." Potiphar's wife immediately called out to other men on the premises and launched a false accusation against Joseph.

"A Hebrew...came in to me to lie with me" (39:14): She accused Joseph of trying to lie with her, and she had his garment to prove it. Notice that by referring to Joseph as a Hebrew, she appealed to a popular ethnic bias and implied that he was not worthy of true respect.

Genesis 39:19-23

Joseph's master...put him into the prison (39:20): Joseph's punishment was light in view of the charge against him. He was put into a royal prison that housed the king's prisoners. This was not the worst prison available. At least Potiphar showed that minimal mercy. Potiphar also showed the mercy of not having Joseph killed. Perhaps he was suspicious about his wife's account.

The Lord was with Joseph and showed him steadfast love and gave him favor (39:21): Regardless of where Joseph was, what his circumstances were, or what anybody did to him, God was always with him. God showed him favor even in prison. In 1 Samuel 2:30 God affirmed, "Those who honor me I will honor." The Lord perpetually honored Joseph as one who had honored Him.

The keeper of the prison put Joseph in charge (39:22): Just as Joseph had been in charge at Potiphar's house, so now the keeper of the prison put him in charge of the other prisoners.

The Lord was with him...the Lord made it succeed (39:23): Just as Joseph had succeeded in running Potiphar's household, so now he succeeded in running the prison. Joseph was like a flower that blossomed wherever he was planted. This is the fourth time that this chapter mentions that the Lord was with Joseph (see verses 2-3,21).

It is important to understand that during the time of Joseph's sufferings—first being enslaved by his brothers, and now being thrown into prison by Potiphar—Joseph had no idea of God's ultimate intentions for his life. He didn't know that God was using these dire circumstances to eventually bring him to a position of prominence in Egypt. That is why it is so important for us—like Joseph—to trust God in every circumstance. In Joseph's case, God truly did bring about a greater good through the pain he suffered.

Major Themes

1. *A man of integrity*. Joseph was clearly a man of integrity. The Bible speaks a great deal about what it means to be a man of integrity: "Better is a poor man who walks in his integrity than a rich man who is crooked in his ways" (Proverbs 28:6). "Better is a poor person who walks in his integrity than one who is crooked in speech and is a fool" (Proverbs 19:1). "The integrity of the upright guides them" (Proverbs 11:3). "The righteous who walks in his integrity—blessed are his children after him!" (Proverbs 20:7). First Peter 3:16 highlights the importance of "having a good conscience, so that, when you are slandered, those who revile your good behavior in Christ may be put to shame."

Joseph was certainly right in line with Paul's words in 2 Corinthians 8:21: "For we aim at what is honorable not only in the Lord's sight but also in the sight of man." Other verses to ponder include Psalms 25:21; 26:1; Micah 6:8; Acts 24:16; Titus 2:1-14; Hebrews 13:18; James 1:22-25.

2. *Bearing false testimony.* Bearing false witness is a great evil (Exodus 20:16). It destroys reputations, puts people in prison, and wrecks relationships. The account of Joseph and Potiphar's wife is a perfect example. Joseph surely felt as David did: "Wicked and deceitful mouths are opened against me, speaking against me with lying tongues" (Psalm 109:2). Proverbs 11:9 warns, "With his mouth the godless man would destroy his neighbor." James 4:11 urges, "Do not speak evil against one another, brothers."

Digging Deeper with Cross-References

Temptresses—Genesis 38:16; 39:7; 1 Kings 11:3; Proverbs 5:3-5; 6:25; Matthew 14:6; Mark 6:22

Resisting temptations—Genesis 14:23; 39:10; 1 Kings 13:8; Job 2:9; Daniel 1:8; Matthew 4:7,10; Luke 4:4-8; Acts 8:20; Revelation 2:26

Life Lessons

1. *Sin is against God.* Joseph was keenly aware that he was accountable to Potiphar but even more accountable to God, who called him to live righteously. When Potiphar's wife attempted to seduce him, Joseph did not ask, "How then can I do this great wickedness and sin against Egyptian law?" He asked, "How then can I do this great wickedness and sin against God?" (Genesis 39:9). Let's never forget that our true and ultimate accountability is to God alone.
2. *A prisoner and a slave.* Joseph had been a slave, and now he

was a prisoner. The good news was that he was not sexually enslaved (addicted) or imprisoned by tormenting thoughts. It is much better to live morally and be falsely in prison than to live immorally and be a free man. Joseph made the better choice (see Job 31:1; Matthew 5:28; 1 Corinthians 5:9-11; Colossians 3:5).

Questions for Reflection and Discussion

1. What does today's lesson teach you about the importance of not letting temptation take root in your mind?
2. Does this chapter in Genesis motivate you to be a person of integrity? What steps can you take to make this a reality?
3. How does Joseph inspire you in your walk with God?

Day 31

Joseph Interprets the Dreams of the Cupbearer and the Baker

Genesis 40

Scripture Reading and Insights

Begin by reading Genesis 40 in your favorite Bible. As you read, stop and meditate on any verses that speak to your heart (Joshua 1:8; Psalm 1:1-3).

In the previous lesson, we investigated Joseph's encounter with Potiphar's wife. Now let's find out about Joseph's encounter with the cupbearer and the baker in prison. With your Bible still accessible, consider the following insights on the biblical text.

Genesis 40:1-8

The king of Egypt (40:1): Biblical scholars identify this Pharaoh as Senusert II.

The chief cupbearer (40:2): The job of the chief cupbearer was important because he brought Pharaoh all his drinks. He had to be trustworthy—the kind of person who would never succumb to poisoning Pharaoh for a bribe from a foreign enemy.

The chief baker (40:2): The chief baker brought Pharaoh his food, meaning that he too had to be trustworthy. His job was to ensure that Pharaoh's food was safe.

The captain of the guard (40:3): This may have been Potiphar,

Joseph's former employer. In Genesis 37:36 Potiphar is called "captain of the guard."

Appointed Joseph to be with them (40:4): Joseph was appointed to watch after the needs of the chief cupbearer and the chief baker. Perhaps Potiphar knew them personally.

They both dreamed (40:5): In ancient Egypt, dreams were thought to provide insights about the future and even determine it. The problem was, the meaning of the dreams was not always clear to those who had them. Professional dream interpreters sought to help people understand the meaning of their dreams. Neither the chief cupbearer nor the chief baker had any idea what their dreams meant. They needed help.

Joseph... saw that they were troubled (40:6): When Joseph stopped by the next morning, he asked why they had troubled looks on their faces. They revealed that they each had a dream and no one could interpret their meaning. They may have wondered, "What does this dream tell me about my future?"

"Do not interpretations belong to God?" (40:8): The truth is, professional dream interpreters had no idea what they were doing. Even if such interpreters were available in the prison, they would have likely given the wrong interpretation. They do not have the power to look into or understand the human mind. God is the one who created the human mind. He alone is omniscient (Psalms 33:13-15; 139:11-12; 147:5; Proverbs 15:3; Isaiah 40:14; 46:10; Hebrews 4:13; 1 John 3:20), so interpretations belong to Him.

Only one other man of God was called on to interpret dreams in the Bible—Daniel, who interpreted a dream for King Nebuchadnezzar. Daniel said, "There is a God in heaven who reveals mysteries, and he has made known to King Nebuchadnezzar what will be in the latter days" (Daniel 2:28). Both Daniel and Joseph gave credit to God as the one who properly understands and interprets dreams.

Genesis 40:9-15

"Pharaoh's cup was in my hand" (40:11): The chief cupbearer's dream related to his specialty—preparing drinks for Pharaoh.

"Joseph said... 'This is its interpretation'" (40:12): Joseph interpreted the dream to mean that the chief cupbearer would be released from prison in three days and restored to his job.

"Remember me" (40:14): Joseph wanted to do anything possible to get out of prison. He knew he was there unjustly. The cupbearer was close to Pharaoh, so perhaps he could put in a good word that would lead to Joseph's release from prison.

Unfortunately, once the cupbearer got his old job back, he completely forgot about Joseph. Later, however, Pharaoh's need for a dream interpreter would jar the cupbearer's memory, and he'd put in a recommendation for Joseph (41:9-14). Joseph didn't know it at the time, but this incident with the chief cupbearer was indeed setting the stage for his release—in God's providential timing. Indeed, a full two years after the cupbearer was released from prison, he would function as a divinely appointed agent whose words to Pharaoh would bring Joseph before Pharaoh to interpret his dream, after which Joseph would be exalted to a high position in fulfillment of his own dreams. We learn a good lesson here. God's timetable may not be the same as our timetable. God's timetable is always perfect. Trust Him!

We can make two more observations. First, Joseph's interpretations of the dreams of the chief cupbearer and chief baker came to pass exactly as Joseph had said. This likely instilled confidence in Joseph that God would one day fulfill his own dreams. Joseph maintained his faith in God despite the fact that he was presently in jail.

Second, we now see that the captain of the guard's appointment of Joseph to watch after the chief cupbearer and chief baker was clearly by God's providence. God Himself brought about the circumstances in which Joseph would connect with these two, thus setting the stage for Joseph's future interpretation of Pharaoh's dreams.

"The land of the Hebrews" (40:15): The land of Canaan—that is, the Promised Land.

"The pit" (40:15): Joseph had been living in luxury in Potiphar's house. Now he was in prison. Comparatively speaking, Joseph was in the pit.

Genesis 40:16-23

The interpretation was favorable (40:16): The chief baker thought that because the cupbearer's dream had such a favorable outcome, perhaps his dream would as well. In high hopes, he informed Joseph of his dream.

"This is its interpretation" (40:18): Unlike the chief cupbearer, the chief baker was in for a rude awakening. The meaning of his dream was that he was to be executed in three days. His body would be plucked by birds—it would be left outside instead of having an immediate burial. In ancient Egyptian thought, this prevented the spirit of the dead from resting in the afterlife.

Some Bible expositors suggest that perhaps the dreams of the chief cupbearer and chief baker set the stage for Pharaoh's dreams as warnings from God about the future. After all, the dreams of these two men were dreams of life and death. Likewise, Pharaoh's dreams deal with the life and death of Egypt (seven years of prosperity followed by seven years of famine).

"Lift up your head" (40:19): We were earlier told that Pharaoh would lift up the cupbearer's head in the sense of setting him free and returning him to his job (verse 13). Now we are told that Pharaoh would also lift up the head of the chief baker by having him executed and left out for the birds to eat. Context always determines what "lift up your head" means. In the psalms, the phrase is most often used in a positive sense (for example, Psalms 3:3; 27:6).

Pharaoh's birthday (40:20): Ancient historical documents reveal that it was the custom to release some prisoners on Pharaoh's birthday. In the present case, one was released to resume his job, and one was released to be executed.

The chief cupbearer did not remember Joseph (40:23): Though the chief cupbearer did not remember Joseph, God never forgets His faithful servants. Joseph would soon be exalted to high authority in Egypt.

We learn an important lesson from Joseph's situation. If we interpret circumstances strictly from the human side of things, Joseph was mistreated by various people and had good reason to be discouraged.

If we interpret things from the divine side of things, we see that God allows us to go through tough circumstances not only to make us more holy but also to prepare us for a future work. Interpreting things from the divine side helps us see that all things do indeed work together for good for those who love God (Romans 8:28).

Major Themes

1. *God providentially controls circumstances.* God controls the circumstances of our lives, for "in him we live and move and have our being" (Acts 17:28). Jeremiah 10:23 affirms, "I know, O Lord, that the way of man is not in himself, that it is not in man who walks to direct his steps." Proverbs 20:24 tells us that "a man's steps are from the Lord." We are told that "the heart of man plans his way, but the Lord establishes his steps" (Proverbs 16:9). God specifically orchestrated the events in Joseph's life to move him from prison to a position of great authority in Egypt.
2. *Perfect timing.* Even after Pharaoh's cupbearer was released from prison, two more years passed before Joseph was freed. From the human perspective, we might lament that good things are too slow in coming. But God always has perfect timing for His purposes. Psalm 139:16 tells us, "In your book were written, every one of them, the days that were formed for me, when as yet there was none of them." Job affirms, "[A man's] days are determined, and the number of his months is with you, and you have appointed his limits that he cannot pass" (Job 14:5).
3. *Be ready to seize the moment.* Joseph trusted in our sovereign God wholly and without reserve. At the same time, he took every opportunity he could to engage in actions that could lead to his release from prison (he asked the chief cupbearer to remember him). He seized the moment whenever he saw an opportunity. Though

we may not fully understand how divine sovereignty and human choices fit together, Joseph's story includes both. Joseph's free choice to seize the moment is somehow a part of God's sovereign plan to bail him out of prison. No wonder the psalmist proclaimed, "Such knowledge is too wonderful for me; it is high; I cannot attain it" (Psalm 139:6).

Digging Deeper with Cross-References

Cupbearers—Genesis 40:1,9; 41:9; 1 Kings 10:5; 2 Chronicles 9:4; Nehemiah 1:11

Bakers—Genesis 40:1,16; 41:10; 1 Samuel 8:13; Jeremiah 37:21; Hosea 7:4

Prisons—Genesis 40:3; 42:16; Judges 16:21; 2 Kings 17:4; Isaiah 42:22; Jeremiah 37:21; 52:11; Matthew 5:25; Acts 16:26

Life Lessons

1. *Helping people is good.* Joseph was a people helper. This is illustrated in his helping both the baker and the cupbearer. The Bible exhorts all believers to be people helpers as well. Hebrews 13:16 urges, "Do not neglect to do good and to share what you have, for such sacrifices are pleasing to God." Philippians 2:4 instructs, "Let each of you look not only to his own interests, but also to the interests of others." In 1 John 3:17 we are asked, "If anyone has the world's goods and sees his brother in need, yet closes his heart against him, how does God's love abide in him?" Perhaps the most cogent exhortation to people helping is found in the words of Jesus. Spend a few moments meditating on Matthew 25:35-40.
2. *Be sensitive to others' emotions.* As Joseph approached the baker and cupbearer, "he saw that they were troubled."

He asked them, "Why are your faces downcast today?" (Genesis 40:6-7). Should not you and I also take notice of the sorrow of others around us? The truth is, all of us suffer. You and I can be vessels of God's comfort. As the apostle Paul said in 2 Corinthians 1:3-4, "Blessed be the God and Father of our Lord Jesus Christ, the Father of mercies and God of all comfort, who comforts us in all our affliction, so that we may be able to comfort those who are in any affliction, with the comfort with which we ourselves are comforted by God." If you ask God to open doors for you to comfort the hurts of others, I can promise you that He will do it.

Questions for Reflection and Discussion

1. Do you consider yourself a people helper? Read Philippians 2:4 and consider how you might start putting that verse into action.
2. Are you sensitive to the way other people feel? Do you typically try to help when you see that someone is sad?
3. Is there a circumstance in your life in which you are still waiting for God to act? What have you learned in this lesson about God's timetable versus human timetables?

Day 32

Joseph Interprets Pharaoh's Dreams

Genesis 41

Scripture Reading and Insights

Begin by reading Genesis 41 in your favorite Bible. As you read, stop and meditate on any verses that speak to your heart (Psalm 1:1-3; Joshua 1:8).

In the previous reading, we considered Joseph's encounter with the cupbearer and the baker in prison. In today's reading, we focus on Joseph's interpretation of Pharaoh's dreams and Joseph's subsequent exaltation in Egypt. With your Bible still accessible, consider the following insights on the biblical text.

Genesis 41:1-13

The Nile (41:1): The most important river in Egypt, whose waters were considered the lifeblood of Egypt. The Egyptians venerated the Nile and all that was associated with it. It was worshipped by the Egyptians under various names and symbols and was considered the father of life. The Egyptians even wrote sacred hymns in honor of the Nile.

Seven cows (41:2): Cows often stayed submerged up to the neck in the Nile river for prolonged periods to keep cool under the Egyptian sun. It was also an effective means of keeping flies off their bodies. The cows would then periodically emerge out of the water to find pasture.

Blighted by the east wind (41:6): The scorching-hot wind easily withers vegetation.

His spirit was troubled (41:8): Convinced that dreams provide insights about the future—and perhaps even determine it—Pharaoh was troubled as to what his dreams may have meant.

The magicians of Egypt (41:8): These were priests who claimed to have occult knowledge (see Exodus 8:18-19; Daniel 2:10-11). They were considered masters of the sacred arts, astrology, interpreting dreams, foretelling events, various forms of magic, and the conjuring of spells. God condemns all forms of occultism, including magic (Exodus 22:18; Leviticus 19:31; Deuteronomy 18:9-13; Ezekiel 13:18).

There was none who could interpret (41:8): The professional dream interpreters proved to be useless. They had no idea what Pharaoh's dreams meant. This was all according to God's providence, for this opened a door for Joseph.

The chief cupbearer said (41:9): The cupbearer suddenly had a flash of memory. He promptly informed Pharaoh about Joseph and how two years earlier he had accurately interpreted his dream and the chief baker's.

"A young Hebrew" (41:12): God would bypass the magicians or wise men of Egypt and choose a young and lowly Hebrew to interpret Pharaoh's dreams. This brings to mind 1 Corinthians 1:27: "God chose what is foolish in the world to shame the wise; God chose what is weak in the world to shame the strong."

Genesis 41:14-36

Pharaoh sent and called Joseph (41:14): Pharaoh's response was immediate because his need was urgent.

He had shaved himself and changed his clothes (41:14): Joseph was cleaned up so he could appear before Pharaoh according to proper Egyptian etiquette. Note that Egyptians were normally clean-shaven, while people in Canaan typically wore beards.

"It is not in me; God will give" (41:16): Joseph is humble, pointing to God as the one who interprets dreams. Joseph's humility and his dependence on God bring to mind 2 Corinthians 3:5, where the apostle Paul states, "Not that we are sufficient in ourselves to claim anything as coming from us, but our sufficiency is from God."

"God has revealed to Pharaoh" (41:25): Joseph, with conciseness and clarity, revealed to Pharaoh what God intended to do with Egypt. In contrast to the Egyptian belief that dreams can determine the future, Joseph indicates what God intends to do with Egypt's future. This was a bit of a paradigm shift for Pharaoh, but he realized Joseph was right.

"Seven years of famine" (41:27): Egypt was to experience seven lean years—much longer than a typical famine.

"The doubling of Pharaoh's dream" (41:32): The fact that Pharaoh had two dreams indicating the same thing indicates the certainty of the famine.

"God will shortly bring it about" (41:32): Just as the chief cupbearer's and chief baker's dreams were fulfilled quickly (just three days had passed), Pharaoh's dreams would soon be fulfilled.

"Discerning and wise man" (41:33): Joseph advised Pharaoh to appoint a wise man to oversee preparations for the seven-year famine. Reserves must be accumulated for seven years prior to the seven-year famine. If done correctly, Egypt could survive. That Joseph was both discerning and wise was evident when he instantly devised a plan to save Egypt from famine.

Genesis 41:37-57

"A man like this, in whom is the Spirit of God" (41:38): Pharaoh saw in Joseph just the man he was looking for. He was discerning and wise, and the spirit of the living God spoke through him. He saw Joseph as having supernatural insight. Of course, the Egyptian Pharaoh had no concept of the Holy Spirit. When he referred to the "Spirit of God," he simply meant that God was with Joseph and that God spoke through Joseph. That was all that mattered.

"I have set you over all the land of Egypt" (41:41): Rarely has anyone escalated in power as rapidly as Joseph did! One day he was in jail. The next day he was exalted over all of Egypt. In modern vernacular, this is definitely a God thing. In hindsight, we see that God had been providentially working behind the scenes in all of Joseph's circumstances to bring him to this point.

Joseph had not been seeking self-exaltation, but God-exaltation.

God thus exalted the faithful and humble Joseph to a position of great authority. This reminds us of James 4:10: "Humble yourselves before the Lord, and he will exalt you."

Also, Joseph had proven himself faithful in small things. He had effectively overseen Potiphar's house. He served effectively in the prison. Now he was elevated to a position of great power throughout Egypt. This brings to mind the words of Jesus in Matthew 25:21: "You have been faithful over a little; I will set you over much."

His signet ring...garments...a gold chain (41:42): Joseph was immediately dressed for success. These items not only made Joseph look good but also represented his authority throughout Egypt. He was now second in command. The signet ring gave Joseph the authority to sign important business documents and conduct business in Pharaoh's name. The signet (or seal) would be impressed on a soft clay document, and once the clay hardened, it left a permanent impression with Pharaoh's seal.

Second chariot (41:43): Joseph was given transportation befitting the second-in-command.

Pharaoh called Joseph's name Zaphenath-paneah (41:45): The meaning of this name is uncertain, though it may mean "God speaks and lives." By giving Joseph a new Egyptian name, Pharaoh "Egyptianized" him for his new work.

Asenath (41:45): Joseph was given an Egyptian wife from a high-ranking family in Egyptian society. Asenath means "she belongs to Neith" (an Egyptian goddess). This was a further effort to assimilate Joseph into Egyptian culture.

Thirty years old (41:46): Thirteen years had passed since Joseph's brothers sold him into slavery at age 17.

Priest of On (41:50): Joseph's wife was the daughter of Potiphera, a priest of On. The city of On was ten miles northeast of modern Cairo.

Manasseh (41:51): The name means "forgetful" or "one who causes to forget." The name is appropriate because Joseph confessed, "God has made me forget all my hardship and all my father's house."

Ephraim (41:52): The name means "fruitful" or "he made me fruitful," for Joseph affirmed, "God has made me fruitful in the land of my affliction." Even though Joseph had received an Egyptian name, he stayed true to his Hebrew roots by giving his children Hebrew names.

Famine in all lands (41:54): The famine spread through all the lands known to the author but not necessarily all the lands in the entire world.

Pharaoh said... "Go to Joseph" (41:55): Once the famine began after seven years of prosperity, Pharaoh continued to trust in Joseph, for he continued to instruct people, "Go to Joseph."

Major Themes

1. *The divine Pharaoh of Egypt*. Egyptian kings were called Pharaoh. They were considered to be divine. Indeed, in Egyptian religion, the chief god was the sun god, Ra. Next in line was Pharaoh, who was considered to be the son of Ra. So the Pharaoh of Egypt was himself considered a god in his own right. And yet this supposedly divine king was unable to interpret his own dreams. Joseph informed Pharaoh, "It is not in me; God will give Pharaoh a favorable answer" regarding the meaning of the dreams (Genesis 41:16). When Joseph was giving Pharaoh the proper interpretation, Joseph said to him, "God has revealed to Pharaoh what he is about to do" (41:25, see also verse 28). Joseph then said that the doubling of Pharaoh's dreams meant that "the thing is fixed by God, and God will shortly bring it about" (verse 32). Pharaoh recognized Joseph's wisdom and said to him, "Since God has shown you all this, there is none so discerning and wise as you are" (verse 39). The bottom line is this: Joseph did not hesitate to point to the one true God before a person who was himself considered a god in Egyptian culture.
2. *Famine in Bible times*. As we have noted previously, threats to the food supply were common in the ancient Near East. An enemy might invade and destroy all the crops (famine almost always follows wars and extensive battle campaigns). Locusts might swoop in out of nowhere and

consume all crops in less than an hour. There might be too little rain for the crops. Because of such factors, famines occurred often in biblical times. God raised up Joseph to help deal with the lengthy famine that was to come in Egypt and the surrounding areas.

Digging Deeper with Cross-References

Grain for food in Genesis—Genesis 41:5,49,57; 42:19,26; 43:2; 47:14

The Spirit of God—Genesis 41:38; Numbers 27:18; Isaiah 63:11; Ezekiel 36:27; 37:14; John 14:17; Romans 5:5; 8:9; 1 Corinthians 2:12; 3:16; 6:19; Galatians 4:6; Ephesians 2:22; 2 Timothy 1:14

Rings in Genesis—Genesis 24:22,30,47; 41:42

Life Lessons

1. *Be prepared with an answer*. In our text, Joseph was pulled out of prison without warning and hauled into Pharaoh's presence, where he was asked to interpret Pharaoh's dreams. You and I will not experience anything so dramatic as Joseph did, but we will have unexpected and sudden opportunities to explain the truth about God and the gospel of salvation. In 1 Peter 3:15 we are exhorted, "Always [be] prepared to make a defense to anyone who asks you for a reason for the hope that is in you; yet do it with gentleness and respect."
2. *Be filled with the Spirit*. Pharaoh recognized that "the Spirit of God" indwelt Joseph (Genesis 41:38). You and I are commanded, "Do not get drunk with wine, for that is debauchery, but be filled with the Spirit" (Ephesians 5:18). The word "filled" in this verse is a present tense imperative verb. The present tense indicates continuing action. The imperative indicates it is a command from God. Day by

day, moment by moment, you and I as Christians are to be filled with the Spirit.

In the context of Ephesians 5, both drunk and spiritual persons are controlled persons—that is, they're under the influence of either liquor or the Spirit, and they accordingly do things that are unnatural to them. They abandon themselves to the influence of either the liquor or the Holy Spirit. So to be filled with the Holy Spirit means that one's life will be controlled or governed no longer by self but by the Holy Spirit. It is not a matter of acquiring more of the Spirit, but rather of the Spirit of God acquiring all of the individual.

Questions for Reflection and Discussion

1. Do you daily make a conscious effort to submit yourself to the Holy Spirit and be controlled by Him?
2. Are you "always being prepared to make a defense to anyone who asks for a reason for the hope that is in you" (1 Peter 3:15)?
3. How's your spiritual life these days? Would you say it is warm, cold, or lukewarm? Do you want to make any new spiritual resolutions?

Day 33

Joseph's Brothers in Egypt—Part 1

Genesis 42

Scripture Reading and Insights

Begin by reading Genesis 42 in your favorite Bible. As you read, notice how the Word of God continues to purify your life (John 17:17-18).

In yesterday's reading, we considered Joseph's interpretation of Pharaoh's dreams and Joseph's subsequent exaltation in Egypt. Now let's watch Joseph's brothers as they travel to Egypt. With your Bible still accessible, consider the following insights on the biblical text.

Genesis 42:1-11

"Why do you look at one another?" (42:1): Instead of taking action to deal with the famine, the brothers sat around staring at the ground in defeat, acting as if they were helpless in the face of dire circumstances.

"Go down and buy grain" (42:2): Jacob took action. We might paraphrase his instructions this way: "Stop wallowing around in pity and defeat. Get up and get going to Egypt. Get us some food, pronto."

"That we may live and not die" (42:2): Desperate times call for desperate measures. Jacob's clan was in danger of starving. Jacob had to risk sending his sons to Egypt for food.

Jacob did not send Benjamin (42:4): Jacob refused to send Benjamin because he was the youngest son. He was also the son of his beloved Rachel. Once Joseph was presumed dead, Benjamin became the new favorite.

The famine was in the land of Canaan (42:5): We were previously told that "there was famine in all lands" (41:54).

Joseph was governor over the land (42:6): Joseph was still held in high regard in Egypt. He had proved himself effective in overseeing the land.

Joseph's brothers came and bowed themselves before him (42:6): We recall Joseph's dream: "My sheaf arose and stood upright. And behold, your sheaves gathered around it and bowed down to my sheaf" (37:7). Note that the complete fulfillment of what he dreamed had not yet taken place—his entire family had not yet come to Egypt under his rulership (see 37:9). As of yet, only his brothers were in Egypt.

Joseph saw his brothers and recognized them (42:7): If Joseph recognized his brothers, one naturally wonders, why didn't they recognize him? There are several reasons. A 17-year-old can change significantly in appearance by the time he's 38. Moreover, Joseph was now thoroughly Egyptian in his clothing, hairstyle, and speech. Hebrews wore full beards, but Egyptians were clean-shaven. And because he had an interpreter present, the brothers naturally assumed that he was an Egyptian, not a Hebrew. Joseph also showed them no familiarity, pretending he didn't recognize them. And besides, from their vantage point, he was no longer alive (see verse 13), so seeing him was beyond the range of possibility.

"You are spies" (42:9,14): Joseph wanted to test his brothers and sift them for information. He did this by accusing them of being spies.

"My lord, your servants" (42:10): Recall that after hearing about Joseph's dream, his brothers responded in resentment: "Are you indeed to reign over us? Or are you indeed to rule over us?" (37:8). As lord over them, Joseph was now in that position.

Genesis 42:12-25

"By this you shall be tested" (42:15): Joseph demanded that Benjamin be brought before him to prove they were telling the truth. Joseph's ultimate goal may have been to find out if Benjamin suffered a fate similar to his own.

"By the life of Pharaoh" (42:15): In ancient times solemn oaths were often taken in the name of the king or ruler of the land.

He put them all together in custody for three days (42:17): Perhaps their imprisonment for three days gave the brothers a small taste of what Joseph had endured for three years in prison. Some Bible expositors suggest that Joseph's goal was to imprison them one day for each year he was in prison.

In any event, Joseph was testing his brothers. Notice that he was treating them much like they had treated him years earlier. They had questioned his motives years earlier, and now he was questioning theirs. They had treated him unfairly, and now was treating them the same way. They had been harsh with him, and now he was being harsh with them. They had treated him as a spy (for their father) years earlier, and now he accused them of spying. They had bound him (first in the pit and then in slavery), and now he bound them in custody.

On the third day (42:18): Joseph initiated a change in plans. He decided to keep only one of the brothers in custody while the other brothers returned home with grain.

"I fear God" (42:18): This is a holy reverence for God that leads to obedience to Him. Solomon tells us, "The fear of the LORD is the beginning of knowledge" (Proverbs 1:7). Exodus 20:20 reveals that people who fear the Lord turn from sin. Job "feared God and turned away from evil" (Job 1:1). When people don't fear the Lord, they think they can get away with anything. Because Joseph feared the Lord, he sought to be obedient to Him.

"If you are honest men" (42:19): Joseph decided to test their honesty. All of them would be released except one, who would remain confined. They were to take grain to their families but bring Benjamin back to him. Once they did this, their words would be verified (verse 20).

"In truth we are guilty" (42:21): The circumstances caused them to reflect on their guilt in selling Joseph into slavery long ago. They had seen "the distress of his soul" when they engaged in the dastardly act. Joseph begged, but they did not listen. They said, "This is why this distress has come upon us."

"Did I not tell you?...Now there comes a reckoning" (42:22): Reuben essentially said, "I told you so, but you wouldn't listen. Now we're going to pay for it." The phrase "reckoning for his blood" likely refers to the death penalty.

Joseph understood them (42:23): An interpreter was present, so the brothers naturally assumed Joseph could not understand what they were saying. But Joseph understood every word.

He turned away from them and wept (42:24): Hearing his brothers admit their guilt and share their remorse for what they had done moved Joseph emotionally. Joseph may have relived in his mind the moment of their betrayal so many years ago. It was difficult for him.

He took Simeon from them and bound him (42:24): Simeon had agreed to selling Joseph into slavery (37:21-31). Joseph did not bind Reuben, who had saved his life years earlier.

Replace every man's money in his sack (42:25): Joseph gave them grain and even returned their money. Later, once they discovered the money in their sacks, "their hearts failed them," and they wondered what God had done to them (verse 28). They thought that perhaps because of what they had done to Joseph, God was now bringing His vengeance against them.

Genesis 42:26-38

They told him all that had happened (42:29-30): The brothers informed Jacob of all that had happened. They had deceived Jacob in earlier years by giving a false account of Joseph's death, but now they truthfully recounted their experience in Egypt. They've experienced a bit of character improvement through the years.

"Now you would take Benjamin" (42:36): Jacob lamented that Joseph was dead, Simeon was in prison in Egypt, and now he would lose Benjamin too. He was overwhelmed. He didn't want to lose another son.

"All this has come against me" (42:36): In reality, all this had come for his benefit. He had no idea that by these circumstances God was about to pour out great blessing on him and his family. We are reminded of Romans 8:28: "We know that for those who love God all things work together for good, for those who are called according to his purpose." As one Bible expositor put it, "A great portion of our present trouble arises from our not knowing the whole truth."[4]

"Kill my two sons" (42:37): Reuben tried to persuade Jacob in an

extreme way, inviting him to kill his two sons if he did not bring Benjamin back. Perhaps Reuben was hoping to get back in his father's good favor by keeping Benjamin safe (see 35:22).

"My son shall not go down with you" (42:38): Jacob could not bear the pain of losing Benjamin. The request was just too much.

"His brother is dead, and he is the only one left" (42:38): Joseph, the son of Rachel, was dead. Benjamin is Rachel's only living son.

"Bring down my gray hairs with sorrow to Sheol" (42:38): If anything happened to Benjamin, Jacob would spend the rest of his days in grief, right up till the time he was buried.

Major Themes

1. *The importance of grain.* Grain—particularly wheat, barley, and spelt—was an extremely important food source in biblical times (Genesis 42:1; Amos 9:9; 1 Corinthians 15:37). The ancients utilized grain in almost every meal. The wonderful thing about grain is that it could be dried and then stored for a very long time. This fact is what enabled Joseph to store dried grain and thereby save the Egyptians from famine.
2. *Joseph's prophetic dream proves true.* The biblical prophets were always 100 percent accurate. In fact, anyone who made a prediction in the name of the Lord that didn't come to pass was to be stoned to death as a false prophet (Deuteronomy 13; 18:20-22). Joseph's prophetic dream of being exalted over his brothers proved to be 100 percent accurate. Joseph said to his brothers, "Hear this dream that I have dreamed: Behold, we were binding sheaves in the field, and behold, my sheaf arose and stood upright. And behold, your sheaves gathered around it and bowed down to my sheaf" (Genesis 37:6-7). In Genesis 42:6, we read of the fulfillment of this dream: "Joseph's brothers came and bowed themselves before him with their faces to the ground."

Digging Deeper with Cross-References

Truthfulness—Genesis 42:16; Exodus 23:7; 1 Kings 22:16; Job 6:28; Psalms 15:2; 24:4; 51:6; 119:29; Proverbs 8:7; 12:19; 14:5,25; 16:13; 30:8; Zechariah 8:16; Mark 5:33; John 21:24; Acts 26:25; Romans 9:1; 2 Corinthians 1:18; 4:2; 11:31; Galatians 4:16; Ephesians 4:15,25; 6:14; Philippians 4:8; James 5:12

Fathers' love in Genesis—Genesis 17:18; 21:11; 22:2; 25:5,28; 27:26; 31:28,55; 32:11; 37:35; 42:4,38; 43:14; 44:20; 45:28; 46:30; 48:10

Life Lessons

1. *No need to boast.* When Joseph was young, he blurted out his dreams without even thinking about the effect they would have on those around him. He was boastful. At that young age, he had no "humility filters." With age, however, Joseph had matured. No longer did he feel the need to boast. Certainly he recognized that his prophetic dream had now come true as his brothers bowed before him. But there was no need for him to remind them of the dream. We learn a good lesson here. As Colossians 3:12 puts it, we all ought to clothe ourselves with humility (see also 1 Peter 5:5-6).

2. *Show mercy despite mistreatment.* Even when others mistreat us, we are always to let Christ shine through us and show mercy. Just as we are to clothe ourselves with humility, so also we are to clothe ourselves with mercy (Colossians 3:12). Never forget that God blesses the merciful (Matthew 5:7). Just as God has shown mercy to us (Deuteronomy 4:31; Lamentations 3:22,24; 2 Corinthians 1:3), so we are to show mercy to others (Matthew 18:33).

Questions for Reflection and Discussion

1. Are you ever tempted to boast? Read 2 Corinthians 10:17 and consider how this verse relates to Joseph. How might you make this verse a reality in your life?
2. Jesus said, "Blessed are the merciful" (Matthew 5:7). Is your life characterized by the kind of mercy Joseph showed to his brothers?
3. Do you fear God? Do you have a holy reverence for Him that motivates you to obedience?

Day 34

Joseph's Brothers in Egypt—Part 2

Genesis 43–44

Scripture Reading and Insights

Begin by reading Genesis 43–44 in your favorite Bible. As you read, notice how the Word of God continues to purify your life (John 17:17-18).

In the previous lesson, we saw Joseph's brothers in Egypt. Now let's look in as they make their second visit to Egypt and Joseph continues to test them. With your Bible still accessible, consider the following insights on the biblical text.

Genesis 43:1-15

"Go again" (43:2): Jacob's clan was out of food. The brothers needed to make a repeat trip to Egypt.

"The man solemnly warned us" (43:3): Jacob instructed his sons to go buy more food. Judah replied that they dare not attempt it unless they take Benjamin with them. That point was nonnegotiable for the young governor of Egypt (Joseph).

"I will be a pledge of his safety" (43:9): Judah pledged to his father that he would indeed keep Benjamin safe and bring him back. Recall that selling Joseph into slavery had been Judah's idea (37:26-27). Now he offers himself as a guarantee—a security—on Benjamin's behalf. Later, in Egypt, Judah will offer himself as a servant to Joseph so that Benjamin could return to his father.

"Carry a present down to the man" (43:11): Jacob suggested that his sons bring a present to the man. It was common in biblical days to bring gifts to a superior (see 1 Samuel 16:20; 17:18; 2 Kings 5:15). The gift would consist of "a little balm and a little honey, gum, myrrh, pistachio nuts, and almonds." Why a little? In the midst of the famine, their reserves were likely growing slim. Balm, honey, myrrh, pistachio nuts, and almonds were not produced in Egypt, so these would have been delicacies to an Egyptian.

"May God Almighty grant you mercy" (43:14): "God Almighty" is *El Shaddai* (see Genesis 17:1; 28:3; 35:11; 48:3; 1 Kings 19:10,14). *El* in Hebrew refers to "Mighty God." *Shaddai* indicates compassion, grace, and mercy. Jacob appeals to this God, who is both Almighty and merciful, for help in the present situation.

They took double the money (43:15): This money would be used to pay for both the original purchase of grain (42:28) and a new purchase.

Genesis 43:16-34

The men were afraid (43:18): Joseph's brothers feared what the consequences would be regarding the money they discovered in their bags of grain.

"Do not be afraid" (43:23): The steward of Joseph's house told them to give the matter no further thought. He affirmed, "Your God and the God of your father has put treasure in your sacks for you." Does this mean the steward was a believer in the true God as opposed to the gods of Egypt? Perhaps so. Or it could be that the steward was simply representing Joseph's view to the brothers.

Bowed down to him to the ground (43:26): This is another fulfillment of the prophetic dreams Joseph had many years earlier (37:5-8).

"God be gracious to you" (43:29): Joseph pronounces a special blessing on his brother from the same mother (see Numbers 6:25; Psalm 67:1). Notice that in this blessing Joseph referred to the one true God as opposed to one of the false gods of Egypt.

He sought a place to weep (43:30): Joseph again found it difficult to rein in his emotions. He wept (see 42:24; 45:2,14-15; 46:29).

The Egyptians could not eat with the Hebrews (43:32): Joseph does not violate the caste system in Egypt, which did not permit eating with Hebrews (considered by Egyptians an abomination). Joseph likely did not consider it an abomination but maintained standard Egyptian protocol until he revealed himself to his brothers.

The men looked at one another in amazement (43:33): The brothers were amazed because the host of their lunch (Joseph, whom they thought was an Egyptian governor) arranged for them to be seated according to proper Hebrew etiquette—in birth order. How did this guy know about that? They were amazed.

Benjamin's portion was five times as much (43:34): Normally a guest of honor would receive a double portion of food. Receiving five times as much food as others indicates honor heaped upon honor.

Joseph favored Benjamin extravagantly. In earlier years, Jacob had favored Joseph, and the brothers greatly resented it. Perhaps Joseph was now watching to see if the brothers would show similar disdain for Benjamin, having now been treated so favorably. The brothers showed no animosity at all.

Genesis 44:1-17

"The silver cup" (44:2): This cup was used for divination (see verse 5; compare with verse 15). This should not be taken to mean that Joseph actually practiced divination. Divination cups were common in Egypt, so it is understandable why such a cup would have been in Joseph's household. As Joseph withheld his true identity from his brothers, he continued to play the role of an Egyptian governor—including the use of the cup. The cup was secretly placed in Benjamin's sack. See Major Themes.

Sent away with their donkeys (44:3): The brothers departed from Egypt with their grain.

"Why have you repaid evil for good?" (44:4): All was going according to plan. The brothers had departed from Egypt without knowing that Joseph's cup had been hidden in Benjamin's bag. He then sent his men to pursue them and ask, "Why have you repaid evil for good?" (see Proverbs 17:13).

"Far be it from your servants" (44:7): The brothers immediately

protested their innocence. We might paraphrase their response in modern vernacular: "No way did we steal it. Why would we return all that money we found in our sacks, only to then steal a cup? We're so sure of our innocence that if the cup was stolen by anyone here, he's a dead man! And the rest of us will be your slaves."

"He who is found with it shall be my servant" (44:10): Joseph's servant softened the penalty. There would be no death sentences. Rather, the one who had the cup would be consigned to servanthood.

Beginning with the eldest (44:12): Each bag of each brother was searched, from the oldest brother to the youngest. Going in this order served as a clue that someone among the Egyptians (Joseph) had inside knowledge about the proper order of family members. The brothers must have wondered how they knew.

The cup was found in Benjamin's sack... They tore their clothes (44:12-13): The brothers tore their clothing as an open expression of grief. They had a perfect opportunity here to turn on Benjamin just as they had turned on Joseph years ago. They could have singled out Benjamin for punishment, but they did not do this. They were brothers in this together, and there would be no betrayal.

They fell before him to the ground (44:14): Yet another fulfillment of Joseph's dream (37:5-8). This time they were begging for mercy.

"What deed is this that you have done" (44:15): Joseph continues to test his brothers. He watches their every response. Continuing his role as the Egyptian governor, he speaks of his ability to practice divination. Again, this should not be taken to mean that Joseph actually practices divination. Joseph is playing a role, responding to their actions the way an Egyptian governor normally would.

And Judah said (44:16): Judah—the spokesman for his brothers—humbly admitted to Joseph, "God has found out the guilt of your servants." He admitted that from now on, he and his brothers would be Joseph's servants. Through it all, however, the brothers never mistreated Benjamin or spoke evil of him. The brothers had clearly changed since they had sold Joseph into slavery years earlier.

"Only the man in whose hand the cup was found" (44:17): Joseph said that only Benjamin need stay with him.

Genesis 44:18-34

"Please let your servant speak a word" (44:18): The brothers had not spoken evil of Benjamin, and now Judah offered a special plea on his behalf. Judah described his father's great love for Benjamin—so great that his father would die if he didn't see his beloved Benjamin again. Judah therefore appealed to Joseph's mercy.

"Please let your servant remain instead of the boy" (44:33): Judah offered himself in place of Benjamin. He begged for his father's sake for Benjamin to be released so he could return to his father. His brothers had indeed changed since the time they sold him into slavery.

Major Themes

1. *The silver cup and divination.* The Egyptians practiced various forms of divination. One method was to pour water into a silver cup and observe the pattern of ripples and bubbles. One who was adept in divination could allegedly predict the future by properly interpreting the ripples in the cup. The Egyptians likely gave Joseph this cup because of his high position in Egypt (Genesis 44:2).
2. *Judah matures.* Earlier in Judah's life, he cared about one person—himself! He was self-centered and self-focused. He certainly did not care about Joseph, nor did he care much about his father (Genesis 37:27,32). Now, years later, things have changed. Judah has matured. We witness a self-sacrificial Judah who was obviously concerned for his father and for his little half-brother, Benjamin (44:18-34).

Digging Deeper with Cross-References

Gifts and presents in Genesis—Genesis 20:14; 24:22,53; 32:13,18; 33:10; 43:11,26; 45:22

Divination—Genesis 44:5,15; Numbers 22:7; 23:23; 24:1; Deuteronomy 18:10,14; 2 Kings 17:17; Jeremiah 14:14; 27:9; 29:8; Ezekiel 12:24; 13:6,23; 21:21; Zechariah 10:2; Acts 16:16

Life Lessons

1. *Honest with money.* When Jacob's sons arrived home, they discovered in their sacks of grain the money that was supposed to have paid for the grain. Jacob therefore had his sons take extra money with them on their return trip to Egypt. He wanted to make sure everything was on the "up and up" in terms of financial obligations. We ought always follow this example. God hates any form of dishonesty (Leviticus 19:13,35; Proverbs 20:23). He blesses those who are honest (1 Chronicles 29:17; Proverbs 11:1; 24:26; Matthew 7:12; Luke 6:31; 2 Corinthians 8:21).

2. *Secret good deeds.* One naturally wonders how the money made its way into the grain sacks. Joseph, as the one in charge, most likely instructed that the money be placed there—but did not take credit for it. Contrary to the ancient Scribes and Pharisees who loved to parade their good works around town, God loves to see His people engage in secret good deeds. God sees those good deeds, and Jesus promised that the Father will one day reward them.

    > When you give to the needy, sound no trumpet before you, as the hypocrites do in the synagogues and in the streets, that they may be praised by others. Truly, I say to you, they have received their reward. But when you give to the needy, do not let your left hand know what your right hand is doing, so that your giving may be in secret. And your Father who sees in secret will reward you (Matthew 6:2-4).

3. *Putting others first.* Judah learned the important lesson of putting others first. He put the needs of his father and Benjamin ahead of his own needs. God desires that you and I learn this important lesson. As Paul put it in Philippians 2:3-4, "Do nothing from selfish ambition or conceit, but in humility count others more significant

than yourselves. Let each of you look not only to his own interests, but also to the interests of others" (see also Romans 12:10; Galatians 5:26; Ephesians 4:2; 5:21).

Questions for Reflection and Discussion

1. Have you ever been falsely accused of something? How did it make you feel? Were you able to respond in a way that honored Christ?
2. What have you learned in this lesson about how old sins can catch up with you? Does this motivate you not to sin?
3. Jacob's trials were actually preparing him for great blessing. Are you presently going through any trials? What is your attitude toward them?

Day 35

Joseph Reveals His Identity

Genesis 45

Scripture Reading and Insights

Begin by reading Genesis 45 in your favorite Bible. Read with the anticipation that the Holy Spirit has something important to teach you today (see Psalm 119:105).

In yesterday's reading, we saw Joseph's estranged brothers return to Egypt and Joseph continue to test them. In today's reading, we see Joseph finally reveal his identity. With your Bible still accessible, consider the following insights on the biblical text.

Genesis 45:1-9

"Is my father still alive?" (45:3): Two urgent needs pressed on Joseph—to reveal his identity and to ascertain his father's status. So he just blurted it all out.

They were dismayed at his presence (45:3): The brothers were terrified. The sudden realization that the very one they had betrayed and sold into slavery was now lord over all Egypt was almost too much to fathom. This was definitely a "deer in the headlights" moment. They would soon learn that Joseph was above vindictiveness and retaliation. Joseph was not an "eye for an eye" kind of man. He was all about mercy and forgiveness and restoration.

"God sent me before you to preserve life" (45:5): Joseph saved not only the Egyptians but also his family members. This was apparently God's providential plan all along.

"Two years" (45:6): This would be a seven-year famine (41:29-30). Two years of the famine had already passed. Five were yet to come. Things would get worse before they would get better.

"God sent me before you" (45:7): Joseph's brothers had sold him to Ishmaelite traders, but God used those dire circumstances in Joseph's life to bring him to Egypt. Notice that Joseph states four times that God is the one who worked providentially to bring him to Egypt: "Do not be distressed or angry with yourselves because you sold me here, for God sent me before you to preserve life" (verse 5). "God sent me before you to preserve for you a remnant on earth, and to keep alive for you many survivors" (verse 7). "It was not you who sent me here, but God" (verse 8). "God has made me lord of all Egypt" (verse 9).

"Preserve for you a remnant" (45:7): This reference to a remnant shows that God's intention all along was to work through Joseph so that the line of the covenant promises would be kept safe. Joseph himself is not in that line, but he was the one God used to ensure that the line stayed alive and thrived. God truly is sovereign. This brings to mind Isaiah 46:9-10: "I am God, and there is no other; I am God, and there is none like me, declaring the end from the beginning and from ancient times things not yet done, saying, 'My counsel shall stand, and I will accomplish all my purpose.'"

"A father to Pharaoh" (45:8): A title of honor given to a vizier—that is, a high-ranking political advisor or minister. Joseph had become "ruler over all the land of Egypt." He was father to Pharaoh in the sense of being his advisor.

"Hurry and go up to my father" (45:9): Joseph didn't want his father to be in the dark about things any longer. He was ready to resume family relations. He couldn't wait.

"God has made me lord of all Egypt" (45:9): Joseph is not boasting here. Notice the first word that comes out of his mouth... *God*. Joseph wants the brothers to tell his father, "Look at this wonderful thing God has done." This is in keeping with the apostle Paul's statement in 1 Corinthians 1:31, "Let the one who boasts, boast in the Lord."

"Come down to me; do not tarry" (45:9): Joseph knew that by now

his father Jacob was a very old man. The sooner Jacob could come to be by his side, the better.

Genesis 45:10-20

"Goshen" (45:10): A fertile territory northeast of the Nile delta, ideal for grazing Jacob's herds. Goshen was only a few days' walk from Canaan.

Recall that in Genesis 15:13 God instructed Abraham, "Know for certain that your offspring will be sojourners in a land that is not theirs and will be servants there, and they will be afflicted for four hundred years." Abraham's offspring became sojourners in Egypt by coming to Goshen to be near Joseph. Later, things would get bad between the Egyptians and the Israelites. But for now, all was good.

"It is my mouth that speaks to you" (45:12): Quite obviously Joseph does not need the interpreter he used before his brothers knew his identity.

"Tell my father" (45:13): Joseph had earlier shared his prophetic dreams with his entire family, including his father. In his second dream, the sun (his father), the moon (his mother), and 11 stars (his 11 brothers) would bow before Joseph (37:9). His father initially rebuked him for his self-exalting dreams, but "his father kept the saying in mind" (37:11). Now the prophetic dreams that Jacob kept in mind have come to pass. Joseph wants his father to see that God has done a wonderful thing. God did just as He said He would do.

Wept... wept... kissed... wept (45:14-15): This was an emotional reunion for the brothers—especially for Joseph, who had been deprived of fellowship with them for the 22 years since they had sold him into slavery. He was now 39 years old. Notice the threefold expression of Joseph's goodwill toward his brothers—weeping with them, explaining things to them, and embracing them.

Pleased Pharaoh (45:16): Pharaoh was more than happy for Joseph's long-estranged relatives to relocate to Goshen. This is in notable contrast to other immigrants to Egypt, who are forced to live in more desolate (far less fertile) areas. Pharaoh no doubt felt strongly about Joseph's relatives out of his gratitude for Joseph saving all of Egypt from famine (45:18; 47:20).

"Best of the land" (45:18): Pharaoh would arrange for Joseph's relatives to receive the best of the land. One recalls the blessings Isaac pronounced on Jacob in earlier years: "May God give you of the dew of heaven and of the fatness of the earth and plenty of grain and wine" (27:28).

Some Bible expositors note that Pharaoh's message to Jacob was an invitation, not a command. Jacob could either accept or reject the offer. Moreover, under this Pharaoh, Jacob and his family could stay as long as they wanted or leave whenever they wanted. It wasn't until this Pharaoh died and a new Pharaoh came into power that new policies were dictated regarding the Israelites. Under a later Pharaoh, the Jews would be enslaved.

Genesis 45:21-28

Three hundred shekels of silver (45:22): This was about seven and a half pounds of silver.

"Do not quarrel on the way" (45:24): Having now been reconciled with Joseph, and with much to think about in terms of the past, present, and future, the field was ripe for conflict to emerge. Joseph instructed them to not let that happen. Joseph wanted them to avoid mutual accusations against each other. To put it in modern vernacular, "All of that is water under the bridge. It's all good now." The bottom line was that since Joseph had forgiven all his brothers, they should also forgive one another (see Jesus's words in Matthew 18:21-35).

His heart became numb (45:26): Jacob was stunned. He had been worried sick that he was losing his sons, but now he finds out that he will be in fellowship with all his sons, including his long-lost beloved Joseph. What an awesome moment it was. A family in dire straits was now a family full of rejoicing.

As we look back on this entire episode, the words of W.H. Griffith Thomas seem appropriate: "Happy is the man whose eye is open to see the hand of God in every-day events, for to him life always possesses a wonderful and true joy and glory."[5]

Israel (45:28): Jacob often had problems believing without seeing. However, he soon became convinced that his sons were telling him the truth—his beloved Joseph was alive. At this juncture, the biblical text (under Moses's writing hand) resumes calling Jacob, Israel. Perhaps we should not read too much into this. But it may be that because Jacob has now returned to a position of trust in God, he again is called Israel.

Major Themes

1. *Joseph's emotional drain.* Notice how often Joseph was brought to tears in his encounters with his brothers: "Then he turned away from them and wept. And he returned to them and spoke to them" (Genesis 42:24). "Then Joseph hurried out, for his compassion grew warm for his brother, and he sought a place to weep. And he entered his chamber and wept there" (43:30). "Then he fell upon his brother Benjamin's neck and wept, and Benjamin wept upon his neck" (45:14). "Then Joseph fell on his father's face and wept over him and kissed him" (50:1). "Joseph wept when they spoke to him" (50:17). The biblical account gives lie to the modern Western view that strong men don't cry!
2. *God sent me.* Once Joseph revealed his identity to his brothers, he said to them, "God sent me before you to preserve life" (Genesis 45:5). He affirmed, "It was not you who sent me here, but God" (verse 8). God also sent others in the Genesis narrative. For example, God instructed Abraham, "Go from your country and your kindred and your father's house to the land that I will show you" (12:1). God said to Jacob, "Arise, go out from this land and return to the land of your kindred" (31:13). In each case God gave someone what might be considered a kingdom assignment.

Digging Deeper with Cross-References

Guilty fear in Genesis—Genesis 3:8-10; 42:28; 43:18; 45:3; 50:15

Preservation—Genesis 7:23; 19:19; 32:30; 45:7; Deuteronomy 4:4; 6:24; 8:4; Joshua 14:10; 24:17; 1 Samuel 30:23; Nehemiah 9:6,21; Job 10:12; Psalms 3:5; 12:7; 16:1; 17:8; 30:3; 31:23; 32:7; 33:19; 34:20; 36:6; 37:28; 40:11; 41:2; 61:7; 64:1; 66:9; 71:6; 79:11; 86:2; 91:3; 97:10; 103:4; 116:6; 118:17; 121:7; 140:1; 145:20; 146:9; Proverbs 2:8; 22:12; Isaiah 31:5; 43:2; 49:8; Daniel 3:25; 6:23; Jonah 1:17; 2:6; Matthew 2:13; Acts 17:28

Life Lessons

1. *The past is the past.* Joseph "sent his brothers away, and as they departed, he said to them, 'Do not quarrel on the way'" (Genesis 45:24). He said this because of the likelihood of some of them quarreling about their past sinful actions. In Joseph's thinking, the past was the past and now was now. In other words, don't fret about the past, but rejoice that we will now have an ongoing family reunion. Not dwelling on the past is also a New Testament emphasis. In Philippians 3:13-14 the apostle Paul said, "One thing I do: forgetting what lies behind and straining forward to what lies ahead, I press on toward the goal for the prize of the upward call of God in Christ Jesus" (see also Luke 9:62).
2. *A good word.* Our text tells us that when the brothers told their father "all the words of Joseph, which he had said to them, and when he saw the wagons that Joseph had sent to carry him, the spirit of their father Jacob revived" (Genesis 45:27). A good report can light up one's life! Proverbs 12:25 tells us that a good word can make a person glad. Proverbs 17:22 tells us that "a joyful heart is good medicine." You

and I have the power to revive people's spirits by the words we use with them. Why not try to find at least one opportunity every day to do this?

Questions for Reflection and Discussion

1. Can you think of a time in your own life when you realized God was acting providentially? How does it make you feel to know that God is absolutely sovereign over the affairs of human beings?
2. Why is it important to leave the past in the past?
3. Joseph's words were a great encouragement to Jacob. Do you know someone who needs encouragement? What are you waiting for?

Day 36

Joseph's Family Relocates to Egypt

Genesis 46–47

Scripture Reading and Insights

Begin by reading Genesis 46–47 in your favorite Bible. Read with the anticipation that the Holy Spirit has something important to teach you today (see Psalm 119:105).

In the previous lesson, Joseph finally revealed his identity to his estranged brothers. In today's lesson, Jacob travels to Egypt and is reunited with Joseph, and Joseph provides for his family. With your Bible still accessible, consider the following insights on the biblical text.

Genesis 46:1-27

Beersheba (46:1): The name of a well dug by Abraham (Genesis 21:31) as well as a city given to the tribe of Simeon (Joshua 19:2; 1 Chronicles 4:28). The journey to Egypt went through Beersheba. Abraham himself had sojourned in Egypt to find relief from a famine (Genesis 12:10). Jacob was following in Abraham's footsteps.

Offered sacrifices (46:1): Beersheba had been a place of worship for both Abraham and Isaac (21:33; 26:25). Now Jacob worshipped there too.

God spoke to Israel (46:2): The first time God spoke to Jacob was through a dream (28:10-12). He now speaks to Jacob through "visions of the night."

Jacob was likely a bit nervous about traveling to Egypt. Was he doing the right thing, leaving the land of promise to go to Egypt? Would the journey be hard? Would his family be saved from the famine? Would Pharaoh be hospitable? One also wonders whether Jacob was aware of God's statement to Abraham that his descendants would be enslaved in a foreign land for 400 years.

The Lord appeared to Jacob to give him assurance, telling him not to be afraid (see 15:1; 21:17; 26:24) and saying, "I myself will go down with you to Egypt" (verse 4). God assured him that while in Egypt, his descendants would become a great nation. We see, then, that all of this is part of the outworking of the original covenant God made with Abraham—"I will make of you a great nation" (12:2).

"Jacob, Jacob" (46:2): The repetition of Jacob's name is an indication of urgency. This was to be an important revelation to Jacob.

"I am God, the God of your father" (46:3): God identified himself in essentially the same way to his father, Isaac: "I am the God of Abraham your father."

"I myself will go down with you to Egypt" (46:4): Notice the repetitive theme of God going with Jacob. God had earlier informed Jacob, "Behold, I am with you and will keep you wherever you go" (28:15). "Wherever you go" now applies to Egypt.

"Bring you up again" (46:4): God would not only providentially be with Jacob and his clan as they went to dwell in Egypt. He would also providentially bring them out of Egypt, a monumental event described in detail in the book of Exodus. Such promises would have been a great comfort to Jacob.

"Joseph's hand shall close your eyes" (46:4): Jacob would not only be reunited with his beloved Joseph but also die in his presence. And once Jacob departed from this life, Joseph would affectionately close his father's eyes with his hand. This was in keeping with the ancient Hebrew custom that the eldest son (or closest relative) would gently close the eyes of the deceased. (Joseph was the eldest son of Jacob's primary wife, Rachel.)

Set out from Beersheba... came into Egypt (46:5-6): The journey was over. Jacob and his clan had arrived in Egypt. Here they would remain for more than four centuries. During that extended time, Jacob's descendants would become a great nation.

Names of the descendants of Israel (46:8): A genealogical record of Jacob's descendants who traveled to Egypt. This grouping of persons would be the seed from which a great nation would be born (see Exodus 1:1).

Sixty-six persons in all (46:26): It is amazing to ponder, but from sixty-six persons would come a great nation.

Seventy (46:27): Adding Jacob, Joseph, Manasseh, and Ephraim into the mix brings the total to 70. Note that Acts 7:14 makes reference to 75 people. This total includes Manasseh's two sons, Ephraim's two sons, and Ephraim's grandson.

Genesis 46:28-34

Sent Judah ahead (46:28): Reuben lost his firstborn privileges when he defiled his father's bed (35:22). Simeon and Levi forfeited their position by killing the men of Shechem (34:25-26). Judah was far from perfect, but after his sacrificial offer to suffer in Benjamin's place (44:18-34), and under God's providence, he emerged to a position of leading and speaking for the family (see 44:16).

Land of Goshen (46:28): A fertile territory northeast of the Nile delta, ideal for grazing Jacob's herds.

Fell on his neck and wept (46:29): Joseph was only 17 when he last saw his father (37:2). Now he was 39. He wept for "a good while" upon reuniting with his father (compare with 42:24; 43:30; 45:2,14-15).

Jacob had experienced another reunion after being separated for many years—with Esau (32:3). Now he had a wonderful reunion with Joseph.

"Now let me die" (46:30): Jacob had said the loss of his sons would cause him to go to his grave in great mourning (37:35; 42:38). Now that Jacob had reunited with Joseph, he affirmed that he could die in peace.

Joseph said to his brothers (46:31): Joseph gave specific instructions to his family to ensure that they would remain separate from the Egyptians. This would keep the Hebrews' cultural identity intact—an important fact considering God's covenant promises to the nation.

Genesis 47:1-12

"Please let your servants dwell in the land of Goshen" (47:4): Under Joseph's guiding hand, representatives of Jacob's clan made their request to Pharaoh. All of this was according to the proper protocol in securing dwelling rights in a land that was under Egyptian sovereignty. Pharaoh approved the request.

Jacob blessed Pharaoh (47:7): Jacob expressed his appreciation when Pharaoh allowed his people to dwell in Goshen. He therefore pronounced a blessing over Pharaoh (compare with Hebrews 7:7).

Jacob's blessing of Pharaoh is another outworking of the Abrahamic covenant, in which God promises, "I will bless those who bless you" (12:3). Pharaoh blessed Jacob and his clan by allowing them to dwell in the land of Goshen. Jacob thus appropriately responded by pronouncing a blessing on Pharaoh. In the verses that follow, we find that Joseph's continued efforts were able to save Egypt from the famine. This seems to be a practical outworking of the blessing Jacob pronounced on Pharaoh.

"The years of my sojourning are 130...Few and evil" (47:9): Jacob had lived 130 years. The word "sojourning" points to the reality that he and his clan would live as foreigners until they finally possessed the Promised Land. His years are few in comparison to those who preceded him—Abraham (175 years) and Isaac (180 years). His time had been evil in a number of ways, including his conflicts with Esau and Laban as well as his impression that Joseph had been dead these many years.

Land of Rameses (47:11): Likely just another name for Goshen (see Exodus 1:11; 12:37; Numbers 33:3,5), though some Bible expositors believe the land of Rameses embraced a larger area of which Goshen was just a part. The word Rameses means "Ra [the sun god] has created it." Ra was the highest god in the Egyptian pantheon.

Joseph provided...food, according to the number of their dependents (47:12): Food supplies were limited, so food was rationed according to how many people were in each family.

Genesis 47:13-31

Joseph gathered up all the money...Give your livestock (47:14-16): The

Egyptians ran out of money as they sought to pay for grain. Subsequently, a bartering system was set up. Livestock became a form of payment. People gave livestock to Joseph in exchange for food.

Nothing left...but our bodies and our land (47:18): Eventually the Egyptians ran out of livestock as they sought to pay for grain. Continuing the bartering system, land became a form of payment. People gave land to Joseph in exchange for food. In this way, all the land of Egypt became the property of Pharaoh (verse 20) except the land allocated to the priests (verse 22).

Give a fifth to Pharaoh (47:24): The people were given seed and were still allowed to work the land. However, to continue battling the famine, a one-fifth tax was imposed on all crop yields.

Were fruitful and multiplied greatly (47:27): Jacob's clan became fruitful and multiplied—just what one would expect if Jacob's descendants were to become a great nation, as God promised (compare with 35:11-12; 46:3). The covenant promises were being fulfilled before their very eyes.

"Put your hand under my thigh" (47:29): In Old Testament times, the gesture of touching in an intimate place (near the organ of procreation) indicated a solemn pledge or oath.

"Do not bury me in Egypt" (47:29): Jacob did not want to be buried in the land of Egypt. He wanted to be buried in the land of promise in the cave of Machpelah, which Abraham had purchased (see 23:1-20; 25:7-10; 35:27-29).

"Burying place" (47:30): A reference to the burial cave in Canaan (49:29–50:5).

Major Themes

1. *Living separately.* When Jacob and his clan moved to Egypt, they were not assimilated into Egyptian culture (Genesis 43:32). The Egyptians would have reacted strongly against such assimilation. Semitic shepherds were held in very low regard, being viewed as a lower caste of human beings. Besides, Jacob and his clan would not have wanted to be

assimilated into Egyptian culture. By living near Egypt but separate from the Egyptians, they could maintain their own cultural identity in serving the one true God.

2. *God begins to fulfill the Abrahamic covenant.* As we have seen, God promised in the Abrahamic covenant, "I will bless those who bless you, and him who dishonors you I will curse" (Genesis 12:3). Pharaoh blessed Jacob and his clan, and in turn Pharaoh was blessed by Jacob (Genesis 47:7). We also note that the Israelites "were fruitful and multiplied greatly" (Genesis 47:27). This, too, was a fulfillment of the Abrahamic covenant, which affirmed that God would make Abraham's descendants innumerable (15:5; 22:17). All was going according to God's plan.

Digging Deeper with Cross-References

God is a promise keeper—Numbers 23:19; Joshua 21:45; 23:14; 1 Kings 8:56

God will not forsake His people—Deuteronomy 31:6; Joshua 1:5; 1 Samuel 12:22

Yearning for home—Genesis 30:25; 31:30; 47:30; Numbers 10:30; 2 Samuel 19:37

Life Lessons

1. *The brevity of human life.* In Genesis 47:9 Jacob said to Pharaoh, "The days of the years of my sojourning are 130 years. Few and evil have been the days of the years of my life, and they have not attained to the days of the years of the life of my fathers in the days of their sojourning." In other words, life is short—a reality often reflected in Scripture. Job 14:1 tells us, "Man who is born of a woman is few of days and full of trouble." The psalmist reflects, "Behold, you have made my days a few handbreadths, and

my lifetime is as nothing before you. Surely all mankind stands as a mere breath!" (Psalm 39:5). In James 4:14 we are told, "What is your life? For you are a mist that appears for a little time and then vanishes." It is therefore good to be mindful of the brevity of life: "O Lord, make me know my end and what is the measure of my days; let me know how fleeting I am" (Psalm 39:4).

2. *Honor your word.* In Genesis 47:29-31, Joseph promised to bury Jacob in his homeland. Jacob had Joseph put his hand under his thigh when making this promise. This was an ancient way of guaranteeing an oath. Of course, Joseph was a man of his word. He did just as Jacob requested (Genesis 50:7). We, too, are called to honor our word. When we say we'll do something, we should do it (see Matthew 5:33-37).

Questions for Reflection and Discussion

1. Does your mortality affect the way you live as a Christian? Do you, like the psalmist, pray, "O Lord, make me know my end and what is the measure of my days; let me know how fleeting I am" (Psalm 39:4)?
2. Joseph was a man of his word. Do you consider yourself a person of your word? Do you think people trust that you are a person of your word?
3. Are there any areas of your life in which you sense God saying to you, "Don't be afraid—I will be with you"?

Day 37

Joseph's Sons Are Blessed

Genesis 48

Scripture Reading and Insights

Begin by reading Genesis 48 in your favorite Bible. As you read, keep in mind that the Word of God brings spiritual maturity (1 Corinthians 3:1-2; Hebrews 5:12-14).

In yesterday's reading, Jacob traveled to Egypt and was reunited with Joseph, and Joseph provided for his family. In today's reading, Jacob blesses Joseph's two sons, Manasseh and Ephraim. With your Bible still accessible, consider the following insights on the biblical text.

Genesis 48:1-7

"Behold, your father is ill" (48:1): Jacob's remaining time on earth was limited. His health was fading fast.

Israel summoned his strength (48:2): Because his illness weakened his body, siting up in bed required great effort. But he managed to do it.

"God Almighty" (48:3): This is the name *El Shaddai*. *El* in Hebrew refers to "Mighty God." *Shaddai* points to God's compassion, grace, and mercy. This mighty God—full of tender mercy—has watched over Jacob through the years.

"Fruitful and multiply... company of peoples... land... everlasting possession" (48:4): Jacob summarizes the key components of the Abrahamic covenant. Jacob may be losing his health, but he has not lost his mental faculties. He repeats with absolute clarity the promises first

made to Abraham and reaffirmed to Isaac and Jacob throughout the years.

"Ephraim and Manasseh shall be mine" (48:5): When Jacob said that Joseph's two sons, Ephraim and Manasseh, were counted as his, he elevated them to the same status as his other sons, in line for an inheritance.

Genesis 48:8-16

"Who are these?" (48:8): The Egyptian Pharaoh gave Asenath—daughter of Potiphera, priest of On—to Joseph as a wife. She bore him two sons, Ephraim and Manasseh. The problem for Jacob is that his eyes were dim with age—perhaps because of cataracts or some other then-untreatable eye disease (48:10). Because of this, many believe that when Jacob said "Who are these?" he was indicating that he couldn't see them well.

Another explanation is possible. Perhaps Jacob knew who they were but was identifying them as part of a legal ritual of adoption and blessing (see 27:18). Both views are possible.

Bowed himself with his face to the earth (48:12): This is a great show of humility on Joseph's part. He is the second-most powerful man in Egypt. And yet to honor his father, he bows with his face to the earth.

Right hand...left hand (48:13): Joseph, anticipating that the firstborn blessing would be pronounced on Manasseh, lined up Manasseh opposite Jacob's right hand and Ephraim opposite his left hand. This would make it easy for Jacob to place his hands on his sons to pronounce the appropriate blessings.

"God...Abraham and Isaac" (48:15): In hindsight, Jacob sees clearly that the God of Abraham and Isaac had providentially guided his life. Just as God had faithfully guided him, so God would continue to guide his descendants.

"My shepherd all my life" (48:15): A shepherd watches over, protects, and makes provisions for sheep with one-on-one attention. This is exactly what God had done for Jacob through his many years. This is the first reference in the Bible to God as a shepherd (see also Psalm

23). Jesus is called the good shepherd (John 10:11), the chief shepherd (1 Peter 5:4), and the great shepherd (Hebrews 13:20).

"The angel who has redeemed me" (48:16): I noted previously that appearances of the Angel of the Lord in Old Testament times were likely appearances of the preincarnate Christ. It is therefore highly significant that Jacob, in blessing Joseph's children, equated the divine Angel with the shepherd. They are one and the same person.

This same Angel of the Lord had appeared earlier to Abraham to prevent him from slaying Isaac on the altar (22:11-18). Now we are told that the Angel watched over and protected Jacob from all harm (48:15-16). The Angel of the Lord also helped Jacob when He informed him that He would prosper him in the face of Laban's unfair dealings with him (see 31:11-13).

This verse contains the first mention of God being a Redeemer. A redeemer is one who buys back or purchases or liberates or sets free. The New Testament often uses this term of Jesus Christ, who has purchased us and liberated us from the slave market of sin (Romans 3:24; 8:23; Ephesians 1:7; Colossians 1:14).

Genesis 48:17-22

Laid his right hand on the head of Ephraim (48:17): Going against the normal protocol of placing the right hand on the head of the firstborn, Jacob crossed his hands and placed his right hand on the younger son, Ephraim, instead of the older son, Manasseh.

"Not this way, my father" (48:18): Joseph thought that his father in his blindness had made an innocent mistake when placing his right hand upon Ephraim. Joseph tried to act quickly because the blessings, once uttered, were irreversible (see Numbers 23:20; Romans 11:29).

His father refused (48:19): Jacob corrected Joseph, indicating to him that Ephraim would be the more influential son of the two. Though the eldest son normally gets the firstborn blessing, we find exceptions throughout Scripture. David was the last one born in Jesse's family, but he is called the firstborn because of the preeminent position God placed him in. Among the descendants of Abraham, the younger son received the birthright blessings for four consecutive generations: Isaac over Ishmael, Jacob over Esau, Joseph over Reuben, and Ephraim over Manasseh. In our present text, Ephraim is treated as the firstborn because he would end up in the preeminent position (see Jeremiah 31:9). Joseph knew, better than most, that God's ways are not man's ways. He accepted Jacob's correction regarding Ephraim's blessing without debate. Jacob was bestowing blessings according to the divine plan, not according to normal human custom.

Notice that this reversal is reflected in verses 1 and 5. In verse 1 we read that Joseph "took with him his two sons, Manasseh and Ephraim." But then Jacob said, "Ephraim and Manasseh shall be mine." This is a subtle communication that Ephraim would receive the firstborn blessing.

There is a slight irony here. Joseph had been wondrously successful in interpreting the dreams of the chief baker, the chief cupbearer, and even Pharaoh. All of this had ultimately led to his great exaltation in Egypt. When it came to the future of his own sons, however, he was without such insight. This lack of insight was cleared up when Jacob informed him that Ephraim would be the greater.

"His younger brother shall be greater" (48:19): Later history reveals that Ephraim did indeed become the greater of the two. Ephraim became the dominant tribe among the ten northern tribes. In fact, the term Ephraim was often used in the prophetic books to refer to the entire northern kingdom (for example, 2 Chronicles 28:12; Isaiah 7:2,5,8-9; 11:13; Ezekiel 37:16-19; Hosea 6:4; 9:13; 12:1,8; Zechariah 9:10).

"I am about to die" (48:21): Though death was near, Jacob could die in peace. He had been reconciled with his beloved Joseph. The promises of God regarding his posterity and land would surely come to pass. All was well.

"God will be with you" (48:21): This is a common statement throughout both the Old and New Testaments.

"Bring you again to the land of your fathers" (48:21): Jacob had virtually no doubt that God would bring his descendants back to Canaan, just as promised.

"Mountain slope" (48:22): No other passage found in the Bible

speaks of Jacob's defeat of the Amorites with sword and bow, so it is unclear what this is referring to. The Hebrew word translated "mountain slope" is *shekem*, which sounds like Shechem. Some Bible expositors suggest that Jacob may have viewed Simeon and Levi's slaughter of the Shechemites as his own taking of the city (34:27-29). That is, Jacob engaged in the slaughter by proxy. Others suggest that Moses used a tense in the original Hebrew that indicated that what is spoken of as being in the past is actually yet future. In this view, it was so certain that the posterity of Jacob would overcome the Amorites in Canaan that it is spoken of as a past event. Still others suggest that perhaps the property Jacob had purchased at Shechem was later repossessed by the Amorites, and that Jacob later forcefully reclaimed the land. In any event, this land is now given to Joseph as a firstborn inheritance.

"The Amorites" (48:22): An ancient Semitic warlike people that lived in Palestine and Syria (see Genesis 15:16; Exodus 34:11; Deuteronomy 1:27). Joshua would later defeat the five kings of the Amorites (Joshua 10:10; see also 11:8).

Major Themes

1. *All is not as it appears.* Notice that Jacob gave the blessing not to Joseph's actual firstborn son, Manasseh, but to the younger son, Ephraim. Joseph sought to intervene, but Jacob would not have it. Under God's providential leading, Ephraim was the right choice. God doesn't make His choices according to human tradition. He bases His choices on His sovereign will (Job 42:2; Proverbs 16:9; 19:21; 21:30; Isaiah 14:24; 46:10). God often accomplishes His sovereign purposes through a person who may appear to be a lesser person from a human perspective. But God does not make mistakes.
2. *Covenant promises reaffirmed.* Yet again we find God reaffirming the original promises He made to Abraham: "Behold, I will make you fruitful and multiply you, and I will make of you a company of peoples and will give

this land to your offspring after you for an everlasting possession" (Genesis 48:4). God is a relentless promise keeper. Keep this in mind the next time you come across a promise in the Bible. As Joshua put it, "You know in your hearts and souls, all of you, that not one word has failed of all the good things that the Lord your God promised concerning you. All have come to pass for you; not one of them has failed" (Joshua 23:14; see also Joshua 21:45; 1 Kings 8:56). God is faithful.

Digging Deeper with Cross-References

Illness in Bible times—Genesis 48:1; 2 Kings 13:14; 20:1; 2 Chronicles 16:12; Job 2:7; Daniel 8:27; John 11:1; Philippians 2:27

Our spiritual inheritance—Romans 8:17; Ephesians 1:11; Titus 3:7

Dimmed vision—Genesis 27:1,23; 48:10; 1 Samuel 3:2; 4:15; 1 Kings 14:4

Laying on of hands—Genesis 48:14; Matthew 19:15; Mark 10:16

Life Lessons

1. *Walk by faith and not by sight.* Even when things seem most hopeless, the God of miracles can come through in ways that we would never have fathomed. Peter was locked in jail, and as far as he knew, he was there to stay. But an angel broke him out (Acts 12:7-12). Daniel was tossed into a lion's den, and from a human perspective, that's about as bad as it can get. But God sent His angel to protect Daniel through the night (Daniel 6). David, from a human perspective, stood no chance against the giant Goliath. But through God's empowerment, David slew the giant (1 Samuel 17). Walking by sight, Jacob was convinced his

son Joseph was dead, but in reality he was still alive. Joseph and Jacob spent more than two decades apart before their miraculous reunion took place. If your miracle hasn't come yet, keep your faith in God strong (Psalms 40:4; 118:8; Proverbs 3:5; Jeremiah 17:7; Matthew 15:28; 21:21-22; Luke 17:5-6; Romans 10:17; 2 Corinthians 5:7; 1 Timothy 1:19; Hebrews 10:35; 11:1; 1 Peter 1:7).

2. *Showing honor to the elderly.* Genesis 48:12 tells us that when Joseph came before Jacob, "he bowed himself with his face to the earth." As great as Joseph was in the land of Egypt, he still bowed and showed respect to his elderly father. The ancient Egyptians revered the elderly, but in modern Western culture, the elderly are often marginalized. They no longer enjoy the respect they once did. As Christians, why not follow Joseph's great example and show respect to the elderly?

Questions for Reflection and Discussion

1. What have you learned in this chapter about the importance of walking by faith and not by sight?
2. Do you make a habit of viewing and treating the elderly with honor?
3. What does it mean to you personally that the Lord is your shepherd?

Day 38

Jacob Blesses His Sons

Genesis 49:1-28

Scripture Reading and Insights

Begin by reading Genesis 49:1-28 in your favorite Bible. As you read, keep in mind that the Word of God brings spiritual maturity (1 Corinthians 3:1-2; Hebrews 5:12-14).

In the previous lesson, we watched as Jacob blessed Joseph's two sons, Manasseh and Ephraim. Now let's listen in as Jacob blesses his own sons. With your Bible still accessible, consider the following insights on the biblical text.

Genesis 49:1-7

Jacob called his sons (49:1): Jacob called his sons together so he could pronounce blessings on them. The blessings were not only for them but also for their descendants.

In the verses that follow—couched in the form of Hebrew poetry—Jacob addresses his sons in this order: Reuben, Simeon, Levi, Judah, Zebulun, Issachar, Dan, Gad, Asher, Naphtali, Joseph, and Benjamin. The sons are grouped according to their mothers: Leah (six sons), Bilhah (one son), Zilpah (two sons), Bilhah (one more son), and Rachel (two sons).

"In days to come" (49:1): In each blessing, Jacob revealed to his sons what would become of them in the days ahead. These blessings were based on Jacob's assessment of their character. You will notice that some

of the blessings do not seem like blessings because they include some negative consequences for bad behavior. Nevertheless, Jacob was righteous and fair in all that he said.

"Reuben, you are my firstborn" (49:3): Reuben was Jacob's firstborn son, but he would not receive the firstborn blessing. Jacob said, "Unstable as water, you shall not have preeminence" (verse 4). Reuben's instability led to his downfall.

Reuben's sexual relations with Bilhah (one of Jacob's wives) defiled his father's marriage bed. That defilement cost him his birthright blessing (35:22). Reuben may have hoped that his father's attitude toward him would soften through the years. As we see, however, Reuben paid dearly for his heinous sin. Israel's later history shows little significance for Reuben's descendants. Bible expositors note that no prophet or judge came from this tribe (see Judges 5:15-16; 1 Chronicles 5:1).

"Simeon and Levi...violence...anger" (49:5-6): Simeon and Levi were violent men. Jacob's "blessing" contains God's moral judgment on their slaughter of the Shechemites (34:25). It affirms that because of their wickedness they would have no independent tribal territory (see Joshua 19:1,9; see also Numbers 35:2,7; Joshua 14:4; 21:41).

Simeon became the smallest tribe (Numbers 26:14) and was omitted from Moses's blessing (Deuteronomy 33:8). Levi's descendants eventually showed loyalty to God. They redeemed themselves by standing with Moses in opposing the idolatry connected with the golden calf: "Moses stood in the gate of the camp and said, 'Who is on the Lord's side? Come to me.' And all the sons of Levi gathered around him" (Exodus 32:26; see also Numbers 3:5-13; 18:6-32). Levi's descendants thus became the priestly tribe.

Genesis 49:8-21

"Judah, your brothers shall praise you" (49:8): Judah was to become a great tribe of national prominence—strong as a young lion. His brothers would praise him in the sense that Judah would become a leading tribe. Judah would enjoy fierce, lionlike dominance over both his brothers and his enemies.

The association of Judah's line with lions communicates sovereignty, strength, and courage (see Ezekiel 19:2; Micah 5:8). Kings would emerge from Judah's line—including David, Solomon, and ultimately the divine Messiah, who is the "the Lion of the tribe of Judah" (Revelation 5:5). Judah was first in line in the march through the wilderness (Numbers 10:14).

"The scepter" (49:10): A symbol of royal command, the right to rule.

"The choice vine...darker than wine" (49:11-12): Many Bible expositors believe these metaphors ultimately point forward to the exuberant blessing, splendor, and abundance of Christ's millennial kingdom (see Isaiah 61:6-7; 65:21-25; Zechariah 3:10). As one Bible expositor put it, "The sense of the imagery is that wine, the symbol of prosperity and blessing, will be so plentiful that even the choicest vines will be put to such everyday use as tethering the animals of burden and vintage wine will be as commonplace as wash water."[6]

"Zebulun shall dwell at the shore of the sea" (49:13): Zebulun's descendants, though not living directly on waterfront property, would enjoy steady contact with seafarers who would travel through their area because it was an important trade route (see Joshua 19:10-16). This was to be a thriving commercial area. As Deuteronomy 33:19 puts it, they will "draw from the abundance of the seas."

"Issachar is a strong donkey" (49:14): Issachar's tribe would be made up of strong people who would be forced to work for others, like a strong donkey. This tribe would often be subjugated by invading armies.

"Dan...a serpent...a viper" (49:16-17): This tribe would produce judges for the nation. Samson, for example, was a descendant of Dan who was a judge for 20 years. However, members of this tribe were morally weak and religiously unfaithful. This tribe would become guilty of idolatry on many occasions and, as a result, would be largely obliterated (see Leviticus 24:11; Judges 18:1,30; see also 1 Kings 12:28-29). Dan's tribe is not mentioned in the list of tribes found in Revelation 7:4-8.

"Gad...he shall raid" (49:19): Being situated east of the Jordan (Joshua 13:24-27), the tribe of Gad was especially vulnerable to border attacks from the Moabites to the south. But Gad would have many

valiant warriors who would repel invasions and retaliate against attackers (see 1 Chronicles 5:18-22; 12:8-15).

"Asher's food shall be rich" (49:20): Asher was blessed by being given the rich seacoast area north of Mount Carmel (see Joshua 19:24-31). Because of the fertile farmlands near the Mediterranean (land with a good water supply), they would enjoy plenty of fine food.

"Naphtali is a doe let loose" (49:21): The descendants of Naphtali would enjoy a free and independent existence in the hill country north of the Sea of Galilee. Just as a doe experiences freedom of movement, so Naphtali's descendants would be a free mountain people.

Genesis 49:22-28

"Joseph...fruitful...blessings" (49:22-26): In this extended blessing, Jacob recaps Joseph's trials and tribulations, but he also points to a sovereign God providentially acting on Joseph's behalf. Because Joseph was obedient to God, Jacob speaks of "the Almighty who will bless you with blessings of heaven above" (verse 25).

Ephraim would initially gain supremacy over the northern tribes (see Joshua 16:9; Isaiah 7:1-2; Hosea 13:1). Sadly, however, the descendants of Ephraim—like the tribe of Dan—would engage in idolatry and paganized worship (see Judges 17; Hosea 4:17). For this reason, Ephraim was omitted from the list of tribes in Revelation 7, just as the tribe of Dan was.

"Mighty One of Jacob" (49:24): God has the power and might to always save His people. God later promised His people, "All flesh shall know that I am the Lord your Savior, and your Redeemer, the Mighty One of Jacob" (Isaiah 49:26).

"The Shepherd" (49:24): God is also the divine shepherd, who rescues, guides, and comforts His people. Earlier Jacob referred to "the God who has been my shepherd all my life long to this day" (48:15).

"The Stone of Israel" (49:24): God is often called the Rock of Israel (for example, Deuteronomy 32:4,15,18,30-31; Psalm 18:2,31; Isaiah 30:29).

"The Almighty" (49:25): God is all-powerful. Some 56 times Scripture declares that God is Almighty (for example, Revelation 19:6). No

one can reverse God (Isaiah 43:13), and no one can thwart Him (Isaiah 14:27). Nothing is impossible with God (Matthew 19:26; Mark 10:27; Luke 1:37).

"Blessings of heaven above, blessings of the deep" (49:25): The soil would be fertile because of rain from above and water springs from below.

"Blessings of the breasts and of the womb" (49:25): People would be fertile and reproduce.

"Benjamin is a ravenous wolf" (49:27): Benjamin's descendants would become a warlike (wolflike) tribe of archers and slingers (see Judges 20:16; 1 Chronicles 8:40; 12:2; 2 Chronicles 14:8; 17:17). Warriors that emerged from this tribe include Ehud, King Saul, and Jonathan.

Blessing each with the blessing suitable to him (49:28): Jacob's blessing on each of his sons was suitable in that he took the character traits and actions of his sons into consideration when pronouncing the blessings. The principle we see illustrated here is that the past affects the future (see Exodus 20:5-6; 34:6-7; Numbers 14:18; Jeremiah 32:18). As *The Bible Knowledge Commentary* puts it, "A fundamental principle in God's economy is that the lives and natures of the patriarchs affected their descendants. God works out the manifold destinies of His people in accordance with their moral distinctions."[7]

Major Themes

1. *Repentance can bring renewed blessing.* The biblical text seems to indicate that Jacob forgave Judah's earlier sins because he repented and later sacrificed himself for Jacob's well-being (44:18-34). Scripture reveals that true repentance shows itself in the way one lives. In the New Testament, John the Baptist urged Jewish leaders to "bear fruit in keeping with repentance" (Matthew 3:8). People are urged to "repent and turn to God, performing deeds in keeping with their repentance" (Acts 26:20; see also 2 Chronicles 7:14; Proverbs 28:13; 2 Corinthians 7:10). Apparently, following his earlier years of folly, Judah eventually performed deeds in keeping with repentance.

2. *The 12 tribes and their eventual land inheritance.* The Israelites were divided into 12 tribes from the 12 sons of Jacob. A different portion of the land of Canaan—the Promised Land flowing with milk and honey—was given to each tribe. Reuben, Gad, and half the tribe of Manasseh settled in the east. Asher, Naphtali, Zebulun, Issachar, Ephraim, and the other half-tribe of Manasseh settled in the northwest. Benjamin, Judah, Simeon, and Dan settled in the southwest (see Joshua 13–19).

Digging Deeper with Cross-References

Messianic scepter—Genesis 49:10; Numbers 24:17; Hebrews 1:8

Old Testament messianic prophecies—Genesis 3:15; 12:3; 49:10; Deuteronomy 18:15; Psalms 2:2; 69:21; 110:1; 118:22; 132:11; Isaiah 7:14; 9:6-7; 11:10; 25:8; 61:1; Jeremiah 23:5; Daniel 7:13; Micah 5:2; Zechariah 11:12; 12:10

Life Lessons

1. *Held accountable for behavior.* Each of Jacob's sons was held accountable for how he lived as Jacob pronounced his blessings one by one. You and I, too, will be held accountable for how we live on earth. All believers will one day stand before the judgment seat of Christ (Romans 14:8-10; 1 Corinthians 3:11-15; 9:24-27). At that time each believer's life will be examined. The scope of the judgment includes our actions (Psalm 62:12; Matthew 16:27; Ephesians 6:7-8), our words (Matthew 12:35-37; James 3:1-12), and even our thoughts (Jeremiah 17:10; 1 Corinthians 4:5; Revelation 2:23). This judgment has nothing to do with whether the Christian will be saved, for believers are eternally secure (John 10:28-30; Romans 8:29-39; Ephesians 1:13; 4:30; Hebrews 7:25). This

judgment rather has to do with only the reception or loss of rewards (see 1 Corinthians 9:25; 2 Timothy 4:8; James 1:12; 1 Peter 5:4; Revelation 2:10).

2. *The forfeiting of blessings*. Reuben, the oldest, was originally entitled to a double portion of the inheritance. That was a privilege for the firstborn in the family. However, because of the way Reuben lived, he forfeited this blessing (Genesis 35:22; 1 Chronicles 5:1-3). Might the same thing possibly happen in our lives before God? It is entirely feasible that the Christian who fails to properly repent of sin may forfeit blessings from God that would have otherwise been his. We know that righteous living yields blessing from on high (see Exodus 19:5; 23:22; Leviticus 26:3-4; Deuteronomy 7:12; 1 Kings 2:3). The choice to live righteously is a no-brainer!

Questions for Reflection and Discussion

1. Have you ever considered the possibility that a believer could forfeit blessings he or she would have received from God had he or she maintained complete obedience to Him? Does this motivate you to change?
2. Since repentance can bring renewed blessing, are there any areas of your life in which you need to make some changes?
3. How does Genesis 49 illustrate the biblical principle that we reap what we sow (Galatians 6:7)?

Day 39

Jacob Dies and Is Buried

Genesis 49:29–50:14

Scripture Reading and Insights

Begin by reading Genesis 49:29–50:14 in your favorite Bible. As you read, remember that the Word of God can help you be spiritually fruitful (Psalm 1:1-3).

In the previous reading, we considered Jacob's blessings of his own sons. Now let's find out more about Jacob's death and the great mourning that followed. With your Bible still accessible, consider the following insights on the biblical text.

Genesis 49:29-33

He commanded them (49:29): Jacob provided detailed instructions regarding his death and burial. Most modern Westerners don't obsess over matters relating to burial, but it was a very big deal among the ancient Hebrews.

At the forefront of Jacob's mind were the land promises given to Abraham, reaffirmed to Isaac, and then reaffirmed to Jacob himself. Jacob wanted to be buried in his appointed homeland—the land of Canaan.

Jacob's words were not couched in the form of a request. He issued a command. It was not an optional matter. Joseph informed Pharaoh regarding Jacob's burial, "My father made me swear" (50:5). Jacob would have his way regarding his burial.

"I am to be gathered to my people" (49:29): This amounts to saying, "I am to join my ancestors in the afterlife." Jacob knew that the moment was near. The participle used in the original Hebrew indicates that death is imminent.

"Bury me with my fathers in the cave" (49:29): The fact that Jacob specifically requested to be buried in this cave represents his firm confidence in the Abrahamic covenant land promises. Because he was unwaveringly sure that his descendants would possess the land of Canaan, that is where he wanted to be buried, along with other family members.

Recall that Abraham purchased the cave of Machpelah from Ephron the son of Zohar (23:8). He paid 400 shekels of silver for the cave—full price. This business deal took place at city gates in front of many witnesses. Such witnesses guaranteed that no one would be able to challenge the transfer of property later. Therefore, this property would be available for Abraham's descendants. Abraham himself was buried there, as were Isaac and Rebekah, as well as Leah, one of Jacob's wives. Now Jacob would be buried there.

Drew up his feet into the bed (49:33): Perhaps Jacob managed to get in a sitting position on the bed, with his feet on the floor, as he issued his final instructions. Once finished, he drew his feet back into the bed, and death was before him. He was going to his death at peace, knowing that all was well and that his descendants would have a glorious future. Jacob was convinced beyond any doubt that God was a promise keeper. God would do just as He said He would do. That being so, he was ready to die so he could join his ancestors in the afterlife.

Breathed his last (49:33): A description of death from a physiological perspective. Physical death involves a cessation of bodily functions. Jacob was 147 years old when he died. Finally his life of struggle and sorrow was at an end. Jacob had earlier told Pharaoh, "Few and evil have been the days of the years of my life" (47:9).

Gathered to his people (49:33): Once his physical body died, his spirit departed the physical body and went straight to heaven. He there joined all his ancestors who were already in heaven. He was literally "gathered to his people." This gathering to his people explains why Jesus later informed some Jewish critics, "He is not God of the dead, but of the living" (Luke 20:38). Abraham, Isaac, and Jacob, though physically dead, were nevertheless alive and well in heaven. One day you and I will be gathered to our people—our Christian loved ones in heaven.

Genesis 50:1-14

Fell on his father's face (50:1): Joseph showed unrestrained sorrow at Jacob's death.

Wept over him (50:1): Yet again, Joseph was so moved emotionally that he succumbed to weeping (see 42:24; 43:30; 45:2,14-15; 46:29).

The physicians (50:2): Joseph avoided having religious embalmers prepare his father's body, for he wanted nothing of the false paganized religion of Egypt marring his father's burial. Joseph therefore had "the physicians" (medical specialists) embalm his father.

Hebrews did not typically embalm dead bodies. Joseph may have allowed the Egyptians to embalm his father because it was a tradition in Egypt, and Joseph likely did not want to rock the boat in this regard. There may have been another reason as well. Most funerals in biblical times were performed quickly. After all, the hot climate would rapidly cause the dead body to decay and stink. So when a person died, he or she would immediately be bathed and then wrapped in strips of linen. Sometimes a gummy combination of spices was applied to the wrappings of the body. It was then carried by stretcher to the place of burial, whether in the ground or in a cave. In Jacob's case, however, a rapid burial would be impossible. Perhaps Joseph allowed Jacob to be embalmed because that would help delay the inevitable decay of the body as they took it to the land of Canaan.

Forty days (50:3): The process of embalming took 40 days to be complete. It involved removing the inner organs, drying the body, and then wrapping it with gums and spices. See Major Themes.

Egyptians wept for him seventy days (50:3): It is likely that the 40 days of embalming overlapped with the 70 days of mourning. The 70-day period of mourning was normal protocol for the death of an important person in Egypt—just two days short of mourning for the death of a Pharaoh.

When the days of weeping for him were past (50:4): Once the 70 days of mourning were complete, Joseph was now free to approach Pharaoh to request permission to go bury his father in the land of Canaan.

"I will return" (50:5): Joseph was aware of his indispensable role in Egypt. The years of the famine were now past, but Joseph's presence had brought great blessing in Egypt. For this reason, it must have crossed the minds of some that if Joseph went to bury his father in the land of Canaan, perhaps he would stay there. Joseph did not want any concern or confusion about this. That's why he told Pharaoh, "I will return." Of course, Joseph had long proven himself worthy of Pharaoh's trust. He had a perfect record, and that gave credence to future promises. Pharaoh had no doubt Joseph would return just as he said.

All the elders of the land of Egypt (50:7): Pharaoh not only granted permission for Joseph to go bury his father in the land of Canaan but also sent along a procession of Egypt's elders (dignitaries). This indicated a strong show of respect for Joseph.

His brothers (50:8): Joseph had earlier experienced conflict and disunity with his brothers, which led to his being forcefully brought to Egypt without them. Now Joseph left Egypt in harmony and unity with his brothers to bury their beloved father.

The Canaanites...saw the mourning (50:11): Even the Canaanites recognized this as "a grievous mourning." The Canaanites likely witnessed quite a spectacle. As one Bible expositor put it, "The Egyptians were a very demonstrative people and vehement in their public lamentations for the dead. They rent their clothes, smote their breasts, threw dust and mud on their heads, called on the deceased by name, and chanted funeral dirges to the sound of the tambourine."[8]

Abel-mizraim (50:11): The funeral procession arrived at the threshing floor of Atad, which is beyond the Jordan, on the border between Egypt and Canaan. The funeral party ceremonially grieved for seven days there. Because the funeral procession included the elders of Egypt, the place was called Abel-mizraim, a term that means "mourning of Egypt."

Sons carried him to the land of Canaan (50:13): Jacob's sons were obedient. They took his body to the land of Canaan and buried him in the cave of the field at Machpelah.

Joseph returned to Egypt (50:14): Following the burial of Jacob, Joseph returned to Egypt, just as he promised. Joseph again proves to be a man of his word.

This was the first time in 39 years that Joseph had been back to his homeland. Though Joseph's visit was temporary, a time would come—following 400 years of enslavement in Egypt—when the Israelites would leave Egypt to return to their homeland (see the book of Exodus). At that time, Joseph's bones would be brought back to the land of promise to be buried there.

Major Themes

1. *Jacob was embalmed.* Embalming the dead was a common practice among the Egyptians. The term "embalm" literally means "to spice," referring to preserving a corpse by means of spices. Egyptians believed the dead needed their bodies preserved so they could live in the world to come. Jacob's family went along with the embalming to avoid offense to the Egyptians. Embalming also helped preserve the body until it could be buried in the land of Canaan. Joseph would also be embalmed following his death (50:26). The biblical view is that bodies are in the world to come (heaven for the believer) by resurrection, not by embalming (see 1 Corinthians 15).
2. *Jacob is buried and mourned.* Jacob was greatly mourned after he died. "Joseph fell on his father's face and wept over him and kissed him" (Genesis 50:1). "The Egyptians wept for him seventy days" (50:3). When the burial party departed Egypt and arrived at the burial site in the land of Canaan, "they lamented there with a very great and grievous lamentation, and [Joseph] made a mourning for his father seven days" (50:10). This indeed was "a grievous mourning by the Egyptians" (50:11).

Digging Deeper with Cross-References

Filial obedience—Genesis 50:12; Proverbs 1:8; 6:20; 7:1; 23:22; Ephesians 6:1; Colossians 3:20; 1 Timothy 3:4

"Seven days" in Genesis—Genesis 2:3; 7:4,10; 8:10,12; 31:23; 50:10

Life Lessons

1. *Bodies buried, spirits in heaven.* In Genesis 49:33 we are told, "When Jacob finished commanding his sons, he drew up his feet into the bed and breathed his last and was *gathered to his people.*" That is, his spirit departed the body and went to heaven, where he rejoined all his departed loved ones. In 2 Corinthians 5:8 the apostle Paul states, "We would rather be away from the body and at home with the Lord." Likewise, in Philippians 1:23 Paul said, "My desire is to depart and be with Christ, for that is far better." When Stephen was being put to death by stoning, he prayed, "Lord Jesus, receive my spirit" (Acts 7:59). These and other verses indicate that at death, the believer's spirit departs from the physical body and immediately goes into the presence of the Lord in heaven. Death for the believer thus leads to a supremely blissful existence.
2. *Faith even in the face of death.* Jacob wanted to be buried in the same cave in the land of Canaan as his grandfather Abraham. This was not just a family sticking together. Rather, the desire to be buried in Canaan is rooted in God's promise to Abraham—a promise that was reiterated to Isaac and Jacob—that the land of Canaan would belong to the descendants of Abraham forever. Even in the face of death, Jacob had faith that God would surely fulfill His promise about the land flowing with milk and honey.

Questions for Reflection and Discussion

1. What is your attitude toward death? Do you have a strong and confident hope, as did Jacob? Do you look forward to resurrection day—a day when you'll gain a "body upgrade" that will never again get sick or die (Philippians 3:20-21)?
2. Jacob was a firm believer in the promises of God. What promises of God do you need to anchor yourself to this coming week?
3. You and I have a "land of promise" too. The Bible calls it a heavenly country (Hebrews 11:16). Does the fact that you are daily en route to the heavenly country affect the way you live?

Day 40

Joseph's Last Days

Genesis 50:15-26

Scripture Reading and Insights

Begin by reading Genesis 50:15-26 in your favorite Bible. As you read, remember that the Word of God can help you be spiritually fruitful (Psalm 1:1-3).

In the previous reading, we focused on Jacob's death and the great mourning that followed. In this final chapter, Joseph reassures his brothers that all is well. Genesis closes with the death of Joseph. With your Bible still accessible, consider the following insights on the biblical text.

Genesis 50:15-21

"Joseph will hate us and pay us back" (50:15): One might recall that Esau originally planned to kill the deceitful Jacob as soon as their father Isaac died (see 27:41-45). Joseph's brothers thought that perhaps Joseph would do likewise.

"Please forgive" (50:17): The brothers, knowing they had engaged in a heinous wrong so many years earlier, pled for forgiveness. They were motivated to make this plea because Jacob's restraining influence was no longer present.

Joseph wept (50:17): Joseph wept because his brothers' sense of guilt still alienated them from him. Joseph had just lost his father in death. More than ever he needed the sense of closeness that comes with a family. The alienation was hurtful to him (see 42:24; 43:30; 45:2,14; 50:1).

His brothers...fell down before him (50:18): Once again we find a fulfillment of Joseph's prophetic dream: "My sheaf arose and stood upright. And behold, your sheaves gathered around it and bowed down to my sheaf" (37:7).

"Do not fear" (50:19): God had exalted Joseph, but Joseph was not in the place of God. We recall Joseph's words in Genesis 45:5-8:

> Do not be distressed or angry with yourselves because you sold me here, for God sent me before you to preserve life. For the famine has been in the land these two years, and there are yet five years in which there will be neither plowing nor harvest. And God sent me before you to preserve for you a remnant on earth, and to keep alive for you many survivors. So it was not you who sent me here, but God. He has made me a father to Pharaoh, and lord of all his house and ruler over all the land of Egypt.

Again, then, God had put Joseph in his current place, but Joseph was well aware that did not mean he was in the place of God. Joseph therefore tells them, "Do not fear."

"God meant it for good" (50:20): Joseph had been sold into slavery by his own brothers (see Genesis 37). This was painful at the time, but God was always in control. God used these negative circumstances to bring Joseph to Egypt, where He elevated Joseph to a position of great authority (Genesis 41). Of course, during the time of suffering itself, Joseph had no idea what God's intentions were. He did not know that God was using these dire circumstances to bring him to a position of great prominence in Egypt. This reality would later become clear to Joseph. Joseph could say with utter clarity and conviction, "You meant evil against me, but God meant it for good" (50:20). This brings to mind Romans 8:28, where the apostle Paul affirms, "We know that for those who love God all things work together for good, for those who are called according to his purpose."

Joseph had come to trust in the sovereignty of God. God is absolutely sovereign in the sense that He rules the universe, controls all things, and is Lord over all things (see Ephesians 1). He may utilize various means to accomplish His ends (such as jealous brothers), but He is always in control. God asserts, "My counsel shall stand, and I will accomplish all my purpose" (Isaiah 46:10). God assures us, "As I have planned, so shall it be, and as I have purposed, so shall it stand" (Isaiah 14:24). God is "the blessed and only Sovereign, the King of kings and Lord of lords" (1 Timothy 6:15). Proverbs 16:9 tells us, "The heart of man plans his way, but the Lord establishes his steps." Proverbs 19:21 says, "Many are the plans in the mind of a man, but it is the purpose of the Lord that will stand." In Proverbs 21:30 (NIV) we read, "There is no wisdom, no insight, no plan that can succeed against the Lord." (This includes the actions of jealous brothers!) Lamentations 3:37 (NIV) affirms, "Who can speak and have it happen if the Lord has not decreed it?"

From our limited vantage point, our lives are marked by an endless series of contingencies. We frequently find ourselves reacting to an unexpected turn of events. We make plans but are often forced to change them. But there are no contingencies with God. Our unexpected, forced change of plans are included in His plan. God is never surprised, never caught off guard, never frustrated by unexpected developments. God does as He pleases, and whatever pleases Him is always for His glory and our good.

This can sometimes be difficult for us. God does not sit us down and say, "Okay, listen, I'm going to allow some bad stuff to happen this next week, but I'm in control, and I'm using this event to bring about a great good. So don't worry about it. Everything's fine." Certainly God did not sit down and explain to Joseph why he would suffer so terribly. You and I are given the privilege of going behind the scenes in Joseph's life by reading the book of Genesis. But we are not able to go behind the scenes of our own lives and discern the mysterious ways that God works in us. That's why we have to trust Him. We generally are not aware of why God engineers our circumstances the way He does. But we may always rest assured that He always has our best interests at heart.

"Many people should be kept alive" (50:20): The brothers intended to hurt one person (Joseph), but they actually rescued countless other people from hurt—Egyptians as well as Jews. In modern vernacular, this was definitely a God thing.

"I will provide for you" (50:21): Joseph reassured his brothers that he would provide for them. They need not fear. All would be well.

Genesis 50:22-26

Joseph saw Ephraim's children...children also of Machir (50:23): Joseph lived long enough to see his great-grandchildren (the children of Machir), a privilege shared by no other patriarchal figure. We recall Proverbs 17:6: "Grandchildren are the crown of the aged" (see also Psalm 128:6).

"I am about to die" (50:24): Because he is about to die, he communicates his final instructions.

"God will surely visit you" (50:25): Joseph knew that God would someday bring His people from Egypt back to Canaan, the Promised Land.

Made the sons of Israel swear (50:25): Joseph had not forgotten his father Jacob's words to him: "Behold, I am about to die, but God will be with you and will bring you again to the land of your fathers" (48:21). When that happened, Joseph wanted his bones to be transferred to the land of Canaan, where they belonged. He lived as an Egyptian, but he was still a Hebrew at heart.

Joseph died (50:26): Joseph trusted in God during life. He also faced death by trusting in God. He was 110 years old when he died. Ancient Egyptian documents reveal the age of 110 to be the ideal life span. With the death of Joseph, the patriarchal age comes to a close. God will now deal with His people Israel as a nation.

Embalmed him (50:26): Like his father Jacob, Joseph was embalmed according to Egyptian tradition.

Put in a coffin (50:26): This was a mummy encasement. Moses would later take Joseph's remains out of Egypt (Exodus 13:19), and even later, Joshua would bury them at Shechem (Joshua 24:32).

As the book of Genesis comes to a close, the land promises of the

Abrahamic covenant remain unfulfilled. But the hope of fulfillment remains alive. The Jews in Egypt await a visitation from God. This visitation will come in the book of Exodus.

Major Themes

1. *God's awesome providence.* I've addressed the issue of God's providence several times in this book. But because it is a constantly recurring theme in Genesis, it is appropriate to touch on it yet again. Daniel 4:35 says of God, "All the inhabitants of the earth are accounted as nothing, and he does according to his will among the host of heaven and among the inhabitants of the earth; and none can stay his hand or say to him, 'What have you done?'" We are told that "in him we live and move and have our being" (Acts 17:28). God even rules over the elements: "Behold, by my rebuke I dry up the sea, I make the rivers a desert" (Isaiah 50:2). God's providence embraces even the smallest details of our existence: "Are not two sparrows sold for a penny? And not one of them will fall to the ground apart from your Father. But even the hairs of your head are all numbered" (Matthew 10:29-30). God's purposes cannot be thwarted (Isaiah 46:10). All this being so, we can easily see how God could have orchestrated the events in Joseph's life so that he was exalted in Egypt and saved people from famine. How awesome is our God!
2. *God brings good out of evil.* God sovereignly uses the forces of evil to accomplish His supreme purposes. God used Joseph's slavery to bring him to Egypt, where He eventually elevated him to a position of great authority. In the New Testament, God allowed the apostle Paul to be put in jail, where he promptly wrote a number of New Testament letters. God allowed His Son to be crucified on a cross to provide the basis of our salvation. God's methods are inscrutable. In the end, evil will be defeated, and all will be perfect (Revelation 21–22).

Digging Deeper with Cross-References

Forgiveness—Genesis 50:17; Matthew 5:39; 5:43-44; 6:14; Mark 11:25; Luke 6:27,37; Romans 12:17,19; Ephesians 4:32; Colossians 3:13

Sovereignty of God—Exodus 15:18; Deuteronomy 4:39; 10:14; 2 Chronicles 20:6; Psalms 9:7; 29:10; 33:8-11; 47:2; 83:18; 103:19; 135:6; Isaiah 40:21-26; 46:10; Daniel 4:34-35; Romans 14:11; Ephesians 1:20-22; Revelation 1:6

Life Lessons

1. *Forgive instead of holding grudges.* Joseph's brothers were worried that after Jacob died, Joseph would seek retribution for their decades-old sin. But the context clearly shows that Joseph had completely forgiven his brothers for their sin against him. Forgiving others is one of the most important lessons we can learn in terms of living the Christian life. Colossians 3:12-13 instructs, "Put on then, as God's chosen ones, holy and beloved, compassionate hearts, kindness, humility, meekness, and patience, bearing with one another and, if one has a complaint against another, forgiving each other; as the Lord has forgiven you, so you also must forgive." Romans 12:17-19 specifically instructs us not to repay evil by evil. Our modus operandi ought to be to forgive and be forgiven (Luke 6:37; Ephesians 4:32). Indeed, we ought to forgive without measure (Matthew 18:21-22).

2. *Trust God in your encounters with evil.* All Christians must come to a place where we finally understand that God indeed can bring good out of evil circumstances. God has the unique ability to overrule other people's evil intentions and bring about His ultimate purposes. Perhaps you are struggling with a health issue. Perhaps you are struggling with finances. Perhaps you are struggling with a relationship. Whatever it is, trust God without reserve in the midst of your difficulties. Wait patiently for Him

to work. Never forget, "for those who love God all things work together for good, for those who are called according to his purpose" (Romans 8:28). Indeed, "the hand of our God is for good on all who seek him" (Ezra 8:22).

Questions for Reflection and Discussion

1. Do you need to forgive anyone?
2. Do you truly trust God with all your circumstances in life?
3. Can you recall a time when God brought good out of evil in your life? If yes, what did you learn in that situation?

Postscript

The Bible begins with paradise lost. This is a primary theme in the book of Genesis. The Bible ends, however, with paradise regained. The book of Revelation explains it all.

It is fascinating to contrast the book of Genesis with the book of Revelation. There is a grand reversal worthy of our deepest contemplation.

- In Genesis, God creates the heavens and the earth (Genesis 1:1). In Revelation, God creates the new heavens and a new earth (Revelation 21:1-2).
- In Genesis, the sun and moon were created as "two great lights" (Genesis 1:16-17). In Revelation, there is no longer any need for such light, for the glory of God lights up the eternal city of the redeemed (Revelation 21:23; 22:5).
- In Genesis, God created the night (Genesis 1:5). In the book of Revelation, there is no longer any night (Revelation 22:5).
- In Genesis, God created the seas (Genesis 1:10). In Revelation, there is no longer any sea on the new earth (Revelation 21:1).
- In Genesis, human beings succumb to Satan's temptations through the serpent (Genesis 3:1-4). In Revelation, Satan is eternally quarantined away from the people of God (Revelation 20:10). He is no longer around to harass God's people.
- In Genesis, the first man and woman succumb to sin (Genesis 3). In Revelation, redeemed humans are free from

sin and live in a perfectly holy environment (Revelation 21:1-2).

- In Genesis, as a result of sin, God pronounces a curse (Genesis 3:17). In Revelation, there is no more curse (Revelation 22:3).
- In Genesis, paradise was lost. The first man and woman were ousted from the garden of Eden (Genesis 3:23-24). In Revelation, paradise is gloriously restored for redeemed humans (Revelation 2:7; compare with Luke 23:43; 2 Corinthians 12:3). Never again will they be ousted from paradise!
- In Genesis, the first man and woman were barred from the tree of life (Genesis 3:22-24). In Revelation, redeemed humans are restored to the tree of life (Revelation 2:7; 22:2,14,19).
- In Genesis, tears, death, and mourning entered human existence (Genesis 2:17; 29:11; 37:34). In Revelation, tears, death, and mourning are forever absent from the redeemed (Revelation 21:4).
- In Genesis, a Redeemer is promised (Genesis 3:15). In Revelation, the victorious Redeemer reigns (Revelation 20:1-6; 21:22-27; 22:3-5).
- In Genesis, a bride is found for the first Adam (Genesis 2:18). In Revelation, we witness the bride (the church) of the last Adam, Jesus Christ (Revelation 19:9).

My friend, you've now completed a study of the book of Genesis. Are you ready for a study of the book of Revelation? If so, I've written *40 Days Through Revelation* just for you. It's available at Christian bookstores and online retailers.

May the Lord bless you and keep you as you continue to study His Word!

Notes

1. H.C. Leupold, *Exposition of Genesis*, vol. 1 (Grand Rapids: Baker, 1968), p. 331.
2. Michael Green, *Illustrations for Biblical Preaching* (Grand Rapids: Baker, 1991), n.p.
3. John MacArthur, ed., *The MacArthur Study Bible* (Nashville: Thomas Nelson, 2010), comment at Genesis 30:1-21.
4. George Bush, *Notes on Genesis*, reprint ed., 2 vols. (Minneapolis: James and Klock, 1976), p. 2.
5. W.H. Griffith Thomas, *Genesis: A Devotional Commentary* (Grand Rapids: Kregel, 1988), p. 379.
6. John H. Sailhamer, "Genesis," in *The Expositor's Bible Commentary, Genesis–Numbers*, vol. 2, ed. Frank E. Gaebelein and Richard P. Polcyn (Grand Rapids: Zondervan, 1990), p. 277.
7. John F. Walvoord and Roy B. Zuck, eds., *The Bible Knowledge Commentary* (Wheaton: Victor Books, 1983), comment at Isaiah 49.
8. John Phillips, *Exploring Genesis* (*John Phillips Commentaries Series*) (Grand Rapids: Kregel Academic & Professional, 2001), n.p.

Bibliography

Barnhouse, Donald Grey. *Genesis: A Devotional Exposition*. Grand Rapids: Zondervan, 1984.

Boice, James Montgomery. *Genesis*. Grand Rapids: Baker, 2006.

Brown, Francis, S.R. Driver, and Charles A. Briggs. *A Hebrew and English Lexicon of the Old Testament*. Oxford: Clarendon, 1980.

Bruce, F.F., ed. *The International Bible Commentary*. Grand Rapids: Zondervan, 1979.

Fruchtenbaum, Arnold G. *The Book of Genesis* (*Ariel's Bible Commentary*). San Antonio: Ariel Ministries, 2009.

Gaebelein, Frank E., ed. *The Expositor's Bible Commentary*. Grand Rapids: Zondervan, 1978.

Gibson, Joyce L., and Larry Richards. *The Book of Genesis* (*The Smart Guide to the Bible Series*). Nashville: Thomas Nelson, 2007.

Hughes, R. Kent. *Genesis: Beginning and Blessing* (*Preaching the Word*). Bloomington: Crossway, 2012.

Jamieson, Robert, A.R. Fausset, and David Brown. *A Commentary, Critical, Experimental, and Practical, on the Old and New Testaments*. Grand Rapids: Eerdmans, 1973.

Keil C.F., and Franz Delitzsch. *Biblical Commentary on the Old Testament*. Grand Rapids: Eerdmans, 1954.

Kidner, Derek. *Genesis* (*Tyndale Old Testament Commentaries*). Downers Grove: InterVarsity Press, 2008.

Leupold, H.C. *Exposition of Genesis*, vol. 1. Grand Rapids: Baker, 1968.

MacArthur, John. *The MacArthur Bible Commentary*. Nashville: Thomas Nelson, 2005.

Pfeiffer, Charles F., and Everett F. Harrison, eds. *The Wycliffe Bible Commentary*. Chicago: Moody, 1974.

Phillips, John. *Exploring Genesis* (*The John Phillips Commentary Series*). Grand Rapids: Kregel, 2001.

Pink, A.W. *Gleanings in Genesis*. Seaside: Watchmaker, 2011.

Ross, Allen P. *Creation & Blessing: A Guide to the Study and Exposition of Genesis*. Grand Rapids: Baker, 1998.

Rydelnik, Michael, and Michael Vanlaningham, eds. *The Moody Bible Commentary*. Chicago: Moody Press, 2014.

Vos, Howard. *Genesis* (*Everyman's Bible Commentary*). Chicago: Moody, 1982.

Waltke, Bruce K. *Genesis: A Commentary*. Grand Rapids: Zondervan, 2001.

Walvoord, John F. and Roy B. Zuck, eds. *The Bible Knowledge Commentary, Old Testament.* Wheaton: Victor, 1985.

Wenham, Gordon J. *Word Biblical Commentary*. Vol. 1: *Genesis 1–15*. Vol. 2: *Genesis 16–50*. Nashville: Thomas Nelson, 1987, 1994.

More Great Harvest House Books by Ron Rhodes

BOOKS ABOUT THE BIBLE

The Big Book of Bible Answers
Bite-Size Bible® Answers
Bite-Size Bible® Charts
Bite-Size Bible® Definitions
Bite-Size Bible® Handbook
Commonly Misunderstood Bible Verses
The Complete Guide to Bible Translations
Find It Fast in the Bible
The Popular Dictionary of Bible Prophecy
Understanding the Bible from A to Z
What Does the Bible Say About...?

BOOKS ABOUT THE END TIMES

8 Great Debates of Bible Prophecy
40 Days Through Revelation
Cyber Meltdown
The End Times in Chronological Order
Northern Storm Rising
Unmasking the Antichrist

BOOKS ABOUT OTHER IMPORTANT TOPICS

5-Minute Apologetics for Today
1001 Unforgettable Quotes About God, Faith, and the Bible
Answering the Objections of Atheists, Agnostics, and Skeptics
Christianity According to the Bible
The Complete Guide to Christian Denominations
Conversations with Jehovah's Witnesses
Find It Quick Handbook on Cults and New Religions
The Truth Behind Ghosts, Mediums, and Psychic Phenomena
Secret Life of Angels
What Happens After Life?
Why Do Bad Things Happen If God Is Good?
Wonder of Heaven

THE 10 MOST IMPORTANT THINGS SERIES

The 10 Most Important Things You Can Say to a Catholic
The 10 Most Important Things You Can Say to a Jehovah's Witness
The 10 Most Important Things You Can Say to a Mason
The 10 Most Important Things You Can Say to a Mormon
The 10 Things You Need to Know About Islam
The 10 Things You Should Know About the Creation vs. Evolution Debate

QUICK REFERENCE GUIDES

Halloween: What You Need to Know
Islam: What You Need to Know
Jehovah's Witnesses: What You Need to Know

THE REASONING FROM THE SCRIPTURES SERIES

Reasoning from the Scriptures with Catholics
Reasoning from the Scriptures with the Jehovah's Witnesses
Reasoning from the Scriptures with Masons
Reasoning from the Scriptures with the Mormons
Reasoning from the Scriptures with Muslims

LITTLE BOOKS

Little Book About God
Little Book About Heaven
Little Book About the Bible

AVAILABLE ONLY AS EBOOKS

Book of Bible Promises
Coming Oil Storm
Topical Handbook of Bible Prophecy

To learn more about Harvest House books and to read sample chapters, visit our website:

www.harvesthousepublishers.com